UNDERSTANDING THE QUR'AN

UNDERSTANDING *The* *Qur'an*

THEMES AND STYLE

Muhammad Abdel Haleem

I.B.Tauris *Publishers*
LONDON • NEW YORK

Published in 1999 by
I.B. Tauris & Co Ltd
Victoria House
Bloomsbury Square
London WC1B 4DZ

175 Fifth Avenue
New York NY 10010

In the United States of America
and in Canada distributed by
St Martin's Press
175 Fifth Avenue
New York NY 10010

A full CIP record for this book is available from the British Library
A full CIP record for this book is available from the Library of Congress

ISBN 1 86064 009 5

Library of Congress catalog card number: available

Typeset in New Baskerville by Hepton Books, Oxford
Printed and bound in Great Britain by The Bath Press, Bath

Contents

Preface

Understanding the Qur'an is intended to help the general reader, and also the scholar, to understand the Qur'an by combining a number of approaches: thematic, stylistic and comparative. Many English studies of the Qur'an tend to regard it as nothing more than a jumble of borrowed and rambling thoughts with no sense of direction. This approach has resulted in a series of unstudied theories which, instead of mapping out the Qur'anic world, have added more confused ideas to an already confused comprehension.

The study of themes in the Qur'an is fairly new in English. This is surprising, as it is the only approach that can give a balanced view of what the Qur'an says on any given topic. In 1976, Fazlur Rahman observed that there was an urgent need for 'an introduction to major themes of the Qur'an', and his book of this title[1] represents an important initiative in using this approach. However, more thematic studies are needed, and the present book is a further step in that direction. Fazlur Rahman has treated some fundamental themes, such as God, prophethood and revelation, Man as individual, man in society, etc.[2] Apart from 'The Face, Divine and Human in the Qur'an', all the themes in this book were suggested as topics for public lectures I have been invited to deliver. In Arab studies, Muslim scholars, particularly in recent years, have been discussing contemporary issues and examining what light the Qur'an throws on them.[3] Perennial themes such as war, marriage, and tolerance in Islam, are among those which Muslims consider to have been seriously misunderstood by Western writers, and they feel that the Qur'an has yet to be explored properly on these themes.

In addition to thematic studies, the book includes a general introduction about the revelation and importance of the Qur'an in the life of Muslims, and a discussion of its style. Certain fundamental aspects of the style of the Qura'n need to be explained for the benefit of general readers and scholars alike. The current translations of the Qur'an, for all their merits, leave the reader puzzled in a number of ways. Chapter 12 of this book, 'The Qur'an Explains Itself', spells out two important methods for understanding the Qur'an and deals with the assertion that Sūra 55 is a mere imitation of Biblical material, for example Psalm 136. Chapter 13 shows that a grasp of certain features of Qur'anic style is essential for proper understanding. For example, what has been assumed to be bad grammar is in fact a well-established and effective feature of Arabic literary writing.

The comparative approach running through many parts of this book was, in fact, suggested by audiences at public lectures who themselves drew the comparisons between the Bible and the Qur'an and asked me to talk about them. It is hoped that my book will help bring more understanding of the Qur'an to readers familiar with the Biblical treatment of similar themes. Fazlur Rahman refers to the tradition of Western scholars who seek to trace the influence of Jewish or Christian ideas on the Qur'an in order to 'prove' that 'the Qur'an is no more than an echo of Judaism (or Christianity) and Muhammad was no more than a Jewish (or Christian) disciple!'[4] Unlike such writings, the comparisons in this book seek only to elucidate the Qur'anic view and approach.

In treating the subjects under discussion, it was felt that, given the controversies that surround it, the Qur'an should be left to speak for itself, albeit in translation. Hence numerous quotations have been included.

Some of the material in this book has appeared as articles in different publications, and I would like to thank the publishers for their permission to reprint them.

My most sincere thanks go to my wife for typing the manuscript, and for her invaluable comments.

Acknowledgements

The author wishes to thank the following for permission to re-use material from his own articles previously published as follows:

G. R. Hawting (ed.) for 'The Qu'ran' in *Sacred Writings in Oriental and African Religions,* SOAS External Services Division (Occasional Paper XII), London 1986, pp. 17–22.
G. Hawting and A.-K. A. Shareef (eds) for 'Context and Internal Relationships: Keys to Qu'ranic Exegesis' in *Approaches to the Qur'an,* Routledge, London, 1993, pp. 71–98.
Macmillan Publishing, London, for 'Life and Beyond in the Qur'an', in *Beyond Death,* ed. Christopher Lewis and Dan Cohn-Sherbok, 1995, pp. 66–79.
The Islamic Cultural Centre, Regents Park, London, for 'Water in the Qu'ran', *The Islamic Quarterly,* XXXIII, 1, London 1989, pp. 34–50.
'The Face in the Qur'an: Divine and Human' *Islamic Quarterly,* London, December 1997, pp. 255–69.
'Tolerance in the Qur'an', *Islamic Quarterly,* London, 1998, pp. 89–98.
The Centre for the Study of Islam and Christian-Muslim Relations, Birmingham, for 'The Story of Joseph in the Qur'an and the Old Testament' in *Islam and Christian Muslim Relations,* I, 2, Birmingham, 1990, pp. 171–91.
The School of Oriental and African Studies, University of London, for 'Grammatical Shift for Rhetorical Purposes: *Iltifāt* and related features in the Qur'an', *Bulletin of the School of Oriental and African Studies* 1992, LV, 3, pp. 407–32.

1

The Qur'an

'Read in the Name of your Lord.' These were the first words of the Qur'an revealed to Muhammad. The revelation came to him during a period of retreat and meditation in a cave outside Mecca in 610 AD. He was already forty-years-old; he was not known to have had any poetic or rhetorical gifts like many of his contemporaries – or to have engaged in any discussion of religion. His account survives of the extraordinary circumstances of this revelation, of being approached by an Angel who commanded him: 'Read!' When he explained that he could not read the Angel squeezed him strongly, repeating the request twice, and then recited to him the first two lines of the Qur'an in which the concepts of 'reading', 'learning/knowing' and 'the pen' occur six times (96:1–5).

The Qur'an does not begin chronologically like the Old Testament, nor genealogically like the New Testament, but – as modern Muslim writers on education point out – by directly talking about reading, teaching, knowing and writing.[1] Nor does the beginning of the Qur'an resemble the beginning of any earlier work known in Arabic literature. Until the first revelation came to him in the cave, Muhammad was not known to have composed any poem or given any speech. The Qur'an employs this fact in arguing with the unbelievers:

Say: Had God pleased, I would never have recited it to you, nor would He have made you aware of it. A whole lifetime I dwelt among you before it was revealed. Will you not understand?

10:16

Never have you read a book before this, nor have you ever transcribed one with your right hand. Had you done either of these, the unbelievers might have doubted. But to those who are endowed with knowledge it is an undoubted sign. Only the wrongdoers deny Our signs.

29:48

The word *qu'rān* lexically means 'reading' and came to refer to 'the text which is read'. The Muslim scripture often calls itself '*kitāb*'; lexically this means 'writing' and came to refer to 'the written book'. Thus the significance of uttering and writing the revealed scripture is emphasised from the very beginning of Islam, and is locked in the very nouns that designate the Qur'an.

The first piece of revelation consisted of two lines in Arabic, which began the Qur'an and the mission of the Prophet, after which he had no further experience of revelation for some while. Then another short piece was revealed, and between then and shortly before the Prophet's death in 632 AD at the age of sixty-three, the whole text of the Qur'an was revealed gradually, piece by piece, in varying lengths, giving new teaching or commenting on events or answering questions according to circumstances. For the first experience of revelation Muhammad was alone in the cave and he reported it. After that the circumstances in which he received revelations were witnessed by others and recorded. Visible, audible and sensory reactions were witnessed by those around the Prophet when he experienced the 'state of revelation'. His face would brighten and he would fall silent and appear as if his thoughts were far away, his body would become heavy as if in sleep, a humming sound would be heard about him, and sweat would appear on his face, even on winter days. This stage would last for a brief period and as it left he would immediately recite new verses of the Qur'an. This state was reported clearly not to be the Prophet's to command: it would descend on him as he was walking, sitting, riding, or giving a sermon, and there were occasions when he waited anxiously for it for over a month to answer a question he was asked, or comment on an event. The Prophet and his followers understood these signs as the experience accompanying the communication of Qur'anic verses by the Angel of Revelation (Gabriel). The Prophet's adversaries explained it as a sign of his 'being possessed', or magic. (In this regard, the Qur'an has itself recorded all claims and attacks made against it and against the Prophet in his lifetime.)

The first word in the Qur'an, and in Islam, was, as seen above, an imperative addressed *to* the Prophet, linguistically making the authorship of the text outside Muhammad. This mode is maintained throughout the Qur'an. It talks to the Prophet or talks about him and does not allow him to speak for himself. The Qur'an describes itself as a book which God 'sent down' to the Prophet: the expression 'sent down', in its various derivations, is used in the Qur'an well over 200 times. In Arabic this word conveys immediately, and in itself, the concept that the origin of the Qur'an is from above and that Muhammad is merely a recipient. God is the one to speak in the Qur'an: Muhammad is addressed, 'O Prophet', 'O Messenger', 'Do', 'Do not do', 'They ask you ...', 'Say' (the word 'say' is used in the Qur'an well over 300 times). The Prophet is censured sometimes in the Qur'an.[2] His status is unequivocally defined as 'Messenger' (*rasūl*) and he is often reminded that his duty is the communication (*al-balāgh*) of the Message to the community.

To the Prophet himself, the Qur'an was 'sent down' and communicated to him by 'the faithful Spirit', Gabriel, and to him it was categorically not his own speech. Stylistically, Qur'anic material which the Prophet recited following the states of revelation described above is so evidently different from the Prophet's own sayings (*ḥadīth*), whether uttered incidentally or after long reflection, that they are unmistakably recognisable as belonging to two different levels of speech. With every new addition to the Qur'anic body, the Prophet would recite it to those around him, who would learn it and in turn recite it to others in an environment which had long been known to be eager to receive any new literary material.[3] Throughout his mission the Prophet repeatedly read the Qur'an to his followers in prayers and speeches. An inner circle of his followers wrote down verses of the Qur'an as they learned them from him. He himself was faithful in having the Qur'an recorded even in the days of persecution and he acquired scribes for this purpose (twenty-nine have been counted in the Medina period).

The book itself as printed today covers less than 500 small pages. It was revealed over twenty-three years, which means a rough average of less than twenty-five pages a year, or two pages a month. Even in our word-processing days, vast numbers of children in Muslim countries learn the entire Qur'an during the early years of their education. In keeping with his care to record and preserve every new piece of the Qur'an, Muhammad tried to ensure that not even his own sayings interfered with this, and ordered, 'Whoever has written anything from me other than the Qur'an, let him erase it.' One consequence of this was that the reports of his own sayings and reported actions later suffered from forgery. Muslim scholars had to sift this *ḥadīth* material through an elaborate system of attestation, rejecting numerous *ḥadīths* on the grounds of forgery, and declaring others weak in their chain of transmission (*mā yuradd li sanadih*) or in the text itself (*mā yuradd li matnih*). All this arose originally from concern for the authenticity of the Qur'anic material. By the end of the Prophet's life (10/632) the entire Qur'an was written down in the form of uncollated pieces. Large numbers of followers learnt parts of it by heart, many learned all of it[4] from the Prophet over years spent in his company. They belonged to a cultural background that had a long-standing tradition of memorising literature, history and genealogy.

With every new piece the Prophet requested his followers, 'Place this in the *sūra* that talks about such and such.' Material was thus placed in different *sūras*, not in chronological order of appearance, but in *sūras* as they were to be read by the Prophet and believers, appearing on examination as if fitting into a pre-existing plan.[5] Over the years, in his prayers and in teaching his followers, he read the material in the order that it appeared in the *sūras* of the Qur'an. The form of the Qur'an still, to this day, follows this original arrangement without any alteration or editing. It is not historical in its arrangement, nor biographical, nor in the form of lectures, nor of a book edited and arranged by scholars.

During the second year after the Prophet's death (12/633) and following the battle of Yamama, in which a number of those who knew the Qur'an by heart died, it was feared that, with the gradual passing away of such men, there was a danger of some Qur'anic material being lost. Therefore the first caliph, Abu Bakr ordered that the Qur'an should be collected in one written copy which was kept with him. This copy remained locked away until the time of 'Uthman, the third caliph, when a problem arose. The urgency is summarised in the appeal of Hudhayfa bin al-Yaman, who demanded of 'Uthman, on returning from battles in Azerbaijan (25/645), 'Quick! Help the Muslims before they differ about the text of the Qur'an as the Christians and Jews differed about their scriptures.' Hudhayfa had become perturbed when he saw Muslim soldiers from different parts of Syria and Iraq meeting together and differing in their readings of the Qur'an, each considering his reading to be the correct one. The only full official written copy had been kept first with Abu Bakr, then with Umar, and after his death with his daughter Hafsa, a widow of the Prophet. Responding to the urgent demand for help, 'Uthman sent word to Hafsa, asking for the copy in her possession to be sent to him. He ordered that a number of copies be made and distributed to different parts of the Muslim world as the official copy of the Qur'an. This prevented the possibility of different versions evolving in time, as Hudhayfa had originally feared. The 'Uthmanic codex has remained as the only canonical text of the Qur'an that exists, recognised by Sunnis and Shi'is alike throughout the Muslim world for the last fourteen centuries.

Muslims have remained so faithful to the 'Uthmanic form' through the ages that although in a few cases certain features of Arabic orthography have changed, it is still adhered to in manuscripts and printed copies of the Qur'an – in spite of calls for change in accordance with what young students are used to in their study of everyday Arabic. Along with modern word-forms, students are taught to recognise the age-old, venerated forms as distinctly belonging to the writing of the Qur'an. It has thus acquired sanctity in its very orthography.[6]

The Qur'anic material that was revealed to the Prophet in Mecca is known as the Meccan material of the Qur'an, while the material that originated in Medina is known as the Medinan. In Mecca the Qur'an was setting out the basic belief system of Islam, parts of which the Arabs found very difficult to accept. They had difficulty in believing in the existence of One God, a belief encapsulated in the first creed of Islam – 'There is no god but Allah' – as they came from a mainly pagan polytheist culture. In their rejection of this, they referred, for instance, to the Christian belief in the Trinity (38:7). The Qur'an in its turn argued that both Heaven and Earth would have collapsed if they were created and governed by more than one god (21:23; 23:91). In response to the belief that God has daughters or had a son, the Qur'an asserts, 'He does not beget, nor was he begotten, neither is anyone equal to Him' (112:1–4). The second belief is in the Prophethood of Muhammad. They could not conceive how someone who eats and goes to the marketplace could be a prophet (25:7). They demanded of Muhammad that he bring an angel with him, or perform all varieties of miracles in order to prove that he was truly a prophet. The Qur'an retorted that if there were angels living on the Earth, then an angel-prophet would have been sent (17:95). The Prophet Muhammad was always commanded to say to them: 'I am only a human being, like yourselves, to whom revelation has come' (17: 90–95; 18:110). The Qur'an cites the example of former prophets, like Noah, Abraham, Moses and Jesus, who preached the same beliefs, the various responses of their communities, and how in the end prophets were vindicated.

But the most insurmountable difficulty for the Arabs was the fundamental belief in resurrection and judgement. Their incredulity at this was frequently recorded in the Qur'an as they could not conceive how, when they had become rotten bones, they could be exhumed, get up and walk again and be judged by God. The Qur'an, in its turn, argued for the possibility and inevitability of Resurrection.[7] Naturally, it would not have been suitable for the Qur'an to introduce to the small Muslim community living under constant persecution in Mecca teachings in the area of civil, criminal and international law, or to command them to fight back to defend themselves. This came in the Medinan part of the Qur'an. Much of the material placed towards the end of the Qur'an is from the Meccan era, whereas much of that in the long *sūras* at the beginning belongs to the Medinan era.

Quantitatively speaking, beliefs occupy by far the larger part of the Qur'an. Morals come next, followed by ritual, and lastly the legal provisions. Thus, the entire Qur'an contains around 6200 verses. Out of these, only 100 deal with ritual practices. Personal affairs take up seventy verses, civil laws seventy, penal laws thirty, judicial matters and testimony twenty verses.[8]

The Qur'an is not like a legal textbook that treats each subject in a separate chapter. It may deal with matters of belief, morals, ritual and legislation within one and the same *sūra.* This gives its teachings more power and persuasion, since they are all based on the belief in God and reinforced by belief in the final judgement. Thus the legal teachings acquire sanctions both in this world and the next. This will be elaborated upon further in discussions about marriage and divorce below, as well as in the chapters dealing with the style of the Qur'an.

Qur'anic material is divided into *sūras*, sections, conventionally translated into English as 'chapters'. This is an unhelpful designation, since a *sūra* might consist of no more than one line, such as *Sūras* 108 and 112, whereas *Sūra* 2, the longest in the Qur'an, consists of just under 40 pages. Each *sūra* consists of a number of verses each known in Arabic as an *āya* (sign from God). There are 114 *sūras* in all. With the exception of *Sūra* 9, each one begins with 'In the name of Allah, the Most Beneficent, the Most Merciful'. Some *sūras* contain Meccan and Medinan *āyas.* The heading of each *sūra* contains its serial number, title, whether it was Meccan, Medinan or mixed, and which verses belong to which era. The order of material in each *sūra* was determined by the Prophet, who is believed to have been acting on the instruction of the Angel of Revelation himself, who delivered the Qur'anic material to him. Western scholars – and even some Muslims in the past – have taken the view that the compilers of the Qur'anic material after the death of the Prophet determined the order of the *sūras* mainly according to decreasing length. However, the stronger evidence shows that it was all done by the Prophet who read it in this order over many years. His companions, judging by their attitude to the Prophet and Qur'anic material, would not have taken the liberty of changing anything that they had learned from him, as the word of God should not be changed in any way.[9]

The Wider Influence of the Qur'an

The collected written text of the Qur'an was the first book in the Arabic language. It was also the starting point around which, and for the service of which, the various branches of Arabic studies were initiated and developed. Thus it was in order to ensure accurate reading of the Qur'an that Arabic grammar was first developed and written down, especially when Islam began to spread outside the Arab region. The same is true of Arabic phonetics, rhetoric, modes of recitation, calligraphy and so on.

It was the Qur'an that took Arabic outside the Arabian peninsula, making it an international language that deeply penetrated important languages like Persian, Turkish, Urdu, Indonesian, Swahili, Hausa and others. Basic religious scholarship in the various countries of the Muslim world is conducted in Arabic. The first *sūra* of the Qur'an, *al-Fātiḥa,*[10] which is an essential part of the ritual prayers, is learned and read in Arabic by Muslims in all parts of the world.[11] This particular *sūra* is read in Arabic by practising Muslims at least seventeen times a day, but other verses and phrases in Arabic are also incorporated into the lives of non-Arabic-speaking Muslims. A Muslim from any part of the world, of whatever linguistic or cultural background, can lead other Muslims in the prayers, as they are performed in Arabic. Such is the far-reaching importance of the Qur'an for the Arabic language that it has in fact preserved the Arabic language. In Egypt, for instance, at the turn of this century there was a call for the adoption of English instead of Arabic, or for the Roman script for writing Arabic, or even the adoption of the Egyptian dialect of Arabic as a written language. All such calls were resisted and then rejected because they meant the demotion of the Arabic of the Qur'an to a mere relic of the past. Muslim children start to learn portions of the Qur'an by heart in their normal schooling: the tradition of learning the entire Qur'an by heart started during the lifetime of the Prophet and continues to the present day. A person attaining this distinction becomes known as a *ḥāfiẓ,* and this is still a prerequisite for admission to certain religious schools in Arab countries.

Nowadays, the Qur'an is recited a number of times daily on the radio and TV in the Arab world, and some Arab countries devote a broadcasting channel exclusively for the recitation and study of the Qur'an. A verse in the Qur'an states, 'When the Qur'an is read, listen to it with attention and keep silent so that you may be given mercy' (7:204). Reading or recitation begins, 'In the Name of God, the Beneficent, the Merciful', and ends with the customary closing phrase, 'The Almighty has spoken the Truth', indicating the sacred nature of the Qur'anic words between these two formulae.

Only those in a state of ritual ablution may touch the Qur'an and a person in a state of major ritual impurity (following sexual intercourse, for instance) may not recite it until a bath has been taken. Muslims swear by the Qur'an for solemn oaths in the law courts and in everyday life.

The Qur'an is the supreme authority in Islam. It is the fundamental and paramount source of the creed, rituals, ethics and laws of this religion. The *sunna* (or *hadīth* – sayings and actions of the Prophet) come second to it. The *sunna* derives its authority from such Qur'anic commands as 'Obey God and obey the Prophet' (v.92). To Muslims, the Qur'an is the speech of God, revealed in word and meaning, and entirely authentic in its divine authority. It is read in acts of worship: the *sunna* is not like that. The relationship between the two, however, is well-defined. The *sunna* either emphasises what is in the Qur'an (*sunna mu'akkida*), explains the manner in which something should be carried out (*sunna mubayyina*) or introduces new teachings modelled on what is in the Qur'an (*sunna muthbita*), but it does not contradict the Qur'an.

The Qur'an and its Translations

The Qur'an was revealed to the Prophet Muhammad in Arabic. Theologically, it is the Arabic version that is considered the true Qur'an, the direct word of God, and read in acts of worship. No translation is considered to be the Qur'an, or Word of God as such, and none has the same status as the Arabic. Translations are considered by Muslims merely as renderings of meanings of the Qur'an. All Muslims, Arab and non-Arab, learn and read the Qur'an, or parts of it, in Arabic, in order to have the satisfaction and blessing of uttering the holy speech, the very same words that were uttered from the mouth of the Prophet and read by his companions, and by successive generations of Muslims, in their different lands and throughout the Islamic era. No translation can claim this status. Christian readers will realise that the Qur'an clearly differs from the Bible in this respect.

The Qur'an was recited first to Arabs whose paramount gift lay in eloquence of speech and who had a rich and elaborate literature, especially poetry. Both followers *and* opponents of the Prophet recognised its literary supremacy and inimitability. Believers hearing it uttered on the spot by the Prophet, and recognising how different it was from the Prophet's day-to-day-speech, saw in this a further proof of its divine origin. One of his opponents who was in awe of the power of the Qur'an's language described it by saying, 'It ascends to the heights and nothing ascends above it, and it crushes what is beneath it.' Thus the Qur'an has a distinct style and noble grandeur that immediately sets it apart from other speech, and which Arabs, Muslims and non-Muslims, recognise. Reflecting on the text, one is constantly struck by its freshness of expression, and yet such is its nature that ordinary Arabs from all walks of life can easily understand and appreciate its powerful effects. The message of the Qur'an was originally, after all, directly addressed to these people without distinction as to class, gender or age, without any officiating priesthood. This is a language that is still in constant use in almost all social and cultural contexts.

The Qur'an has its own self-created features which unfortunately have not been fully studied in English. Knowledge of Qur'anic stylistics is essential for scholarship in this field. The Arabic science of rhetoric owes its existence to the desire of Muslim scholars to appreciate and interpret the literary aspects of the Qur'an. Yet while we find numerous books on Arabic grammar written in English over the centuries, there are in fact no parallel books on Arabic rhetoric. Important commentaries in Arabic on the Qur'an, which elucidate its rhetorical excellence, such as those by Zamakhshari (d.1143) and Fakhr al-Din al-Razi (d.1209), have not yet been translated into English. When sufficient books on these subjects are written in English they will help to solve the problems Western readers find in appreciating the Qur'an's existing English translations.

Arabs themselves find English translations of the Qur'an disappointing, unconvincing, and lacking in the cohesion, clarity and grandeur, as well as the rhythm and power of the original Qur'anic verses. A comparison between the history and manner of translation of the Bible and the Qur'an into English is useful in this regard. The Authorised Version of the Bible was translated by a group of forty-seven including clerics, scholars and men of letters working together to produce a work for King James I. The New English Bible was retranslated into modern English by a similarly large group of English-speaking people. On the other hand, the first translation of the Qur'an into English was made by Alexander Ross and printed in 1649. He called it *The Alcoran of Mahomet, the Prophet of the Turks ... newly Englished for the satisfaction of all that desire to look into the Turkish vanities.* Ross was not a specialist in the Qur'an or *hadīth,* and he did not know Arabic, but based his translation on a French version. He added a letter 'From the Translator to the Christian Reader', justifying his translation of the 'heresy of Mahomet' to satisfy his critics who almost prevented the publication of this 'dangerous book'. This was the beginning of a long tradition of translations and studies of the Qur'an in English. Some – Rodwell (1861) and Bell (1937) – sought to refute it in the light of the Bible, while others – Sale (1734), Palmer (1880), Pickthall (1930) and Arberry (1955) – brought increasing levels of scholarship in Arabic and appreciation of Arabic literature, and decreasing levels of prejudice to bear on their translations – no prejudice being apparent in the last two. There are now numerous translations in English, but not one has been made by more than one person at a time, and no Arab Muslim specialist in Qur'anic studies has made a translation. The Qur'an's unique qualities in the Arabic need to be analysed in English, and a new approach adopted towards its translation. Even the best of the available translations pose very serious difficulties in the proper appreciation and understanding of the Qur'an. The Arabic original, however, will remain to the Muslims the sacred speech 'a sublime scripture' (41:41).

Features of Style

As already mentioned, the Qur'an has its own style, and the reader should be acquainted with some important features of this style. In the remaining part of this chapter, we will discuss some of these features. The reader should not expect the Qur'an to be arranged chronologically, or in subject order. In many *sūras* it combines a number of subjects, for instance beliefs, rituals, morals and law, in order to reinforce its basic teachings. Legal matters are given more force through being related to beliefs, rituals and morals. The impressive Throne Verse (2:255), for example, about the majestic attributes of God, follows an instruction to the believers to part with their money for charity before the day comes when no money or friendship would avail them before God in all His majesty. Those who do not understand how the Qur'an presents its material for its own ends, criticise this as being jumbled.[12] Similarly in discussions about settlements in divorce, often accompanied with bitterness or over-possessiveness, the Qur'an suddenly (2:237) reminds people to 'preserve the prayer and stand before God in devotion' (2:238) before resuming discussion on the original subject.

If the Qur'an were arranged in chronological order it would have become a biography or historical record. If it were to combine different material, say about God or prayer, in one separate chapter, and insert another chapter on paying to charity and a third chapter on settling marriage disputes; if there had been a chapter on water, and one on the afterlife and one on Adam, it would not have had the powerful effect it does by using these themes to reinforce its message in various places. The Qur'an is not an academic thesis, but a book of guidance and has its own methods of *targhīb* (instilling desire) and *tarhīb* (instilling fear) so that they act together. This is an important feature of the Qur'an. Thus you find contrast in the material: wherever it speaks of Paradise and the rewards of the righteous, always next to it, it also mentions Hell and the punishment of the evildoer, since it recognises that there will always be people who do good and others who do evil (76:3). Those who feel that the Qur'an talks too much about punishment should remember that it talks also about the rewards of the righteous: God forgives and punishes (15:49–50).

Although the Qur'an was not written in the form of an edited text, and the Prophet did not interfere in its revealed order, adding connecting sentences here or there, the connection between material within each *sūra*, is understood in Arabic either by short conjunctions or pronouns, or certain words repeated, referring to the earlier material, or contrasting with it, or giving an example. It may also put material in historical order, an earlier prophet being followed by a subsequent one without a conjunction like 'then' or 'thereafter' as the order itself shows a clear connection. Sometimes the conjunction is left out but the cohesion remains. This is known in books on Arabic rhetoric as *faṣl* (disjoining). In certain situations by not joining with a conjunction you establish a certain relationship with the previous material. Verses 2:1–5 speak about the believers; verses 6ff speak of the unbelievers, without using a conjunction. The English language, which has different patterns of cohesion, may add something like 'as for the unbelievers ... such and such happens to them.' In *Sūra* 96, vv. 1–5 talk about God's grace to man in creating and teaching him. Verses 6–8 are connected by repeating the word *al-insān* (man) and by being a contrast: whereas man should have shown gratitude, he is actually arrogant and oppressive. Bell[13] saw the rest of the *sūra* as having 'hardly any connection' with the first part, when in fact it is simply giving an example of the arrogant and oppressive unbeliever who is trying to prevent a believer from worshipping his Lord. Razi, in his *tafsīr,* always shows the linguistic and logical connection, and if Bell had read him he would have changed his opinion over a vast number of examples in his translation and his commentary on the Qur'an.[14] Translators should be aware of this and should attempt to convey the Arabic into an English equivalent, supplying the expected English form. Much work has to be done in English on the cohesive devices in the Qur'an as they work in Arabic.

The early Qur'anic scribes put all the material of one *sūra* together from beginning to end without paragraphing. English translators sometimes fail to see where a section should properly begin and where it ends, and thus they disjoin material that should go together. For example, in discussions about war in *Sūra* 2, some translators start the section from v. 190, when in fact it should start from 189 and continue up to 196, not 195. This would show the connection between asking the Muslims to fight, and their being prevented from reaching the Holy Mosque of Mecca to perform the pilgrimage. The same applies in *Sūra* 22. Verse 25 talks about the unbelievers barring the Muslims from reaching the Holy Mosque, and this is where the section should begin, and continue up to v.41. Those who separate v.41 from 40 cause a disruption of the meaning, since 41 is an adjectival clause talking about people already mentioned. Those who do not put the translation into paragraphs but follow the old Arabic system also cause difficulties to the modern reader. Others, by simply putting the *āyas*, rather than the paragraphs, into separate lines, and by not being fully aware of the cohesive devices in Arabic, again cause problems.

As we shall see in discussions on the *Fātiḥah* the Qur'an has an internal logic for developing its material, even though this is not introduced in a scholastic manner. Moreover, the Qu'ran always offers justification for its message, supporting it with logical arguments, for example in explaining the unity of God (e.g. 21:21–2; 23:91; 36:78–83). More examples may be seen in the chapter on 'Life and Beyond'. The Qur'an also supports its statements with reference to the past (the history of earlier nations and prophets), to the present (nature as a manifestation of God's wisdom, power and care) and to the future (life hereafter and Judgement), in addition, of course, to constantly reminding people of God and His attributes, for example the Throne verse (2:255) and the Light verse (24:35), and 59:22–4; 57:1–10.

The Qur'an couches legal matters in language that appeals to the emotions, conscience and belief in God. Examples will be seen in the discussions on divorce. In the verses dealing with retaliation (2:178–9), once the principles are set out it goes on to soften the hearts of both parties, offender and victim. In introducing the obligation of the fast of Ramadan (2:183–7), the aim throughout is to make the fast seem easy and highly desirable. As a book of guidance, if the Qur'an reports on people's wrong views, attitudes or situations, it always comments on them by way of refutation or correction, even if this appears to interrupt the flow: there is continual dialogue. For example, 'When it is said to them, "Follow what God has revealed," they say "We will only follow what we found our fathers doing"', the answer comes in the form of a question: 'Even though their fathers were senseless men, lacking in guidance?' (2:170). Again, when man says, 'When I am once dead, shall I be raised to life' the answer comes, 'Does man forget that We created him out of the void?' (19:66–7). The unbelievers say to the believers, 'Follow our way and we will carry your sins for you'; the answer is 'They shall not carry any of their sins, they are liars, they shall bear their own burdens, and will be questioned on the Day of Resurrection about their falsehoods' (29:12–13).[15]

Another important feature of the Qur'an that should be mentioned here is that, with few exceptions such as prophets and angels, it does not name individuals, as we shall see in the story of Joseph. It consistently uses techniques of generalisation, which indicate what actually justifies a statement. One method of achieving this is the use of *ta'mīm* – words of general application like 'those who' 'whoever', giving the message universal application. Thus, in giving permission to the Muslims to defend themselves, it gives it generally to 'Those who have been driven out of their homes ...' (22:39 ff.). This will apply at any time or place. When it urges the Prophet to deliver the message, even when dealing with his own personal situation and feelings, instead of saying 'You should deliver the message and fear none but God,' it says, '... Those who deliver God's message, fearing God and fearing none beside Him, sufficient is God's reckoning' (33:39). Reformers, preachers and anyone standing for the truth can apply this readily to him or herself, because such statements are put in a proverbial manner and they are used to influence people in Muslim society. They are often quoted and hung on the walls of offices, houses, courtrooms and so on as reminders.

In the Arabic text, the removal of names does not necessarily make the verse enigmatic or difficult to follow because the contexts, some verbal connections, and the sentence structure give enough clues for the message to be understood. The Qur'an is above all a book of guidance. There is no interest in whether a particular named individual did something: if that thing is good, it is singled out as good; if it is bad it is condemned and the message is obvious to the reader. Those who are interested in academic treatment can refer to a body of literature around the Qur'an called *asbāb al-nuzūl* (normally printed in the footnotes or marginal notes) which identifies the circumstances of the revelations and refers to names and details of what actually happened. Since moving the material from its Arabic setting to another language like English removes it further from what instigated the passage, translators too need to provide these explanatory footnotes. Similarly, they need to identify the pronominal references, especially as modern English grammar does not make distinctions in the second person between singular, plural, masculine or feminine and the Qur'an sometimes shifts between persons as we shall see in the discussion on its dynamic style.

The separate alphabetical letters

At the beginning of 29 *sūras* there are sets of separate letters of the alphabet which, in translation, are normally rendered as they are. Scholars have attempted to explain the significance of these. One theory is that the Arabs were challenged that 'The Qur'an consists of letters of your own alphabet that you know well, and yet you cannot imitate it.' Others would merely say: 'God knows best'. The fact is that these letters are normally followed by statements about the Qur'an being sent down from God. They come at the beginning to alert the reader to listen to what follows, just as, in classical Arabic poetry, the poet sometimes began with an interjection, like 'Hey!' to make his audience immediately listen and pay attention.[16]

The titles of sūras

Titles of *sūras* were allocated on the basis of the theme, or an important event that occurs in the *sūra* or a significant word that appears within it, and which enabled reciters to identify the *sūra. Sūrat Yūsuf* (Chapter 11 below) and *Sūrat al-Raḥmān* (Chapter 12 below), are both thematic titles and refer to important words at or near the beginning of the *sūra*, whereas the title *al-Fātiḥa* (see Chapter 2) refers to the function of the *sūra* in opening the Qur'an.

We have discussed here a number of stylistic features that will, it is hoped, help the reader in embarking on the study of the Qur'an. To this more will be added in the course of the book and especially in the last four chapters, which deal with style.

2

Al-Fātiḥa: The Opening of the Qur'an

1. *In the name of God, the Most Beneficent, the Most Merciful*
2. *Praise belongs to God, the Sustaining Lord of all the Worlds*
3. *The Most Beneficent, the Most Merciful*
4. *The Master of Judgement Day*
5. *It is you we worship, it is you we ask for help*
6. *Show us the right way*
7. *The way of those whom you have blessed, who incur no anger and are not astray*

The Opening of the Qur'an

The above passage, *al-Fātiḥa,* is the opening *sūra* of the Qur'an. It comes also at the beginning of each *rak'a* (section) of the Islamic formal daily prayers; without it the prayer is not complete. On account of these first two functions, it has developed a third, more wide-ranging function in the social and cultural life of Muslims. Chronologically, these three functions came into being in this order and it is in this order that we shall deal with them.

This compact passage, an independent *sūra* of the Qur'an, consists of seven verses, divided into three groups: invocation, affirmation and petition, in a sequential progression that exemplifies the conclusively convincing logic of Qur'anic material. As will be demonstrated, the passage embodies the essence of Islam, which is *tawḥīd* (oneness of God).

1. The invocation: Bismillāhi-l-Raḥmāni-l-Raḥīm: In the name of God, the Most Beneficent, the Most Merciful

The invocation 'In the name of Allah', is a dedication to God. In Arabic it is also an expression on the part of the reader that s/he begins his/her act with the invocation of God, so that the act begins with, and is accompanied by, His name. The Arabic preposition *bi* has several meanings: beginning, dedication, accompaniment, and instrumentality. In this passage all these are applicable, so the preposition has multiple meanings. Unfortunately there is no equivalent word in English that carries the same range of meanings, and consequently, there is an inevitable loss in translation: the translator has to opt for one word that carries only one of these. Coming at the beginning, the preposition *bi* demonstrates one of the major problems in translating the Qur'an: the limited possibilities of conveying the wealth of the original that resides even in the smallest word. There are several examples of this even in this short *sūra.*

In Islam, 'Allah' is the name of God in the absolute sense, the only 'personal' name. All other 'beautiful' names are adjectives or attributes. In this Qur'anic verse we meet the first description of God as *al-Raḥmān, al-Raḥīm* in Arabic, the Most Beneficent, the Most Merciful. They are the most frequently recurring attributes of God in the Qur'an. Both are intensive forms of the adjective in Arabic. *Al-raḥmān* in particular is used in Arabic exclusively for God. Translators give a variety of renderings: Gracious and Merciful, Compassionate and Merciful, Beneficent and Merciful, the Merciful, the Compassionate. Both words derive from the same root in Arabic *r-h-m* the general meaning of which is 'mercy'. From the same root comes the word *raḥim* – 'womb'. Thus there is a *ḥadīth* in which God says:

> I have created the *raḥim* and given it a name derived from my name. Whoever keeps the bond (of the womb/kinship) connected I will keep him connected to me and whoever severs it I will sever him from me.

Because *raḥmān* and *raḥīm* derive from the same root, translating them into two words with different roots, like 'Compassionate and Merciful' loses the connection. Exegetes of the Qur'an have given different opinions of the meanings of these words. Some take *raḥmān* as 'showing mercy in this world and the next', with *raḥīm* applying only to the next. Others see *raḥmān* applying to believers and non-believers, and *raḥīm* to believers only; or *raḥmān* as 'Provider of Mercy' in relation to large-scale things and *raḥīm* to small scale things; or *raḥmān* as provider of mercy which only God can provide while *raḥīm* can also be provided by humans. In my opinion, the most likely meaning of *al-Raḥmān* can be derived from *Sūra* 55 named *al-Raḥmān*[1] where manifestations of God's beneficence and bounty are illustrated. In any case, the combination *al-Raḥmān al-Raḥīm* – frequent in the Qur'an – is used only for God and together they encompass all meanings of mercy and are therefore the most fitting first attributes of God in the Qur'an.

2. Al-Ḥamdu li-Llāhi, Rabbi-l-ʿĀlamīn, Praise belongs to God, the Sustaining Lord of all the Worlds:

Following the dedication, the reader's relationship with God is shown as one of praise. The generic *al-* in Arabic makes the word *ḥamd* encompass all praise.

The Qur'an explains elsewhere:

The seven heavens, the earth, and all who dwell in them glorify Him – All creatures celebrate His praise. Yet you cannot understand their praises.

17:44

In such a compact passage as the *Fātiḥa*, used at the beginning of the Qur'an and the ritual prayer, the choice of this word, *al-ḥamd*, is very fitting. This is reinforced in Arabic by the choice of the nominal rather than verbal sentence which would have limited it to a certain person or tense. (*al-*) which has this generic, general sense can also be understood as referring to a pronoun (my or our) i.e. my praise is to God. *Ḥamd* is followed by *li* the first meaning of which is: 'belongs to', but it can also mean 'is due to'. It is a declaration, an affirmation, rather than a tentative wish like the subjunctive 'be' in 'Praise be to him'. The literary multiplicity of meaning observed in the very first letter of the passage is discerned here too, as *ḥamd* in Arabic means both 'praise' and 'thanks'. The reader of Arabic understands both meanings, whereas the English translation again narrows the word to one single sense.

Praise belongs to God who has three attributes:

1. *Rabb al-ʿālamīn: Rabb* is normally translated as 'Lord' but this is rather limiting, since the Arabic word carries within it the root meaning of 'caring' and 'sustaining'. Again there is no equivalent single word in English carrying all these meanings. *Al-ʿālamīn* is translated as 'the worlds' being the plural of *ʿālam.* The exegetes state that God is the Lord of the worlds of humans, plants, earth, heavens, this world and the next, the

physical and spiritual, etc. In short, He is the Lord of everything: *Rabbu kulli shay'* (6:164). *Al-'ālamīn* occurs sometimes in the Qur'an meaning only 'all human beings'. Again, whoever reads the words in Arabic understands a multiplicity of meaning. Through praising the Cherishing Lord of all beings, one becomes aware that one is, like everything else, part of this vast creation of God, under the Lordship and care of God. The word *'ālam,* is defined in Arabic and Islamic theology as meaning *mā siwa Allāh* (what is other than God). Therefore *Rabb al-'ālamīn* singles God out as the one and only God, encapsulating in a short compact phrase this most central belief in Islam, for which the Qur'an gives many proofs.

2. *al-Raḥmān al-Raḥīm* (the Most Beneficent the Most Merciful) repeats, for emphasis, this important epithet which is central to the description of God in this *sūra.* All *sūras* (except for 9) begin with *Bismillāh al-Raḥmān al-Raḥīm* but here the description is also incorporated into the *sūra* itself. Placing mercy in the middle makes it extend to encompass His Lordship and His mastery of the Day of Judgement.
3. *Māliki Yaum al-Dīn* – Master/Sovereign/King/Ruler/Owner/Wielder of the Day of Judgement.

Here again the central theme of oneness is emphasised since no sovereignty will stand on the Day of Judgement other than God's (40:16).

Dīn is translated variously as judgement, reckoning, requital, doom, recompense. This last attribute of God is so fundamental in the Qur'an and Islamic theology and so frequently recurring, (see 'Life and Beyond' below) that a prominent place was reserved for it in this brief *sūra.* It is natural that 'Master of the Day of Judgement' comes chronologically as the last of the three attributes of God.

Adjectives are prominent in the structure of this *sūra.* We have three attributes of God here in this first part of the *sūra.* There will be two adjectives describing the path or the 'way' in the latter part of the *sūra,* and three describing the followers of that path. This adjectival scheme is important for the progression of ideas. The passage (like others in the Qur'an) has its own internal logic: God is praised, because He is Lord of all the Worlds, Most Beneficent, Most Merciful, Master of the Day of Judgement. Who, then, should be more worthy of praise than the One described in this way?

3. Affirmation: Iyyāka na'abudu wa iyyāka nasta'īn, It is you we worship and it is you we ask for help

This comes at the centre of the passage, and follows logically from the earlier part. Only when the first part has been conceded can the second follow naturally. Who is more worthy of being singled out for worship, and in seeking help, other than the caring Lord of all the Worlds, the Most Beneficent, the Most Merciful, the Master of the Day of Judgement? Because there is judgement, the judgement should be prepared for by worship. Placing the object 'you' (*iyyāka*) before the verb singles God out for worship and makes Him the only source of help, again the essence of worship and religion in Islam. In the first part of the *sūra*, praise in general is affirmed as belonging to God, whether the specific reader or worshipper is there or not. It is confined neither to a verbal subject or tense. It can be affirmed by humans, the angels or even by God Himself, at the beginning at the Qur'an. Moving to the second section, however, the reader or the servant has to affirm that he/she worships God exclusively and seeks His help. The first section prepares him for this and brings him nearer to God, to address Him. Here we have the shift from the third person to the second person – an example of *iltifāt* as an important feature of the style of the Qur'an discussed later under 'Dynamic Style'. In this central section, God is worshipped, but He also provides help. A remote God from whom help cannot be expected is not the Islamic conception of God. This is also psychologically helpful to those who are inclined to always expect something for anything they give.

4: The petition: Ihdinā ṣirāṭ al-mustaqīm, show us the right way

Having invoked God and affirmed his attributes, and his worship, and sought His help, the reader can naturally move on to seek that help more specifically in the final part of this *sūra*. Here we have one single, but crucial, request – guidance – and who can give it better than God whose praise and worship have already been affirmed? The request is not for worldly gain, but relates fundamentally to the function of the Qur'an – guidance (2:2). The single request is for guidance to the right way, and this is expressed in the concrete, tangible and definite image of *ṣirāṭ* (path or way). This image shows the believer to be moving forwards and coming to a crossroads, where only one road leads to the desired destination – God and His pleasure. It thus connects the text and leads the believer to God. The believer is active in searching and praying for divine guidance to show him that path.

The path is not described as that of Islam but it has two attributes: firstly, it is straight/right, this is the surest and shortest way to the destination; secondly, it has been tested before and proved right, taking the person to the good company of 'those whom you have blessed'; these are described elsewhere in the Qur'an (4:69) as the prophets, those who do not deviate from the Truth, martyrs and the righteous ones, 'and how goodly a company are these!' (an illustration of the principle: 'Different parts of the Qur'an explain each other'). The sequence of material makes the *sūra* convincing throughout. Who is more worthy of being praised than the Lord of the Worlds, the Merciful, the Master of the Day of Judgement? Who is more worthy of being worshipped and asked for help than Him? In the same way, who would reject a path described as being straight, leading to proven success with excellent company?

The followers of the path are described in three ways: (i) they are blessed/favoured by God. Consequently (ii) they are not the objects of anger and (iii) they are not astray. This is the persuasive nature of Qur'anic language, which in this passage does not include anything repellent or discouraging. Every section, in the way it is presented, is acceptable in itself and leads naturally to the subsequent section. The request of the believer, then, appears to be significant and perfectly acceptable to right-minded people. Blessing the followers of the path is attributed to God: 'the path of those You have blessed'. Being the object of anger and being astray are not related to God in this way. The second group is those who incur anger. Anger can be from God, the angels, human beings or other creatures. It is wrong to say: 'With Whom you are angry or wrathful', as many translators do, since this deviates from the original Arabic and adds a quality of God which does not appear anywhere in this passage. In fact the entire picture of God in *Sūrat al-Fātiḥa* is benign and beautiful, the Beneficent, Most Merciful, Caring Lord. Even as the Master of the Day of Judgement,[2] He is the Source of Help, who gives guidance and blessings. He is not said to be angry or leading people astray. Non-Muslim believers can without difficulty appreciate such a picture God, and the sentiments expressed throughout the *sūra* are equally acceptable to believers in God whether they are Muslims or non-Muslims.

Some translators render v.6 as 'Guide us into/along the straight path' meaning Islam. This is a possible meaning, with the believer (already guided to Islam as a religion) asking to be confirmed within that path, and guided along it, but it does not have to be confined to that meaning. *Hidāya*, or guidance to the right course, is required at any moment in any person's life. It is not only moral or religious guidance but the correct way of taking any action. It occurs in this sense in certain verses of the Qur'an.[3] It is those who are already Muslims who plead to God in their prayers, seventeen times spaced throughout the day, to be shown the right way in any situation. In the same way as a believer at the beginning of the *sūra* is aware of the whole creation of God. At the end of the *sūra* he is aware of the company he prays to be joined with, but also aware of others to whom he does not wish to be joined. His vision is not confined simply to his own group, and the three groups at the end of the *sūra* actually encompass all people, since anyone is either blessed on the right course or not blessed and astray from the right course.

The *Fātiḥa*, opens the Qur'an and contains its Essence. The Prophet called it *Umm al-Qur'ān* (the Mother/Essence of the Qur'an). It is seen by Muslim scholars as encapsulating the Qur'an's whole message – on God and his attributes, the relationship between Him and the world, the message that comes from Him through prophets and is to be followed, and the variety of responses and destinations of the different groups. It is natural, therefore that this 'table of contents' comes at the beginning of the Qur'an, to open it. The request, 'Guide us to the right way' in this first *sūra* is answered immediately at the beginning of the second: 'This is the book, there is no doubt about it, a guide for all the God-conscious' (2:2), and the rest of the Qur'an goes on to explain this. With the *Fātiḥa* at the beginning, the Qur'an does not begin chronologically like the Old Testament or genealogically like the New Testament.

The Function of the *Fātiḥa* in Islamic Prayers

It was the Islamic formal daily prayers that gave the Fātiḥa its most prominent role in Islamic worship and life. Reciting it is essential to the prayer, as the Prophet said: 'A prayer performed by someone who has not recited the Essence of the Qur'an in it is deficient [and he repeated the word three times], deficient, deficient, deficient.'

As it encapsulates the essence of the Qur'an, and of Islam, it is a most fitting passage as an obligatory part of Islamic prayer. It became part of the prayer very early in Islam and with the introduction of the five daily prayers during the Prophet's mission in Mecca, the *Fātiḥa* had to be recited by practising Muslims at least seventeen times a day – one of the names of the *Fātiḥa* is *al-sab' al-mathāni* (the often repeated seven verses). The prayer is the second pillar of Islam after the confession of faith, and as such it remains an obligation on all Muslims from early life right to the point of death.

As part of the prayer, the Prophet reported that God, Almighty and Sublime, has said: 'I have divided prayer between Myself and My servant into two halves, and My servant shall have what he has asked for.' When the servant says: 'Praise be to God, Lord of the Worlds,' God (mighty and sublime be He) says: 'My servant has praised Me'. And when he says: 'The Merciful, the Beneficent', God (mighty and sublime be He) says: 'My servant has extolled Me', and when he says: 'Master of the Day of Judgement', God (mighty and sublime be he) says: 'My servant has glorified Me' – and on one occasion He said: 'My servant has submitted to My power.' And when he says, 'It is you we worship and it is You we ask for help', He says: 'This is between Me and My servant, and My servant shall have what he has asked for'. And when he says: 'Guide us to the straight path. The way of those whom you have blessed; not those who incur anger or those astray', He says, 'This is for My servant, and My servant shall have what he has asked for.' (*Ḥadīth*: Muslim)

This shows the *Fātiḥa* to be a remarkable experience of worship indeed, involving believers and God throughout. The believer recites each of these short verses, knowing that God responds to every statement s/he makes in this way. The believer repeats, 'Master of the Day of Judgement; You alone we worship' – the Prophet affirmed that the first act to be evaluated at the Judgement will be the prayers.

The request, 'Guide us to the straight path', makes the prayer of daily and hourly significance in the life of the believers as they plead repeatedly to be guided in their beliefs, in their morals and practical judgements. This makes the *Fātiḥa* vital both as a plea and as a spur to seek and follow the right way.

In their prayer, the believers see themselves as part of all humanity – indeed all creation – under the caring hand of God, the *Rabb al-'ālamīn* (Lord of all the worlds). They pray to be part of the company of the blessed servants of God from the beginning of the world and in the future; to be guided, along with other blessed servants of God to the straight path. This is not just the path of the Muslims, followers of Muhammad; indeed God speaks in the Qur'an as having favoured Moses and Aaron and guided them to the straight path (37:118). The Qur'an speaks of eighteen earlier prophets in one passage (6:83–87) having been chosen by God and guided to a straight path, as well as their ancestors, descendants and brethren. This large company of believers, which Muslims pray in the *Fātiḥa* to join, is reinforced at the end of the Islamic formal prayer (*ṣalāh*), with the formula: 'Peace be to us and to the righteous servants of God.' This is followed by another invocation of the blessing of God on the Prophet Muhammad and his family, saying, 'as You have blessed Abraham and his family *fi 'l-'ālamīn* (among all humankind)'. The singularity of God is emphasised throughout: in the dedication, praise, in His names and attributes, and in being the sole object of worship and of seeking help. In contrast, the affirmation and petition are put in the plural, not the singular, so that even if an individual is praying on his own, he sees himself as part of a company of believers. The Muslim theologian and interpreter of the Qur'an, Fakhr al-Din al-Razi (606/1209) expressed this in a pleasant way, stating:

> The believer in effect is saying to God: 'I have heard Your Prophet say, "Being together is a mercy and being separated is a grief, so when I intended to praise you, I mentioned the praise of everybody, and when I wanted to worship you, I mentioned the worship of everybody, and when I asked for guidance, I asked for guidance for everybody, and when I prayed to be kept away from those rejected, I fled from all those who incur anger and all those who are astray."'[4]

The Prophet stated that 'Praying together is twenty-seven times better than praying alone.' Thus, if a Muslim enters the mosque and finds one person praying, he stands behind him taking him as 'leader', each finishing in his/her time and each gaining the special reward for praying together.

Style of the *Fātiḥa*

The passage comes in a style that suits its important functions both as a condensed summary of the Qur'an and as the centrepiece of the Islamic prayer and devotion. It is short, comprising 29 words in Arabic, and it is divided into seven short verses, written in rhythmic rhymed prose. The second sentence, for instance, consists of four words comprising God's name, praise, power, and status as Caring Lord of everything. The centrepiece, v.5, written as four words in Arabic, sums up the entire relationship of the servant to God: 'You alone we worship and of you we ask for help'.

The choice of words and structures allows for remarkable multiplicity of meaning difficult to capture in English. All existing translations show considerable loss of meaning. The words are very simple and familiar. In the first part about God they are composed of soft-sounding consonants which contrast with the latter part about human beings, especially as it reaches those who incur anger and those who are astray. There is a high degree of voicing and nasality, which gives a pleasing effect, including consonants such as l, m, n, and long u. The rhyme scheme alternates between '... *īm*' and '... *īn*' throughout. The quality of consonants and vowels does not allow for the passage to be hurriedly pronounced, and the rhymes come at crucial points, to make the reader pause where God will comment on the statement as mentioned above in the prophetic *ḥadīth.* In congregational prayer this is recited aloud by the *imām* in a resonant voice. The congregation listen to the recitation and do not join him in reciting aloud, until he comes to the end of the passage, when they all respond with a long, drawn out, resonant '*āmin*', which has the same quality of sounds and length as the preceding rhymed words. The total effect makes the *Fātiḥa* particularly fitting for the atmosphere of prayer and devotion. Its brevity and auditory qualities make this passage, which has to be recited by all Muslims of any linguistic background, easy to learn by heart and recite.

The *Fātiḥa* and the Lord's Prayer

1. Our Father, Which art in Heaven
2. Hallowed be Thy name
3. Thy Kingdom come
4. Thy will be done in earth as it is in Heaven
5. Give us this day our daily bread
6. And forgive us our trespasses
7. As we forgive them that trespass against us
8. And lead us not into temptation
9. For Thine is the Kingdom
10. The Power and the Glory
11. For Ever and Ever, Amen

Christian scholars in the West have often compared the *Fātiḥa* with the Lord's Prayer, some seeking to belittle Islam, and to show the Christian origins of Islamic teaching. H. Winkler (1928) tried to show that the Fātiḥa on the whole was 'modelled on the Lord's Prayer', although Paret (1965) considers Winkler's attempt to have failed'.[5] Muslims, on the other hand, at least in the Arabic tradition, do not show any interest in comparing these two prayers. Muslims experience no difficulty if they find similarities – in fact quite the reverse – since the Qur'an repeatedly affirms that it has come to confirm previous scriptures, all of which have the same central message. The Qur'an uses this argument with non-Muslims and with Muslims to endorse its teachings, and reinforce the faith of Muslims.

However, before going into comparisons, it should be noted that there are some textual problems. First the *Fātiḥa* is known to us in the Arabic original, and Muslims repeat the very words of the prayer read by the Prophet

Muhammad, his companions, and successive generations of Muslims up to now. The Lord's Prayer, on the other hand, is know to us only in translation. Second, whereas there is only one version of the *Fātiḥa*, there are two of the Lord's Prayer, one in Matthew 6:9–14 and a second in Luke 11:2–4, the first being longer than the second. According to Sperl, they appear to have derived from diverse liturgical origins and to have undergone a period of evolution and change before entering the gospel.[6] Sperl goes on to say that 'A reconstruction of the Aramaic originals as attempted, among others by Lohmeyer (1946) is therefore problematic.'

Moreover, it should be remembered that the contexts of the *Fātiḥa* and the Lord's Prayer are very different. The *Fātiḥa* was revealed first as part of the Qur'an, as its name indicates: the opening part, encapsulating its whole essence. In their prayer, Muslims read the *Fātiḥa* as the opening chapter of the Qur'an. As we have seen, the petition 'guide us to the straight path' is answered immediately in the following *sūra*: 'This is the book ... wherein is guidance ...' The fact that it was adopted for the daily prayer does not change its original function.

The context of the Lord's Prayer is completely different. In St Matthew's gospel, Jesus had been directing his disciples to pray in a different way from those who make a show of it or pray at great length, thinking that by doing this they will have their prayers answered. Differences in context between the *Fātiḥa* and the Lord's Prayer must have a bearing on the intention and text of each prayer, leading to differences even in shared elements that defy any claim of similarity and influence. The similarities that have been noted by earlier scholars appear to have more to do with form and quantity.

A Muslim would view the content of the *Fātiḥa* as being acceptable to Christians. There are, however, elements in the Lord's Prayer that pose difficulties for a Muslim nurtured on the *Fātiḥa*, which is universal. 'Our', limits God to a particular community and to a particular relationship of fatherhood, compared to 'The Sustaining Lord of All Creation' not the Lord of the Muslims, or the Arabs. And although 'father' is a very intimate term to Christians, Muslims would not speak of God as a 'father' or a 'son'. 'Which art in heaven' distances God from the earth as compared to the 'Sustaining Lord of all Creation'. Being in heaven does not in itself justify praise in the same way as His being Sustainer, Merciful and Master of the Day of Judgement does.

Then a Muslim will find a problem with the mood of the verbs as they occur in English: 'Hallowed be thy name, thy kingdom come, thy will be done'. In English this is all placed in the subjunctive which is rather tentative and sounds to a Muslim as if you are praying *for* God, not *to* Him. The description of God in the *Fātiḥa,* in Arabic and in English, is more affirmative: praise *belongs* to God, He *is* the Sustaining Lord of All, Master of the Day of Judgement. The affirmation at the core of the *Fātiḥa* – 'It is you we worship and it is you we ask for help' – central to the Islamic experience of worship and prayer, is not contained in the Lord's prayer. The petition is also different: there is one request in the *Fātiḥa* – for guidance – compared to 'Give us our daily bread, forgive our trespasses, lead us not into temptation'. Guidance is forward-looking, required by anyone in any action to be done, whereas forgiveness is more to do with sins already done. Moreover, 'Guide us' is positive; by comparison 'Lead us not into temptation' is not so positive: it merely keeps them away from temptation, but does not advance from there. 'Forgive us our trespasses as we forgive them that trespass against us, (rendered by C. W. F. Smith[7] 'as we have also forgiven them') could appear to turn the human action into an example to be followed by God. In the Qur'an, 'God's is the highest example' (16:60). It is of course more binding for the believer to think that in order to be forgiven by God, he himself should first forgive others. The Qur'an states this in 24:22 and 4:149, but it does not use the form, as it appears in the English text of the Lord's Prayer, which seems to make humans an example for God to follow.

A Muslim who is used to the logical and conclusive sequence of ideas in the *Fātiḥa* would not understand the final part of the Lord's prayer in Matthew: 'for Thine is the Kingdom, the power and the Glory', coming as it does after, 'As we forgive them that trespass against us'. According to the logic of the *Fātiḥa,* this line should have come right at the beginning, together with 'hallowed be thy name', not as a reason for forgiving us our trespasses as in the English version. Justification in the *Fātiḥa* is more obvious: you praise God because He is the 'Lord of ...', and only after such praise does it come naturally that He is the One to be worshipped and from whom help is to be sought. Only after this is it natural to ask for help. The request for guidance to the path is justified by its being straight and proven, wishing to be with that particular company is justified by its being blessed, and not the object of anger, or astray. The sequence is logical and conclusive. This does not come out clearly in the English version of the Lord's prayer. The *Fātiḥa* also contains belief and worship and the way of living, the path; it is a summary fitting for the beginning of the scripture as well as for repetition by the believers in daily life.

The Lord's Prayer has a different purpose and is different in scope from the *Fātiḥa.* The frequency of use of the *Fātiḥa,* and its social function, are wider than those of the Lord's Prayer. In the end, it is salutary to repeat

Muslim scholars' affirmation at the end of discussions *wa'llāhu a'lam* (and God knows best). As stated above, Muslims do not take an interest in comparing the two prayers. Nor should comparison be pursued with disregard to the different contexts of the two texts. Each prayer has sustained, in its own way, and will continue to sustain, the spiritual life of countless believers throughout their history; and both have in common the earnest desire to glorify God and eagerness to please Him.

The *Fātiḥa* in Muslim Life

As it is the first *sūra* in the Qur'an and the centrepiece of Muslim daily prayer, this concise passage plays a much wider role in Muslim life. It is the first part of the Qur'an that children learn – and it opens their education. In schools they can be heard chanting it in groups. Learning it in Arabic gives it a unifying function between Muslims throughout the world, and inspires non-Arabs to start learning more Arabic later in life. Its blessing is sought on numerous occasions in Muslims' lives. Before contracting marriages, when the two parties have agreed, they have a *Fātiḥa* reading ceremony to seal the agreement – and this opens the marriage. Going back on such a reading of the *Fātiḥa* is thought to have serious consequences. No other man is allowed to think of proposing to a girl, once 'her *Fātiḥa* has been read'. In commercial deals it has a similar function: it is read for its binding force, and the blessing it gives to the undertaking. Before entering exams, students may read the *Fātiḥa* to give them strength and hope for success.

Other names of the Fātiḥa are *al-Shafi'a* (the Healer), and *al-Kāfiya* (the Sufficient). When asking God earnestly to heal a sick person, or to lighten a difficulty, Muslims resort to the *Fātiḥa.* Even after a person's death, the *Fātiḥa* continues to be recited, to invoke mercy on his/her soul. In fact funeral receptions are called, in some Middle-Eastern countries, 'the reading of the *Fātiḥa*'. When people are talking about a departed person – even a long-departed one – they may read the *Fātiḥa li-rūḥihi* (for his soul). When seeking the blessing of saints, people read the *Fātiḥa* and then ask God to answer their prayer, for the sake of the saint.

In art the *Fātiḥa* figures prominently. In calligraphy, it offers a central motif, inspiring artists in endless variety, and is hung in houses and offices like a prized possession or used for decorating mosques. This decoration can be either the whole of the *Fātiḥa*, or a single verse, usually verse one (referred to in Arabic as the *bismillāh*) or two (the praise), or five: 'It is You we worship and from You we seek help'.

Circular design of the 'Fātiḥa'

The 'Basmalah' in a mirror design

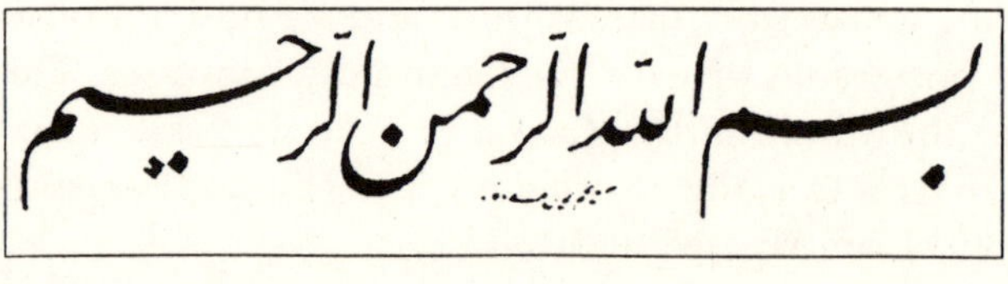

The 'Basmalah' in Ta'liq script

The 'Basmalah' in calligraphic design 'Ṭughra'

Osman Waqialla

The 'Basmalah' in modern stylised calligraphy

The concept of 'opening' in the name of the *Fātiḥa* is ever present in the life of a Muslim. It has become a favourite source of personal names in various forms – Fātiḥ, Fatḥi, Fattūḥ, Fatḥiya, Fatiḥa – all with the connotation of opening. Short prayers such as 'May God open for you' (*Allāh yiftaḥ 'alayk*) are part of everyday language, and the Prophet recommended, when entering the mosque to pray, 'Lord open the gates of Your mercy for me' (*Allāhumma iftaḥ lī abwāb raḥmatik*). If a deal falls through, in a shop for instance, the vendor will say '*yaftaḥ Allāh*' when declining to sell, meaning 'God will open other opportunities for me'.

Individual verses, or parts of a verse, play an important role, especially '*bismillāh*' (in the name of God). As the Prophet said, any serious matter that does not begin with '*bismillāh*' would be imperfect and incomplete. On the instruction of the Prophet it is the grace before eating, before speaking in public (even as a panellist on TV), on leaving the house in the morning, or returning to it, before sleeping, or sexual intercourse with one's spouse. Indeed, as Razi explains in a beautiful passage, quoting prophetic authority:

> When the midwife receives a new baby she should say *bismillāh,* or the deceased is being laid to rest, those doing it should say *bismillāh.* On rising from the grave, and again on reaching the place of Judgement, each person should repeat *bismillāh.*

Reciting this phrase invokes the help and protection of God in every task. The *Fātiḥa* is the opening to all good things.

3
Water in the Qur'an

We made from water every living thing (21:30)

In this concise and powerful statement, the Qur'an sums up the importance of water and draws attention to it, and in perusing the Qur'an one finds that water is a major theme. The word 'water' occurs over sixty times, 'rivers' over fifty and 'the sea' over forty, while 'fountains', 'springs', 'rain', 'hail', 'clouds' and 'winds' occur less frequently. The Qur'an, however, is not a science text-book, and it does not discuss the chemistry and physics of water. Rather it is a book 'for the guidance of mankind'. As we shall see, it treats the theme of water in its own way and for its own objectives. Water is seen not merely as an essential and useful element, but as one of profound significance, and with far-reaching effects in the life of individual Muslims and for Islamic society and civilisation. From the Qur'anic treatment of the theme of water we also learn much about the patterns of persuasion in the Qur'an as well as its characteristic language and style.

In discussing water as one of the most precious resources on earth, the Qur'an speaks of two kinds of water, fresh water and sea water, 'one palatable and sweet, the other salt and bitter' (29:53), pointing out some of their qualities and benefits, a division which we will conveniently follow.

Fresh Water

As will be seen, there are extensive references to fresh water in the Qur'an. Although the Qur'an states that, 'God is the Creator of all things and He is guardian over all things' (39:62) and that 'He created everything and ordained it in due proportion' (25:2) – both axiomatic in Islam – it does not just state that He *created* fresh water: that would be rather remote from the reader. Instead, the Qur'an involves people in what they can observe of the processes that generate water and produce its benefits, and invites them to look and reflect:

It is God who drives the winds that raise the clouds and spreads them along the sky as He pleases and causes them to break up so that you can see the rain issuing out from the midst of them.

30:48

The Qur'an frequently speaks of the winds and the heavy clouds that God raises (13:12):

In the marshalling of the winds, and in the clouds that are driven between earth and sky: surely in these there are signs for people who have sense.

2:164

It is He Who drives the winds, glad tidings heralding His mercy, and We send down pure water from the sky.

25:48

Do they not see how we drive the rain to the barren land and bring forth therewith crops of which their cattle eat, and they themselves? Have they no eyes to see with?

32:27

Such statements frequently begin with 'It is God ..., It is He Who ...', as a reminder that the origin of fresh water is with God and not man. This is further emphasised by the significant words, 'from the sky ...', immediately removing the source of water from the terrestrial realm, where men could claim they have made it, and pointing out how God brings it down from that higher source. The unbelievers are thus challenged in the Qur'an:

Consider the water which you drink. Was it you that brought it down from the rain cloud or We? If We had pleased, We could make it bitter: why then do you not give thanks?

56:68–70

The repetition of 'from the sky' also draws attention to the surface paradox that the sky contains water held there by His power and at will He 'brings it down'; the Qur'an never says 'it falls'. Since water is of such vital importance, human beings are reminded, '... you are not the holders of its stores ...' (15:22). Rather:

There is not a thing but with Us are the storehouses of it, and We do not send it down except in a known measure.

15:21

God 'drives' the water-laden clouds (7:57) to a certain land; causing the water to fall for whomsoever He wishes, and diverting it away from whomsoever He wishes (24:43). Thus, both the sources and disposal of fresh water are exclusively in the hand of God while we are only invited to observe, reflect and rejoice in the benefits of this life-giving substance.

Benefits

The benefits of this gift from God are often pointed out. Drinking is naturally a high priority:

And We send the water from the sky and give it to you to drink.

15:22

We provided you with sweet water.

77:27

We send down pure water from the sky, that We may thereby give life to a dead land and provide drink for what We have created – cattle and men in great numbers.

25:48–49

Interestingly, in this instance, and in others, cattle occur first, showing God's mercy to animals and grace to man – a humbling thought, since animals are a source of food and drink for man. God uses 'We', the plural of majesty, in drawing attention to all these acts. With water He gives life to animals, humans and to the earth itself:

There is a sign in the water which God sends down from the sky and with which he gives life to the earth after its death, dispersing over it all manner of beasts.

2:164

He sends it down in due measure (43:11). The earth is revived to produce what benefits man and beast, and the Qur'an repeatedly enumerates such products, detailing the observable phases they go through, and inviting the reader to look upon them:

It is He Who sends down water from the sky and with it brings forth the buds of every plant. From these We bring forth green foliage from which We bring forth the thick-clus-

tered grain, palm-trees laden with clusters of dates within reach, vineyards and olive groves and pomegranates [which are] alike and different. Look upon their fruits when they bear fruit and upon its ripening, surely in these there are signs for true believers.

6:99

Water is *driven* to the dead land, *caused* to fall on it '... and with it we bring forth all manner of fruit (7:57) ... fruits of different hues ... (35:27) Watered with one water, yet We make some excel others in taste' (13:4). Water has, moreover, a dramatic and beautifying effect on earth which men are directed to observe:

Do you not see that God sends down water from the sky and then the earth becomes green on the morrow?

22:63

You see the earth barren and lifeless, but when We send down water upon it, it thrills and swells and puts forth every joyous kind of growth.

22:5

The Qur'an deals with material very intimate to human beings, things taken perhaps too much for granted for them to reflect upon. By pointing such things out and emphasising their phases and stages, the Qur'an refreshes people's sensitivity to them and invites reflection on them:

Let man reflect on the food he eats: how We pour down the rain in torrents; We open the soil for the seed to grow; how We bring forth the corn, the grapes and the fresh vegetation, the olive trees and the palm trees, the thickets, the fruit-trees and the green pastures, for you and your flocks to enjoy.

80:24–32

Cleanliness

For Muslims, water serves another important daily function: cleansing and purification for worship and for reading or touching the Qur'an. Performing the daily prayers, spread as they are throughout the day, requires cleaning of the body, clothes and place of prayer. This is done by ablution (*wuḍū'*), which in Arabic suggests brilliance and glow, especially in the face. The Prophet states that those who do it well for their prayers will come on the Day of Judgement with light on their faces and ankles. *Wuḍū'* is the minor ablution, but there is also the requirement of a major ablution, *ghusl*, full washing of the body after sexual intercourse, at the end of menstruation and confinement. It is described in the Qur'an as a means of physical, psychological and spiritual purification and uplift (8:11). Thus we read in the Qur'an that God, 'sends down water from the sky to cleanse you' (8:11). Muslims are ordered, 'Cleanse your garments' (74:4) and the Qur'an stresses: '[God] loves those who purify themselves' (9:108). As the Prophet said, 'Cleanliness is part of faith,' and in the Qur'an the instruction to cleanliness is a favour that warrants thanksgiving:

O you who believe, when you rise to pray, wash your faces and your hands as far as the elbow, wipe your heads, and your feet to the ankle. If you are polluted, cleanse yourselves ... God does not wish to burden you, but desires to purify you and to perfect His favour to you and that you may give thanks.

5:6

The Prophet urged his followers to cleanse themselves particularly for such a gathering as the Friday prayer 'even if a glass of water would cost a dinar'. Cleanliness, then, means completing one's faith, perfection of God's favour, brilliance in this world and the next; it is the gateway to prayer and reading the Qur'an and a means to attain God's love.

Ground-water

Understandably, there is a noticeable emphasis on water from the sky as a source of water for drinking, irrigation and cleanliness, but water on and in the ground also figures prominently:

... channels flow, each according to its measure.

13:17

He led it through springs in the earth.

39:21

One of the stores of fresh water provided by God is in the ground. He 'lodged it in the earth' (22:18), a gift made clear through contemplation of what would happen if it were to sink too far down to make it recoverable:

Say: 'Think: if all the water that you have were to sink down into the earth, who would give running water in its place?'

67:30

The main channels of fresh water are rivers, and they recur over fifty times in the Qur'an. They are described as the vessels of abundant 'running' water; the epithet forms a collocation with 'river' in the Qur'an, emphasised by the noticeable juxtaposition of the mountains, 'standing firm' on earth, with the rivers (16:15; 27:61).

The fundamental importance of rivers for cooling, irrigation and aesthetics is borne out by the frequent statements in the Qur'an about Paradise 'underneath which rivers flow' (5:119 and *passim*).[24] Paradise is almost always connected with running rivers and 'is better and more lasting' than this world (87:17). Its inhabitants will drink of a cup 'from a fountain, making it gush forth plenteously' (76:5–6). They will drink to their hearts' content, a reward for what they did in their life on earth (76:24). All this gives water a particular and more lasting significance for Muslims.

Sea Water

In the language of the Qur'an and classical Arabic in general a large perennial river is called *baḥr*, and the same word as is used for 'sea'. In a number of cases the Qur'an compares fresh and sea water, speaking of them as *al-baḥrayn* (the two *baḥrs*). The majority of translators render this as 'the two seas', which is confusing to the reader. Yusuf Ali opts for 'the two bodies of flowing water', which is to be preferred. Both of them are signs of God's power and grace, subjected by God to human beings for the common benefits they derive from them.

From each you eat tender fish and bring up ornaments to wear, and you see the ships plough their courses through them, so that you may seek His bounty and may be thankful.

35:12

These benefits are mentioned many times in the Qur'an. The vital difference between fresh water and sea water is emphasised:

The two are not alike, the one fresh, sweet and pleasant to drink from while the other is salt and bitter.

35:12

Had he wishes, he would have made drinking water bitter.

56:65

The two kinds of water meet, yet He has set a barrier between them which they do not overrun.

25:53

The benefit of using the sea for transportation is strongly emphasised in the Qur'an, as a sign of honour from God:

We have honoured the sons of Adam; and provided them with transport on land and sea.

12:70

This is fitting for Muslims who are urged in the Qur'an to travel and seek the bounty of God (4:100; 73:20). Islam, which encourages travel, has set aside for the wayfarer a share in the *zakāt* (welfare due). The Qur'an reminds people:

It is He Who conveys you on the land and the sea.

10:22

Ships float and run by His command and He keeps the ships from sinking and the sky from falling, except by His own will.

22:65

The sea is used as a metaphor for the vastness of God's power. It is 'kept filled' to perform its functions (52:6). It contains a proverbial volume of water:

Say: 'If the waters of the sea were ink with which to write the words of my Lord, the sea would surely be drained before His words were finished'.

18:109

This boundless sea, with all that it contains, is encompassed by God's knowledge:

And He has knowledge of all that land and sea contain.

6:59

The vast volume of water, originally a sign of God's power and grace, can be a source of peril from which His mercy alone can save people. He delivers them from darkness and harm on the sea when they call out to him humbly and in secret:

Say: Who delivereth you from the darkness of the land and sea? Ye call upon Him humbly and in secret, [saying]: If we are delivered from this [fear] we will be truly thankful.

6:63

And when harm toucheth you upon the sea, those that ye call upon (for succour) fail, save for Him (alone).

17:67

Here again, all the material serves to emphasise the central belief in Islam: *tawḥīd* (the oneness of God). It is He who created the sea, it is He who made it suitable for human benefit and it is He who delivers people from its dangers.

Language

It will have become clear from the earlier part of this chapter that the language the Qur'an employs in speaking of water is lively and full of movement. Water is vital to life, and the language the Qur'an employs for it is full of vitality. The winds 'drive' the clouds; God 'sends down' water which 'revives' the earth. He 'leads it through' springs and 'flowing' rivers, He 'splits' the earth and with water 'brings forth' plants and fruits, etc. The movement indicated is quick, using the conjunction of speed (*fa*) and the conjunction of surprise (*idhā*) (30:48; 41:39). He sends down water and the earth 'becomes green on the morrow'. This is intensified by personification: the earth is 'barren and lifeless' and 'lowly', but when God sends down water on it 'it thrills and swells', the effects of the rain are 'the marks/prints of God's mercy':

He sends the winds, harbingers pacing along close in front of/between the two hands of His approaching mercy.

25:48

He sends down saving rain for them when they have lost all hope and spreads abroad His mercy.

42:28

The same intensity used in drawing attention to fresh water is also shown in references to the sea:

It is He Who conveys you on the land and sea, until when you are in the ships, and they sail, carrying them in a pleasant wind, a violent wind overtakes them, and billows surge upon them from every side, and they fear that they are encompassed, then they pray to God with all fervour: Deliver us from this peril and we will be truly thankful.

10:22

The intensity and richness of the language is enhanced by the employment of *iltifāt*, a prominent feature of the Qur'an as will be seen later.[25] It is frequently used with water and involves a sudden grammatical shift for a desired effect, in this case from the singular to the plural, while continuing to refer to the same person. The shift occurs at a significant point in the sentence. Thus we read:

It is He who drives the winds, glad tidings heralding His mercy, and We send down pure water from the sky, that We may give life thereby to a dead land and provide drink to what We have created – cattle and men in great numbers.

25:48–9

Qur'anic statements about water remind people of its importance to their very survival, their drink, their food, the survival of their animals, plants and crops. Sometimes they are made to contemplate the terrible opposite:

We could take it [drinking water] all away.

23:18

If We willed, We could make it bitter.

56:70

In contrast with the benign nature of water manifested in such adjectives as 'purifying', 'blissful', 'fresh', 'saving', 'mercy', man is sometimes reminded of the destructive side of water, when, instead of being sent down in due measure it is 'loosed', made to 'rise high', and 'billows surge from every direction', 'when nothing could provide protection from the flood' (11:43)

When We opened the gates of heaven with pouring water and caused the earth to gush forth with springs.

54:11

People are regularly directed to 'look', 'observe', 'think' and 'contemplate'. On numerous occasions, verses end with 'In this there are signs for people who think/ who hear/ who have sense'. 'Can they not see, will they not give thanks?' (7:58; 13:2–4; 32:27; 36:34–5). Thus in discussing water, man's senses, emotions and reason are constantly brought into play.

Purposes of Referring to Water

Unlike a text-book, the Qur'an does not discuss water in a separate chapter, but in the course of many *sūras* in a way that serves three main purposes.

Firstly, it is used as a proof of God's existence, unity and power. This is indicated by such phrases as 'of His signs', 'in this there are signs' 'It is God/He that'; and questions like:

Who is it that sent down water for you from the sky with which We caused to spring forth joyous orchards? Try as you may you cannot cause such trees to grow, was it another god beside God?

27:60

And consider the water which you drink. Was it you that brought it down from the cloud or We?

56:68

The Qur'an employs a well-defined set of verbs in the Arabic causative form, showing how God originates both water and its effects – verbs like 'sent down', 'revived', 'brought forth', 'gave to drink', 'to purify you with', 'subjected the sea ...' (45:12). Water is not simply there, it does not fall by itself, nor does the earth revive itself or plants come out by themselves. It is God who does all these things *bi'l-mā'* ('with' or 'by means of' water), and this preposition, *bi*, recurs regularly. So also does *min* 'from' water, emphasising over and over again that this vital element is instrumental in His act of creation.

Secondly, it is used as a proof of God's care. This is always indicated by the prepositions 'for you', 'to you', which accompany statements about sending down, bringing forth, or subjecting, 'for you and your flocks to enjoy', 'out of His mercy', and is implied in the contemplation of the opposite (56:65, 67:30):

Thirdly, water, with its effects, is further used in the Qur'an as a proof of the Resurrection. The unbelievers frequently argue in the Qur'an: how, when they have died and been turned into 'dust and bones', can they be restored to life? (56:47). Amongst the answers the Qur'an gives to this type of logic is the effect of water on the dry and barren earth.

He that gives it life will restore the dead to life.

41:30

Likewise you shall be brought forth.

30:19

In fact the Qur'an uses the very same verb, *akhraja*, for 'bringing forth' people out of their mother's womb (16:78), 'bringing forth' plants from the earth (32:27) and 'bringing forth' people from the earth at the resurrection (7:75). Likewise the same verbal root, *ḥayaya*, is used in 'making every *living* thing from water', '*giving life* to earth' and 'He who *gave* it *life* will *give life* to the dead'. Such a linguistic method enhances the pattern of persuasion used in the Qur'an.

The belief in God's existence, unity, power and care and in the resurrection are fundamental in Islam. Using water as proof of these lends it a deeper significance and explains why it is so frequently referred to in the Qur'an.

Guidance on the Use of Water

The Qur'an provides practical teaching about the use of water. Since it is God who 'made from water every living thing', and it is He who sent down fresh water from the sky out of His grace and mercy and gave it lodging in the earth, this vital resource should not be monopolised by the powerful and privileged and kept from the poor. References in the Qur'an to water distribution, for example, 'Tell them that water is to be divided between them' (54:28),[26] 'provide the basis upon which much legal thought was formulated' in Islamic law.[27]

Accordingly, the Prophet said, 'People are co-owners in three things: water, fire and pasture' and 'God does not look with favour upon three kinds of people'. One of these is '... a man who has surplus water near a path and denies the use of it to a wayfarer.' The Prophet told this story:

> While a man was walking, he became thirsty. He went to a well and drank from it. Afterwards he noticed a dog sniffing at the sand because of thirst. The man said to himself, 'This dog is suffering what I have suffered', so he filled his shoe with water and held it for the dog to drink. He then thanked God who bestowed upon him forgiveness for his sins. The Prophet's companions asked, 'Are we also rewarded for (kindness to) animals?' He answered, 'There is a reward for (kindness to) every living thing.'

The Prophet said, 'He who withholds water in order to deny the use of pasture, God withholds from him His mercy on the day of resurrection.'

Muslim jurists in general recognise man's urgent need for water as well as the necessity of providing water for animals. A man who is thirsty is permitted to fight another, though without the use of any weapon, if the other has water and denies him the right to quench his thirst.[28] A tradition records that 'Umar made some owners of water pay the *diya* (blood money) for a man who died of thirst after they had refused his request for water.'

In addition to the prohibition on monopoly of water, there is the prohibition on excess and wastefulness in using water. Readers are reminded by the Qur'an that water resources are not inexhaustible:

We sent down water from the sky according to a determined measure.

23:18

Eat and drink but do not be excessive; He loves not the extravagant.

7:31

To train his followers in using water economically, the Prophet said: 'Excess in the use of water is forbidden, even if the user has the resources of a whole river at his disposal.' Wasting such precious resources is strongly condemned:

Do not squander [your substance] wastefully, for the wasteful are the devil's brothers.

17:26

It is forbidden, moreover, to pollute water. Out of His grace, God sent it down from the sky 'pure', 'for you', 'to cleanse you with it' (25:47; 8:11), to give drink to animals and humans in great numbers (25:49). Thus in Islamic law it is forbidden to urinate in water. Polluting rivers and seas goes against the functions and purposes stated for them in the Qur'an, it is corruption:

Corruption doth appear on land and sea because of [the evil] which men's hands have done.

35:41

God created the earth:

And blessed it and measured therein its sustenance.

4:10

Pollution that disturbs plant, animal, or sea life disturbs the balance in 'measurement' and is a long way from 'rendering thanks' for the blessing of water. Thus in Islam, refraining from monopolising water, wasting or polluting it is not merely a matter of being wise, civilised, or showing good conduct as a citizen – it is, above that, an act of worship.

Water in Islamic Society

It is natural that Qur'anic teaching should have a far-reaching effect on Islamic life, as shown in the attitude of Muslims to water, whether related to this world or the world to come, in the rituals, the law, in Islamic art and architecture and in Islamic civilisation in general. We have already mentioned the emphasis on cleansing one's body and clothes which is a condition observed several times a day for the five-times-daily prayer, one of the 'pillars' or basic duties, of Islam. It is no wonder that before the advent of modern civilisation, public baths were an important feature of Islamic cities and recorded in great numbers in classical writings. Drinking fountains (*sabīl*) also became an architectural feature of Islamic cities, their facades adorned with calligraphic Qur'anic references to drinking in Paradise; so did watering places for animals. Religious endowments, with elaborate and exquisitely detailed Deeds of Trust, many of which have survived, were made to ensure the continued maintenance of such institutions.[29] Traditional Islamic gardens were inspired by the Qur'anic descriptions of Paradise, underneath whose trees 'rivers flow'.[30]

In powerful language, the Qur'an impresses on the minds of its readers that it is water that sustains plants, animals and humans with all their cultures and civilisations. This vital sign of God's existence, power and grace is truly worthy in the Qur'an of thankful recognition and gratitude to its Maker who used it to make 'every living thing'. An instrument of cleanliness and beauty; it is not to be monopolised, wasted or polluted and it is an essential feature of the best that Muslims aspire to in the life to come.

4
Marriage and Divorce

Islam is the religion of marriage and only allows divorce in order to create better marriages. The Qu'ran encourages marriage in many ways and makes it the only avenue for satisfying the sexual instinct.[1] It urges society to bring about the marriages of unmarried men or women,[2] and instructs unmarried people to remain chaste until God provides for them out of His bounty.[3] They become married and share in this blessing which figures prominently in Qur'anic discussions of God's blessings to mankind:

One of his signs is that He created for you from among yourselves spouses so that you may find repose in them and He ordained affection and mercy among you. Surely in this there are signs for people who reflect.

30:21

It reminds men, 'Your wives are a garment to you and you are a garment to them' (2:188), suggesting that marriage provides warmth, comfort and protection. It also strengthens human relationships by acquiring relatives through marriage (25:54) and provides a means of acquiring offspring. 'God has made for you spouses from among yourselves and through them has given you children and grandchildren and provided you of the good things' (16:72). Such is the importance of marriage that it is part of the ultimate reward believers hope for: going to Paradise where both spouses will be joined together, along with the righteous ones among their parents and offspring (13:23; 52:20–21; 25:74).

In line with Qur'anic teachings the Prophet Muhammad, who is the model for all Muslims to follow, had a rich, successful married life and said marriage was part of the way of life he brought, and whoever shunned that way of life did not belong with him. Christ does not provide such a model of marriage for Christians, nor did he urge his followers to marry in a similar way. Whereas celibacy is meritorious for those who devote themselves to religious life in Christianity, the Qur'an denounces it as a human invention.[4]

Because Islam attached such importance to marriage it makes it easy to enter into. There is no bureaucracy involved in getting married and the wedding ceremony is short and simple, requiring no more than a proposal and acceptance spoken in front of two witnesses, and a the payment of the dowry to the woman. There is no requirement for an official place or person or any specified time.

In common with the treatment of other themes, the Qu'ran mainly talks about marriage in general terms, giving some recommendations as stated above. It is not a detailed text guiding people in the conduct of daily lives, and goes into detail only in the following areas: (1) when it talks about what is forbidden, or situations that lead to forbidden things; (2) when it talks about people's rights; (3) when it replies to specific questions that have been asked.

Thus the Qu'ran lists all classes of people that one is not allowed to marry, then declares: 'beyond that is made lawful for you to marry' (4:24). It lists individuals' inheritance rights in great detail (4:11–13; 4:176) and the rights of women are protected – the right to the dowry, lodging and maintenance, and the legitimacy of offspring. The Qur'an sets out rights for the wife and then allows her to willingly waive some, such as the dowry if she chooses (4:4, 24).

The general statements in the Qu'ran are normally elaborated in the *ḥadīth* of the Prophet. For instance, the Qur'an recommends that men should consider the importance of piety when choosing a wife (2:221) and the Prophet elaborates on this in the *ḥadīth.* He explains that a woman may be sought for marriage for four reasons: her wealth, her beauty, her family or her piety, but the Prophet recommends that a man choose a woman of piety otherwise he will end up empty-handed. This stresses the importance of starting families on solid foundations, so that the marriage can last.

According to the teachings of the Prophet, no one should be forced to marry anyone that they do not desire. It is the husband's responsibility to pay the dowry and to provide for his wife and family. The way that both husband and wife should conduct themselves in marriage is set out in the Qur'an. Marital relationships should involve the qualities of affection, repose and mercy, and the example of the Prophet is the recommended norm. He says 'the best of you are those who are best to your families'. Consultations which are enjoined on all Muslims in conducting their common affairs become important in marriage, and we find mutual acceptance and consultations occurring frequently, always in the reciprocal form: *tarāḍ, tashāwur* (2:234; 65:6; 2:232). Another frequent term or expression is *ma'rūf,* which means what is good and commendable. Indeed, this occurs four times in one page (2:232–236). Thus compulsion within marriage is prohibited (2: 231,232).

The marriage contract is considered to be a very strong bond, which should stop injustice or ill-treatment.[5] The physical relationship is considered very important, and God commands the believer to partake in it, saying: 'Seek what God has ordained for you'.[6] Accordingly, the Prophet considered this a meritorious act. When one of the companions said, 'How can this be so?' the Prophet explained, 'If you did it with someone other than your wife, would you not be punished for it? Equally you will be rewarded for it when it will be with your wife.'

The Prophet recommended that men should approach the physical relationship with proper affection and the right mood for both parties, saying, 'Let none of you fall upon his wife like a donkey falls upon a she-donkey'. When women are menstruating, husbands should not have intercourse with them as it is painful and unclean (2:222). We know from *ḥadīth* that there is no ban on anything other than full intercourse.

When the Muslims migrated from Mecca to Medina the men found the women of Medina bashful and only willing to sleep with their husbands lying on their side. So the Muslim men asked the Prophet if there was anything wrong with such sexual positions. The answer came in the Qur'an, 'Women are your fields. Go then into your fields whence you please. Forward good deeds for yourself (for the Judgement day). Be conscious of God and know that you shall meet Him and give good tidings to the believers (2:223).' So even in this intimate situation, they are reminded that they should 'forward good deeds' for themselves. The good deed here is to make the marriage as God has intended, full of affection and mercy, and any misbehaviour in this intimate situation will be recorded and they will face the consequences of their bad or good acts on Judgement Day when they will meet God. The Prophet was asked if it was lawful for men to practice the only form of contraception that was available to them, coitus interruptus, and Muslim jurists have said that this should only be done if the wife consents to it.

Both husbands and wives are reminded that they should literally 'guard their private parts' from approaching others or being approached by other than the lawful person (33:35). Believers are described in the Qur'an as,

'Those who pray: "Our Lord, give us full contentment and joy in our spouses and offspring and make us an example to be followed by the pious"' (25:74). The Prophet advised that if a man sees a woman and feels any desire for her he should rush to his wife. The Prophet says that the best pastime for a husband is to play with his wife, or to train his horse, and the best money spent is money spent on your wife. Placing some food in the mouth of your wife is a meritorious act. The husband who is responsible for maintaining his family should not squander his money or even give it away in charity to the disadvantage of the family. When a companion of the Prophet asked him whether he should give away all his wealth to charity, the Prophet said no. The man said 'Can I give half?' The Prophet said no. 'A third?' and even that was too much. It is better for you to leave your family well provided for if you die rather than leave them to beg from people. He also said, 'Only a good man treats women well, and only a mean man treats them badly'.

Islam protects married life in many ways. It enjoins chastity on everybody and stipulates a deterrent penalty for violation and defamation of character. No-one should go into other people's houses without the owner's permission; and men and women who are not married and are outside the family circle should not mix freely within houses when they are alone together (33:27–31, 58–61).

Polygamy is permitted in the Qu'ran. Unlike marriage and divorce, it is only mentioned once, and only incidentally rather than having a separate section or verse devoted to it. It is only permitted with the proviso that if you feel you may not be equitable to co-wives then you may only marry one (4:3). So it is neither obligatory or highly recommended, merely allowed in certain circumstances.

Muslim scholars have written in justification of this institution.[7] They argue that in some marriages it can be advisable if, for instance, the first wife is unwell or has lost interest in marital relations, or cannot bear children. If the husband is barred from marrying another wife he may find no alternative to divorcing the present wife. In such circumstances, if polygamy was not allowed, men could be driven towards having an illicit relationship. In situations where women outnumber men, polygamy also provides a solution in a religious morality that does not allow sexual relationships outside marriage.

Women cannot be forced into polygamy, as the second wife enters into the marriage freely and the first wife, or any wife, could stipulate in the marriage contract that the husband may not enter into another marriage without her consent. This is practised by some women in Muslim countries today. Polygamy can actually increase the number of marriages in society, and properly entered into, can protect marriage and lessen the need for divorce.

Difficulties in Marriage

The Qu'ran instructs men to live with their wives *bi'l-ma'rūf*, with kindness, according to the accepted norms and advises them that if they dislike their wives, they should remember that they may dislike something in which God has placed much goodness (4:19). The Prophet said, 'A good believer should not loathe his wife. If he dislikes one characteristic of her – there are other characteristics which will be pleasing.' In difficult situations society is urged to care for families, and send an arbiter from the husband's side and one from the wife's side to try to bring about reconciliation (4:35). But serious situations may require firmness. We will discuss this now before we discuss the subject of divorce.

'... and you may hit them'

In discussing the position of women in Islam, an important Qur'anic verse, 4:34, is frequently referred to, often in a sensational way, as it is seen to give men the right to beat women.

However, a close examination of the verse in question shows that it has been subjected, both in the popular understanding and even by some exegetes, to selective and subjective interpretation, decontextualisation, exaggeration and blatant disregard for the Prophet's own interpretation of certain elements of this verse. English translations of the Qur'an have contributed to the popular picture of the treatment of women in Islam, and in some translations, most of the words of the passage have been misunderstood and mistranslated. Misinterpretation is usually based on male chauvinism, copying the views of others without close examination of the passage itself, age-old prejudice and media sensationalism.

Our understanding of the verse will be based on three things:

1. Linguistic analysis of the passage itself. The Qur'an is the supreme authority in Islam, and since this is a text from the Qur'an it has to be understood on the basis of accepted linguistic criteria; an understanding reached by this method needs no apology or further justification.
2. The Prophet Muhammad's own interpretation of key elements of this verse. The *Ḥadīth* is the second authority in Islam. The first role of the

Prophet was to deliver the Qur'an and his second was to explain it. It would be presumptuous of any one to claim to know the meaning of the Qur'an better than the Prophet.

3. What the Qur'an itself says in other verses about difficulties in the marital relationship and how to deal with them and what the Prophet said about how wives should be treated.

Opinions of Muslims or non-Muslims, scholars or laymen cannot be accepted as having higher authority than the Qur'an and *Ḥadīth* in determining the meaning of this verse on marital relations or relations between men and women in Islam.

Let us start by examining one popular translation of the passage:

Men have authority over women because God has made the one superior to the others, and because they spend their wealth to maintain them. Good women are obedient. They guard their unseen parts because God has guarded them. As for those from whom you fear disobedience, admonish them and send them to beds apart and beat them. Then, if they obey you, take no further action against them. God is high, supreme.
If you fear a breach between a man and his wife, appoint an arbiter from his people and another from hers. If they wish to be reconciled, God will bring them together again. God is wise and all-knowing.

4:34–5 DAWOOD

In the first verse, I have listed about a dozen words which have been misinterpreted or give rise to misunderstanding in the existing translations.

Let us consider some terms in this verse. First we have 'men' and 'women'. They mean 'husbands' and 'wives' as the passage goes on to mention intimate relations between couples and arbitration that may lead to divorce. Why does the verse not say 'husbands and wives'? Because the word *zawj* (which in modern Arabic means 'husband') applies in classical Arabic to both sexes. It has no feminine; it is like the English word 'spouse', and it would not have made sense to say 'spouses are given more than spouses'. This can also be seen in other parts of the Qur'an where husbands and wives are mentioned; the same terminology of 'men' and 'women' is used.

The verse is thus talking about husbands and wives, not men and women in general. This distinction is important because those who misunderstand the verse take it to mean that God has given 'men' in general 'more than women' in general, applying that very extensively and interpolating what they think men are given more of e.g. strength, intelligence, wisdom; even having a beard is listed by some! They then go on from this to say that women cannot be judges, heads of state, or in any position of leadership over men.

Secondly, we come to the key word *'qawwāmūna 'alā'.* In English translations you find such renderings as 'have authority over them' 'in charge of the affairs of' 'protectors and maintainers of'. In Arabic lexicography, the expression *qāma 'alā* means merely 'maintain her and attend to her affairs'.[8] The *ḥadīth* also elucidates the meaning of *qawāma* at the time of the Prophet. A companion of the Prophet explains that he chose to marry an older, experienced woman because he had young orphaned sisters and he wanted a woman *taqūmu 'alayhinna* and to gather them and comb their hair'.[9] However, judging by the rest of the verse, it appears that there is another role, one which makes the husband the chairman of the family, so to speak:

> Every one of you is a shepherd and will be held responsible for his charges: the man is a shepherd in his house and is responsible for his charges; the woman is a shepherd and she is responsible for her charges; the servant is a shepherd over his master's property and he will be responsible for his charges.

Good Group Management in Islam

Islam attaches great importance to people being together in a group with a leader. Praying together led by an *imām* increases the reward for each individual twenty-seven times. The Prophet had a distinct desire for good management, and said: 'If there are three of you on a journey, let them appoint one of them as *amīr* (the one in charge).' And when he sent a group of people away for any purpose he would see that they had an *amīr*, though not to bully them, because he said: 'The *sayyid* (chief) of a group of people is their servant.'[10]

Similarly, he advised that the pace of a travelling company should be set to suit the weakest among them, the *imām* in prayer should set his pace to suit the old and the mothers who need to attend to their babies.

So in the family, which is the fundamental unit of society, there must be a head or a chairman. In the Qur'an, this role is assigned to the husband, who has the responsibility to maintain the family, whereas the wife is not obliged to maintain the family or even herself.

The *qawama* or stewardship of the family that is assigned to the husband does not give him open or unlimited authority. It is limited by the Qur'anic principle of *ma'rūf* and works according to the principle of *shūra* – *qawāma* is part of *mu'ashara* (living together). Husbands are ordered:

Consort/live with them bi'l ma'rūf [in a good manner in accordance with what is honourable and commendable]

4:19

Al-ma'rūf is taken for granted in the marriage contract. In the Qur'an, by virtue of the marriage contract, husbands make a strong pledge to their wives (4:21), understood by exegetes to be 'living together according to what is honourable and commendable'.

As for the principle of *shūra,* the Qur'an describes the believers as those whose affairs '... are conducted by consultation' (4:38).

This is a general and permanent description that was revealed in Mecca before political life was started in Medina. Naturally it applies to the most basic social unit, the family. It has been seen above that such expressions of reciprocity as *mu'ashara, tashāwur* (mutual consultation), *tarāḍi* (mutual acceptance) are frequent in Qur'anic discussions of family matters.[11]

The role of *qawāma,* which involves the husband's responsibility to maintain and look after his wife, is different from merely 'ruling over' the wife as is made explicit in the Book of Genesis. There, as a punishment for making Adam eat from the fruit, Eve was told that her pains would be multiplied in conception and 'in sorrow shalt thou bring forth children, and thy desire shall be to thy husband and he shall rule over thee'.

A third concept that has been misinterpreted is the Arabic expression *bimā faḍḍal Allāh* ... which explains the basis of *qawāma.* There is one translator (Yusuf Ali) who says: 'Because God has given the one more [strength] than the other ...' Others say: 'Because God has preferred in bounty one of them over another ...' (Arberry); 'Because God made the one of them to excel the other...' (Pickthall) and 'Because God has made the one superior to the other...' (Dawood).

The root of the concept of *faḍl* in Arabic means 'to give more'. Lexically *faḍl* is *ziyāda* i.e. more. That is why some exegetes understood it to be the extra in the share of inheritance, thinking that this is corroborated by 4:32, while others thought it was strength, intelligence and so on, or the beard. However, this is all based on a hasty, incorrect reading of the text which assumes that *mā* (in *mā faḍḍala*) has the same grammatical function in 4:32 and 4:34. It does not. In the former, it is a relative pronoun meaning 'that which God has given more of to some than to others'. As such it requires an additional preposition and a pronoun *bihi.* In 4:34, on the other hand, *mā* is *maṣdariyya.* It merely turns the verb into a verbal noun (*bi tafḍīl Allāh* – 'by the appointment of God'). Thus in 4:32 men have something extra given to them (the share of the inheritance) while in 4:34 there is only the assignment of the role of *qawāma* – assignment of the chairmanship of the family to the husband. The verse thus means: 'Men maintain and attend to their wives because God has assigned this extra role to them and because of what they spend of their money on the family.' The Qur'an 2:228 mentions the rights and obligations of wives: 'They have rights similar to the rights men have over them according to what is *ma'rūf*, but men have a *daraja* (degree) over them'. Like the above 'more/extra', this word *daraja* (degree) has been interpreted by some as referring to the extra share of the inheritance. However, since within the marriage of two living people the question of inheritance does not arise, the 'degree' clearly refers to the role of *qawāma* circumscribed in the way described above.

It is interesting to note that the Qur'an does not say, 'Because God has given *men* more than *women* ...' but 'God has given *some* more than *others*'. This expression occurs a number of times to refer to the nature of things, namely that in this world some have been given more wealth (16:71) and some more of other things. In our verse, for husbands this 'more than others' is the stewardship of the family. Each will be judged according to how they conducted themselves with what they have been given (6:165).

Having established for the husband the role of *qawāma*, or maintenance and stewardship of the family, the Qur'an goes on to divide wives into two classes: the good ones who are described as *ṣāliḥāt* (righteous) and bad ones who are not. The *ṣāliḥāt* does not simply mean good as wives: *ṣalāḥ* is a general term to describe men or women who are righteous in observing the tenets of religion. These good wives are described in two ways, as: (i) *qānitāt*, which translators render as 'obedient' – this is misleading because it give the impression that they are obedient to their husband whereas the term is used in the Qur'an solely as being 'devotedly obedient to God' (33:35; 39:9); (ii) *ḥāfiẓāt*, a term used in the Qur'an for women (*ḥāfiẓūn* for men) who guard their private parts, so equivalent to 'chaste' (23:5; 33:34). This includes guarding their private parts from approaching or being approached by anyone other than the spouse.

Li'l-ghayb means that the wife is chaste 'in his absence' (when he is away from her). She is expected to guard her chastity because 'God has ordered these things to be guarded.' In the Qur'an, God's order in this respect is for men and women alike (24:30–31). Thus, being obedient to God and being chaste are the only two qualities by which a good wife is described, and we can see that they are not an excessive requirement. They are required of any Muslim of either sex.

On the other side comes the other class of women, whose *'nushūz'* (translated mainly as 'rebellion' though Dawood gives 'disobedience')[12] is feared by the husband. It is with these that the husbands are instructed to go through three stages. Here again, we have a misinterpretation of the concept of *nushūz* and misinterpretation and mistranslation of the three stages recommended in dealing with a wife in *nushūz*. The proper meaning should be derived on the basis of the three criteria listed above, namely: linguistic analysis of the text of the Qur'an; what the Prophet said and did; and what the Qur'an says elsewhere about dealing with wives in difficult situations.

Let us briefly consider *nushūz* in the light of these considerations:

1. It is clear that the contrast in this passage between the first and second type of women cannot be disregarded. If we say now, 'Good students attend regularly and submit their essays on time; as for others, they may be warned and barred from entering the exam,' the others must be understood in contrast with those who are said to attend and submit essays. Similarly, the second class of wives here is the opposite of those who are devoutly obedient to God and guarding their private parts, which God has ordered to be guarded. So what we have here is a woman whose husband fears her unfaithfulness and disregard for the commands of God.
2. This linguistic understanding is corroborated by the interpretation of the Prophet in his Farewell Speech, heard by thousands of people: 'You have rights over your wives and they have rights over you: you have the right that they should not defile your bed, and that they should not commit flagrant lewdness.[13] If they do, God allows you to put them in a separate room, and to beat them, but not with severity.'[14] 'To put them in a separate room' is a mistranslation by Guillaume; as we shall see later, it should read: 'to refrain from speaking to them in the bedroom'. The Prophet did not say here that husbands have the right of absolute obedience or to discipline for any kind of offence. He defined the exact circumstances in which the sanctions apply. We should also point out here that the different stages of treatment are given as a 'permission' not an 'order', as the Prophet made clear in his speech: *adhina lakum* 'God has allowed you', so husbands may choose not to apply the sanction.
3. In at least six *sūras* the Qur'an mentions difficulties in marriage, divorce and even the aftermath of divorce. Even when husbands dislike their wives they are instructed:

Consort with them in a good manner [bi'l ma'rūf], for if you dislike them it may happen that you dislike something in which God places much goodness

4:19

Even if they have experienced hostility from their wives and children, men are warned merely to beware of it, but advised that to pardon, overlook and forgive is better because God is forgiving and merciful (64:14). Even in divorce proceedings, with all the attendant bitterness, husbands are forbidden to harass their wives or make their life difficult (65:1,6; 4:19). It should be done 'with kindness' (2:229), *bi'l ma'rūf* (67:1). However there is a significant exception from this magnanimity (4:19; 65:1 also 4:15, 25): 'Except when they commit a flagrant lewdness' (4:19; 65:1). This again corroborates our understanding that the *nushūz* in our present verse means a serious offence of infidelity.

In dealing with a wife in *nushūz*, the three stages that are permitted are:

1. *'Iẓūhunna* which translators render as 'admonish them' but this is not correct. *Wa'ẓ* in Arabic is 'reminding of God and His teachings'. This meaning of the word is used in the Qur'an and this 'reminding' is the core of the lexical meaning in Arabic, so that the person who is reminded may take heed of the message.
2. *Wahjurūhunna fi'l maḍāji'*, which translators render variously as: 'Send them to beds apart ...' (Dawood); 'Banish them to beds apart ...' (Pickthall); 'Banish them to their couches ...' (Arberry); 'Refuse to share their beds ...' (Yusuf Ali); 'Leave them alone in bed ...' (Asad). Those who say 'send them' or 'banish them' have a basic misunderstanding of the verb. Even if it is understood as 'leaving', it is men who are asked to leave, not the women. It is mysterious how translators understood the verb to mean 'sending' or 'banishing' women. Misunderstanding also arises from the term *hajr* which people seem to relate to *hijra* (emigration) but *hajr* also means a verbal boycott. As the Prophet said, 'It is not lawful for a Muslim to have *hajr* with his brother for more than three days. They meet each other; one turns his face one way, the second to the other way. The best of them is the one who first greets the other.' These are people who meet and the term *hajr* still applies to them because the one does not speak to the other, and this is what it implies in our verse. This sulking or boycott is suggested only in bed *fi'l maḍāji'* not in front of the children or others. It is remarkable that a husband who fears that his wife may have been unfaithful in his own house and in his absence, should be blamed by some for boycotting her for a while in bed. It must also be remembered that it is the duty of any Muslim, man or woman, if they see someone misbehaving, to go through the stage of *wa'ẓ* (verbal reminding) and if this does not work, to show disapproval by boycotting them. It is an obligation on every Muslim, in accordance

with the Prophet's *ḥadīth*: 'Whoever sees a *munkar* (something objected to by religion) should change it with his hand, and if he cannot then with his tongue, and if he cannot, then with his heart, and this is the least degree of faith.' So the husband here is like any Muslim.

3. The third stage is 'beating' – *waḍribuhunna.* This is done only if the first two stages do not work. The husband has no right to jump from one stage to another, or to put them in the wrong order, as al-Shafi'i said: 'Start with what God started with.' This applies to any Qur'anic injunction which lists options in this way.

It should be remembered that the Qur'an mentions 'beating' only once, even though it talks about serious difficulties in marriage in several chapters. It should also be remembered that the Prophet, who is the model for all Muslims, never hit any of his wives.[15] He also said:[16]

'The best of you are those that are best in treating their wives.'
'It is only a magnanimous man who will show respect to women, and only a base one who will humiliate them.'
'Is any one of you who beats his wife not ashamed to beat her and then sleep with her?'

It may well be asked, 'How could the Prophet (who was the most obedient person to the instructions of the Qur'an) condemn beating so much when the Qur'an said 'and beat them' unless he understood beating here to be only for the serious offence he himself mentioned in the Farewell Speech?'

All Muslim exegetes agree that the husband is not allowed to beat the wife severely, since the Prophet said 'without severity'. In fact most say that it has to be so light as to be a something like a toothpick. The basis for this appears to be in the story that the Prophet was once angered by a servant girl whom he sent on an errand, but she was inordinately late. When she returned he raised his toothpick and said, 'If I did not fear God I would hit you with this.'

The word 'beat' causes difficulty. In my efforts to find a suitable word, I looked at dictionaries and found the English language rich in expressions like 'hit', 'strike', 'slap', 'beat', 'bash', 'wallop', 'belt', 'beat up', 'thump', and now 'batter', in wife-battering. Compared to English, Arabic has only a very limited range indeed, including the word *ḍaraba.* This may be why translators opt for 'beat'; but you don't 'beat' someone with a toothpick in English. Moreover, a *ḥadīth,* said by some to have been the cause of this verse, mentions a husband who slapped the face of his wife once. Thus 'beat' is not suitable translation; hit is nearer to the mark. The authority of the husband to hit his wife is circumscribed by a number of things: by the Prophet's own practice – he is the model for all Muslims to live their lives by – and by the ending of the Qur'anic verse, 'God is high and great'. Characteristically, this reminds men that if they misbehave God is watching over them and will deal with them. It is relevant here to mention the story of how the Prophet once saw Ibn Mas'ud with his hand raised, about to hit his slave. The Prophet cried out, 'God has more power over you than you have over him,' so he dropped his hand and set the slave free. In the theme under discussion it is important to observe that four successive verses end in the following ways: 'God knows all things ... '(4:32), 'God is ever witness over all things ...' (4:33). 'God is ever high, exalted and great ...' (4:34). 'God is ever-knowing and aware ... ' (4:35).

There are still more circumscriptions round the permission to 'hit'. Many Muslim scholars are also of the opinion that hitting is only permissible if the husband is sure that it will bring the right results, otherwise it should be avoided.

The verse ends by saying, 'If they obey you, you have no way against them' – obey at any stage – and 'obey', coming in its place here, means 'refrain' from the act which caused this problem, as in the Qur'anic verse: 'listen and obey' (64:16) (that is, obey what you have heard in that context). The Prophet himself, in his Farewell Speech, explained the Qur'anic phrase *fa in aṭa'nakum* (if they obey you) by using a different word, *fa in intahayna* (if they desist), in its place. Thus 'obedience' here does not mean being submissive to the husband, but refraining from a serious offence. To refrain in this way is an obligation on every believing person. In any case, any obedience is restricted, in Islam, by the Prophet's statements: 'There is no obedience for any creature in disobedience to the Creator'; and 'Obedience is only in *ma'rūf*, which means accepted, decent and commendable norms. As already pointed out, this expression, *bi'l ma'rūf*, occurs more frequently in situations of difficulties between married couples and in the treatment of wives, than anywhere else in the Qur'an. The 'obedience' is not *carte blanche* and Islamic marriage does not include the vow to 'love, cherish and obey'.

Following this verse we have 4:35 addressed to the relatives and all those surrounding the family, including legal authorities:

If you fear a breach between the couple, appoint an arbiter from his people and one from her people. If they desire amendment, God will make them of one mind. He is ever-knowing and aware.

In Islamic society, volunteering to bring reconciliation is a meritorious act (4:114). This is on an individual level, but the state is also under an obligation to create a body responsible for implementing Qur'anic teachings. An attitude of 'It is none of my business' runs counter to the teachings of the Qur'an and the Prophet. Even at the stage of fearing a breach, the Qur'an states: 'If they desire amendment, God will bring reconciliation ...' (4:35).

If, on the other hand, the arbiters find that it is not possible to reconcile a couple, then such a family is not worth preserving. Indeed God promises couples who part amicably that he will give each something more suitable, and ends the verse with: 'The scope of His provision is boundless, and He is all wise' (4:130).

It should be observed that with the two types of wives mentioned above, the husband is not mentioned at all in relation to a righteous wife; he only comes in when the situation of a serious offence is under discussion. In this situation, Muslim authors ask,[17] 'if the Qur'anic teaching in this matter is not fair and sensible, then what should be the alternatives'? Either the husband has to allow himself to become a cuckold or he has to take the wife to court which would affect the whole family and add to the bitterness, or divorce her and thus break up the family completely. Surely it is better to remind the wife of her duty, or sulk for a while, or even strike her lightly and then bring in arbiters who could, if all attempts at reconciliation fail, rule in favour of a divorce. According to the Qur'an it is not fair that a husband who maintains and pays for everything and is under Qur'anic instructions to live with his wife in an honourable, kind, commendable way, should also be asked to put up with acts that undermine the whole family.

As mentioned earlier, verse 4:34 has been subjected to misinterpretation, decontextualisation and sensational exaggeration. For Muslims, all the Qur'an is a revelation from God and husbands should obey God in this verse and in all other instructions given in the Qur'an – not misinterpret this verse and ignore all other teachings of the Qur'an and *Ḥadīth* on the subject.

As explained earlier, the Qur'an has set the proper norms for marital relationships: that the couple may repose in each other in an atmosphere of love and mercy (30:21).

Divorce by the Husband

Divorce has been said by the Prophet to be the most disliked lawful thing in the sight of God. However, it is available and easily carried out by the husband pronouncing it. There is a retarding mechanism of a menstrual cycle, but divorce can be effected after this. Then there is a further waiting period of three months, or until childbirth for pregnant women, within which the married couple could reconsider and the wife remains in the marital home. As the Qu'ran says, you do not know, 'God may bring a change of situation' (i.e. there could be a change of hearts). Within this waiting period the husband can revoke the divorce he pronounced by word or deed (65:1–7). After the waiting period, the divorce becomes final. But if the couple reconcile and then later on divorce is resorted to again, the same procedure as described above will pertain. If divorce is pronounced for a third time, it has been proved beyond doubt that this unhappy marital situation should not continue any longer. The husband may not marry his divorced wife again unless she happens to marry someone else in between. If that second husband were to die or to divorce her, it becomes possible for the first husband to enter into marriage with her again (2:229–30).

So there is freedom of action within limits, and this is also the Qu'ranic position during marital difficulties. Thus we find: 'There is no blame on you for doing such and such', and on the other hand, 'these are the bounds which you must not cross'. In two pages, for example, we have the statement 'There is no blame on you' repeated seven times but also there are bounds mentioned (2:229–240, Ch. 65). This gives freedom of action to deal with the numerous situations that can arise at different times and under different cultures.

The flexibility of Islamic law in this respect is remarkable. In fact, whenever divorce is mentioned in the Qu'ran, revocation is recommended, and whenever revocation is recommended we find the statement 'If they can uphold the limits set by God' (2:229, 231). This is conditional upon no harm being caused (2:229, 231). A continuation of marriage must involve the original objective of affection and mercy, establishing rights and observing the limits set by God. If this is not possible, then it is better for husband and wife to leave each other, and if they separate God will give to each out of his boundless resources something that would be better for them (4:130). This is stated in the Arabic in a conditional sentence which is understood in the Qu'ran to be a promise from God, and He does not break his promises. Divorce, thus, will be effected in order to start solid marriages, and to strengthen the marriage institution itself. After divorce the original state obtains, that marriage becomes highly recommended for any Muslim, and becomes an obligation for those who cannot live without exercising their sexual drives.

During marriage difficulties the Qu'ran keeps repeating 'If you believe in God and the Day of Judgement' or 'Remember that God is watching over you. Remember that he knows better than you'. 'Be conscious of God and know that he has knowledge of everything' (2:230–242; 4:32–36; Ch. 65). In the middle of divorce negotiations and financial settlements etc., when people can be bitter, the Qu'ran interrupts the discussions to state, in one verse, 'Keep up your daily prayer, and stand before God in obedience' before it resumes the discussion again (2:238).

Divorce, then, carries no stigma whatsoever in Islam, nor does any attach to divorcees who wish to remarry and resume their married sex life. The Qu'ran considers that to prevent them remarrying would drive them to doing what is forbidden, and as Islam wishes to build a moral society it provides the institution that would help towards achieving that end. Thus the Qu'ran recognises that those who have been used to married life are particularly likely to need it more and forbids women's families from interfering and preventing divorced women from remarrying their previous husband.

Do not prevent her from remarrying her husband if they have come to an honourable agreement. This is enjoined on those of you who believe in God and the Last Day; it is more honourable for you and more pure. God knows and you do not.

2:32

When a woman or a man becomes divorced, the same original instructions to get married and for society to bring about the marriage of unmarried members obtains.

In this respect there is an obvious difference between the Qu'ran and the Gospel. In Mark 10, vv.11 and 12, Christ says 'Whoever divorces his Wife and marries other than her, he will be committing adultery, and if a woman divorces her husband and marries someone else she will have committed adultery'. In Matthew 5:32: 'But I tell you that anyone who divorces his wife, except for marital unfaithfulness, causes her to become an adulteress, and anyone who marries the divorced woman commits adultery'. Also in Luke 18:16. In spite of these clear statements, since 1983 the Anglican church has allowed divorcees to be remarried in Church, influenced by the result of changes in English divorce laws in the late 1960s.

Women and Divorce

So far we have discussed men's rights to divorce. However, women can also instigate divorce. They can obtain divorce by mutual consent (2:229–31), or in cases of cruelty, abandonment or harm, or if a husband fails to meet his obligations of maintenance. In these latter cases the woman should apply to the court. The husband is responsible for maintenance during marriage and for a period after the marriage. He is also responsible for his children's maintenance. This in itself places some restrictions on his exercising his right to divorce lightly, without going to court. The delayed dowry payment, which can be a considerable sum, falls due on divorce, and can act as a deterrent to hasty proclamations of divorce.

In any case, a woman can stipulate in the marriage contract her right to divorce her husband at any time without his consent. This is recognised in Islamic law and practised in certain parts of the Muslim world.

When discussing family life, marriage and divorce, the Qu'ran does not simply produce regulations couched in dry legal language. Legal instructions are couched in religious, emotional language, employing a powerful use of linguistic techniques of persuasion and dissuasion such as those already mentioned: 'If you believe in God and know that you are going to meet him' or 'Remember that God is watching over everything and He has full knowledge and full power over you. That is better and purer for you'. 'He knows and you do not know'. Marriage and divorce in Islam are protected by law, by society and by the strong appeal to the belief in God and the hereafter.

5
War and Peace in the Qur'an

The Sources of Islamic Law

As explained in Chapter 1, The Qur'an is the supreme authority in Islam and the primary source of Islamic Law, including the laws regulating war and peace. The second source is the *ḥadīth,* the traditions of the Prophet Muhammad's acts and deeds, which can be used to confirm, explain or elaborate Qur'anic teachings, but may not contradict the Qur'an, since they derive their authority from the Qur'an itself. Together these form the basis for all other sources of Islamic law, such as *ijmā' (consensus* of Muslim scholars on an opinion regarding any given subject) and *qiyās* (reasoning by analogy). These and others are merely methods to reach decisions based on the texts or the spirit of the Qur'an and *ḥadīth.* The Qur'an and *ḥadīth* are thus the only binding sources of Islamic law. Again, nothing is acceptable if it contradicts the text or the spirit of these two sources. Any opinions arrived at by individual scholars or schools of Islamic law, including the recognised four Sunni schools, are no more than opinions. The founders of these schools never laid exclusive claim to the truth, or invited people to follow them rather than any other scholars. Western writers often take the views of this or that classical or modern Muslim writer as 'the Islamic view', presumably on the basis of assumptions drawn from the Christian tradition, where the views of people like St Augustine or St Thomas Aquinas are often cited as authorities. In Islam, however, for any view of any scholar to gain credibility, it must demonstrate its textual basis in the Qur'an and authentic *ḥadīth,* and its derivation from a sound linguistic understanding of these texts.

Ijtihād – exerting one's reason to reach judgements on the basis of these two sources – is the mechanism by which Muslims find solutions for the ever-changing and evolving life around them. The 'closing of the door of *ijtihād*' is a myth propagated by many Western scholars, some of whom imagine that 'the door' still remains closed and that the Muslims have nothing to fall back on except the decisions of the Schools of Law and scholars of the classical period. In fact, scholars in present-day Muslim countries reach their own decisions on laws governing all sorts of new situations, using the same methodology based on the Qur'an and *ḥadīth* and the principles derived from them, without feeling necessarily bound by the conclusions of any former school of law.

In the Qur'an and *ḥadīth*, the fundamental sources of Islamic teachings on war and peace are to be found.

Normal Relations

The Islamic relationship between individuals and nations is one of peace. War is a contingency that becomes necessary at certain times and under certain conditions. Muslims learn from the Qur'an that God's objective in creating the human race in different communities was that they should relate to each other peacefully (49:13).[1]

The objective of forming the family unit is to foster affection and mercy, and that of creating a baby in its mother's womb is to form bonds of blood and marriage between people:

It is He Who created the human being from fluid, making relationships of blood and marriage.

25:54

Sowing enmity and hatred amongst people is the work of Satan:

Satan wishes to sow enmity and hatred between you with intoxicants and gambling.

5:91

Division into warring factions is viewed as a punishment that God brings on people who revert to polytheism after He has delivered them from distress:

... He is able to divide you into discordant factions and make you taste the might of each other ...

6:65

War is hateful (2:216), and the changing of fear into a sense of safety is one of the rewards for those who believe and do good deeds (24:55). That God has given them the sanctuary of Mecca is a blessing for which its people should be thankful (29:67). Paradise is the Land of Peace – *Dār al-Salām* – (5:127).

Justifications and Conditions for War

War may become necessary only to stop evil from triumphing in a way that would corrupt the earth (2:251). For Muslims to participate in war there must be valid justifications, and strict conditions must be fulfilled. A thorough survey of the relevant verses of the Qur'an shows that it is consistent throughout with regard to these rulings on the justification of war, and its conduct, termination and consequences.

War in Islam as regulated by the Qur'an, and *ḥadīth* has been subject to many distortions by Western scholars and even by some Muslim writers. These are due either to misconceptions about terminology or – above all – using quotations taken out of context.[2] Nowhere in the Qur'an is changing people's religion given as a cause for waging war. The Qur'an gives a clear instruction that there is no compulsion in religion (2:256). It states that people will remain different (11:118), they will always have different religions and ways and this is an unalterable fact (5:48). God tells the Prophet that most people will not believe 'even if you are eager that they should' (12:103).[3]

All the battles that took place during the Prophet's lifetime, under the guidance of the Qur'an and the Prophet, have been surveyed and shown to have been waged only in self-defence or to pre-empt an imminent attack.[4] For more than ten years in Mecca, Muslims were persecuted, but before permission was given to fight they were instructed to restrain themselves (4:77) and endure with patience and fortitude:

Pardon and forgive until God gives his command.

2:109; *see also* 29:59; 16:42

After the Muslims were forced out of their homes and their town, and those who remained behind were subjected to even more abuse, God gave His permission to fight:

Permission is given to those who fight because they have been wronged, and God is indeed able to give them victory; those who have been driven from their homes unjustly only because they said, 'Our Lord is God' – for had it not been for God's repelling some men by means of others, monasteries, churches, synagogues and mosques, in which the name of God is much mentioned, would certainly have been destroyed. Verily God helps those that help Him – lo! God is Strong, Almighty – those who, if they are given power in the land, establish worship and pay the poor-due and enjoin what is good and forbid iniquity.

22:39–41

Here, war is seen as justifiable and necessary to defend people's right to their own beliefs, and once the believers have been given victory, they should not become triumphant or arrogant or have a sense of being a superpower, because the promise of help given above and the rewards are for those who do not seek to exalt themselves on earth or spread corruption (28:83).

Righteous Intention

Righteous intention is an essential condition. When fighting takes place, it should be *fī sabīl illāh* – in the way of God – as is often repeated in the Qur'an. His way is prescribed in the Qur'an as the way of truth and justice, including all the teaching it gives on the justifications and the conditions for the conduct of war and peace. The Prophet was asked about those who fight for the booty, and those who fight out of self-aggrandisement or to be seen as a hero. He said that none of these was in the way of God. The one who fights in the way of God is he who fights so that the word of God is uppermost (*Ḥadīth*: Bukhari).

This expression of the word of God being 'uppermost' was misunderstood by some to mean that Islam should gain political power over other religions. However, if we use the principle that 'different parts of the Qur'an interpret each other', we find (9:40) that by simply concealing the Prophet in the cave from his trackers, after he had narrowly escaped an attempt to murder him, God made His word 'uppermost', and the word of the wrongdoers 'lowered'. This could not be described as gaining military victory or political power.

Another term which is misunderstood and misrepresented is *jihād*. This does not mean 'Holy War'. 'Holy War' does not exist as a term in Arabic, and its translation into Arabic sounds quite alien. The term which is specifically used in the Qur'an for fighting is *qitāl*. *Jihād* can be by argumentation (25:52), financial help or actual fighting. *Jihād* is always described in the Qur'an as *fī sabīl illāh*. On returning from a military campaign, the Prophet said to his followers: 'We have returned from the minor *jihād* to the major *jihād* – the struggle of the individual with his own self.'

Jihād as an Obligation

When there is a just cause for *jihād*, which must have a righteous intention, it then becomes an obligation. It becomes an obligation for defending religious freedom (22:39–41), for self-defence (2:190) and defending those who are oppressed: men, women and children who cry for help (4:75). It is the duty of the Muslims to help the oppressed, except against a people with whom the Muslims have a treaty (8:72). These are the only valid justifications for war we find in the Qur'an. Even when war becomes necessary, we find that there is no 'conscription ' in the Qur'an. The Prophet is instructed only to 'urge on the believers' (4:64). The Qur'an – and the *ḥadīth* at greater length – urge on the Muslim fighters (those who are defending themselves or the oppressed) in the strongest way: by showing the justice of their cause, the bad conduct of the enemy, and promising great rewards in the afterlife for those who are prepared to sacrifice their lives and property in such a good cause.[5]

Who is to be Fought? Discrimination and Proportionality

In this regard we must discuss two verses in the Qur'an which are normally quoted by those most eager to criticise Qur'anic teachings on war: 2:191 ('slay them wherever you find them') and verse 9:5, labelled the 'Sword Verse'. Both verses have been subjected to decontextualisation, misinterpretation and misrepresentation. The first verse comes in a passage that defines clearly who is to be fought:

Fight in the way of God those who fight against you, but do not transgress. God does not love the transgressor.

2:190

'Those who fight against you' means actual fighters – civilians are protected. The Prophet and his successors, when they sent out an army, gave clear instructions not to attack civilians – women, old people, religious people engaged in their worship – nor destroy crops or animals.

Discrimination and proportionality should be strictly observed. Only the combatants are to be fought, and no more harm should be caused to them than they have caused (2:194). Thus wars and weapons of destruction that destroy civilians and their towns are ruled out by the Qur'an and the word and deed of the Prophet, these being the only binding authority in Islamic law. The prohibition is regularly reinforced by, 'Do not transgress, God does not love the transgressor'. Transgression has been interpreted by

Qur'anic exegetes as meaning, 'initiation of fighting, fighting those with whom a treaty has been concluded, surprising the enemy without first inviting them to make peace, destroying crops or killing those who should be protected' (Baydawi's commentary on Q. 2:190).

The orders are always couched in restraining language, with much repetition of warnings, such as 'do not transgress' and 'God does not love the transgressors' and 'He loves those who are conscious of Him'. These are instructions given to people who, from the beginning, should have the intention of acting 'in the way of God'.

Linguistically we notice that the verses in this passage always restrict actions in a legalistic way, which appeals strongly to Muslim's conscience. In six verses (2:190–5) we find four prohibitions (do not), six restrictions: two 'until', two 'if', two 'who attack you', as well as such cautions as 'in the way of God', 'be conscious of God', 'God does not like aggressors', 'God is with those who are conscious of Him', 'with those who do good deeds' and 'God is Forgiving, Merciful.' It should be noted that the Qur'an, in treating the theme of war, as with many other themes, regularly gives the reasons and justifications for any action it demands.

Verse 2:191 begins:

Slay them where you find them and expel them from where they expelled you; persecution [fitna] is worse than killing.

'Slay them wherever you find them,' has been made the title of an article on war in Islam.[6] In this article 'them' is removed from its context, where it refers back to 'those who attack you' in the preceding verse. 'Wherever you find them' is similarly misunderstood: the Muslims were anxious that if their enemies attacked them in Mecca (which is a sanctuary) and they retaliated, they would be breaking the law. Thus the Qur'an simply gave the Muslims permission to fight those enemies, whether outside or inside Mecca, and assured them that the persecution that had been committed by the unbelievers against them for believing in God was more sinful than the Muslims killing those who attacked them, wherever they were. Finally, it must be pointed out that the whole passage (2:190–5) comes in the context of fighting those who bar Muslims from reaching the Sacred Mosque at Mecca to perform the pilgrimage. This is clear from v.189 before and verse 196 after the passage. In the same way, the verse giving the first permission to fight occurs in the Qur'an, also in the context of barring Muslims from reaching the Mosque to perform the pilgrimage (22:25–41).

The 'Sword' Verse

We must also comment on another verse much referred to but notoriously misinterpreted and taken out of context – that which became labelled as the 'sword verse':

Then, when the sacred months have passed, slay the idolators wherever you find them, take them and besiege them and prepare for them every ambush.

9:5

The hostility and 'bitter enmity' of the polytheists and their *fitnah* (persecution) (2:193; 8:39) of the Muslims grew so great that the unbelievers were determined to convert the Muslims back to paganism or finish them off.

They would persist in fighting you until they turn you back from your religion, if they could.

2:217

It was these hardened polytheists in Arabia, who would accept nothing other than the expulsion of the Muslims or their reversion to paganism, and who repeatedly broke their treaties, that the Muslims were ordered to treat in the same way – to fight them or expel them.

Even with such an enemy Muslims were not simply ordered to pounce on them and reciprocate by breaking the treaty themselves; instead, an ultimatum was issued, giving the enemy notice, that after the four sacred months mentioned in 9:5 above, the Muslims would wage war on them. The main clause of the sentence: 'kill the polytheists' is singled out by some Western scholars to represent the Islamic attitude to war; even some Muslims take this view and allege that this verse abrogated other verses on war. This is pure fantasy, isolating and decontextualising a small part of a sentence. The full picture is given in 9:1–15, which gives many reasons for the order to fight such polytheists. They continuously broke their agreements and aided others against the Muslims, they started hostilities against the Muslims, barred others from becoming Muslims, expelled Muslims from the Holy Mosque and even from their own homes. At least eight times the passage mentions their misdeeds against the Muslims. Consistent with restrictions on war elsewhere in the Qur'an, the immediate context of this 'sword verse' exempts such polytheists as do not break their agreements and who keep the peace with the Muslims (9:7). It orders that those enemies seeking safe conduct should be protected and delivered to the place of safety they seek (9:6). The whole of this context to v.5, with all its restrictions, is ignored by those who simply isolate one part of a sentence to build their theory of war in Islam on what is termed 'The Sword Verse' even when the word 'sword' does not occur anywhere in the Qur'an.

Cessation of Hostilities

Once the hostility of the enemy ceases, the Muslims must stop fighting (2:193; 8:39):

And if they incline to peace, do so and put your trust in God. Even if they intend to deceive you, remember that God is sufficient for you.

8:61–2

When the war is over, the Qur'an and *ḥadīth* give instructions as to the treatment of prisoners of war and the new relationship with the non-Muslims. War is certainly not seen as a means in Islam of converting other people from their religions. The often-quoted division of the world into *dār al-ḥarb* and *dār al-Islām* is seen nowhere in the Qur'an or *ḥadīth*, the only authoritative sources of Islam. The scholars who used these expressions were talking about the warring enemies in countries surrounding the Muslim lands. Even for such scholars there was not a dichotomy but a trichotomy, with a third division, *dār al-ṣulḥ*, the lands with which the Muslims had treaty obligations.

The Qur'an and *ḥadīth* talk about the different situations that exist between a Muslim state and a neighbouring warring enemy. They mention a state of defensive war, within the prescriptions specified above, the state of peace treaty for a limited or unlimited period, the state of truce, and the state where a member of a hostile camp can come into a Muslim land for special purposes under safe conduct.[7]

Treaties

The Prophet and his companions did make treaties, such as that of Hudaybiyah in the sixth year of the *hijrah* and the one made by 'Umar with the people of Jerusalem.[8] Faithfulness to a treaty is a most serious obligation which the Qur'an and *ḥadīth* incessantly emphasise:

Believers, fulfil your bonds.

5:1

Keep the agreements of God when you have made them and do not break your oaths after you have made them with God as your bond ...

16:91

Covenants should not be broken because one community feels stronger than another.

16:92

Breaking treaties puts the culprit into a state lower than animals (8:55). As stated above, even defending a Muslim minority is not allowed when there is a treaty with the camp they are in.

Prisoners of War

There is nothing in the Qur'an or *ḥadīth* to prevent Muslims from following the present international humanitarian conventions on war or prisoners of war. There is nothing in the Qur'an to say that prisoners of war must be held captive, but as this was the practice of the time and there was no international body to oversee exchanges of prisoners, the Qur'an deals with the subject. There are only two cases where it mentions their treatment:

O Prophet! Tell the captives you have, 'If God knows goodness in your heart He will give you better rewards than have been taken from you and forgive you. He is forgiving, merciful.' And if they intend to be treacherous to you, they have been treacherous to God in the past and He has put them into your hands.

8:70–1

When you have fully overcome the enemy in the battle, then tighten their bonds, but thereafter set them free either by an act of grace or against ransom.

47:4

Grace is suggested first, before ransom. Even when some were not set free, for one reason or another, they were, according to the Qur'an and *ḥadīth*, to be treated in a most humane way (Q.76:8–9; 9:60; 2:177). In the Bible, where it mentions fighting, we find a different picture in the treatment administered to conquered peoples, for example:

When you march up to attack a city, make its people an offer of peace. If they accept and open their gates, all the people in it shall be subject to forced labour and shall work for you. If they refuse to make peace with you in battle, lay siege to that city. When the Lord your God delivers it into your hand, put to the sword all the men in it. As for the women, the children, the livestock and everything else in the city, you may take these as plunder for yourselves. And you may use the plunder the Lord your God gives you from your enemies. This is how you are to treat all the cities that are at a distance from you and do not belong to the nations nearby.

However, in the cities of the nations the Lord your God is giving you as an inheritance, do not leave alive anything that breathes. Completely destroy them – the Hittites, Amorites, Canaanites, Perizzites, Hivites, and Jebusites – as the Lord your God has commanded you. Otherwise they will teach you to follow all the detestable things they do in worshipping their gods, and you will sin against the Lord your God.

DEUTERONOMY 20:10–189

Resumption of Peaceful Relations

We have already seen in the Qur'an 22:41 that God promises to help those who, when He has established them in a land after war,

'*... establish worship and pay the poor-due and enjoin what is good and forbid iniquity*'.

In this spirit, when the Muslim army was victorious over the enemy, any of the defeated people who wished to remain in the land could do so under a guarantee of protection for their life, religion and freedom, and if they wished to leave they could do so with safe-conduct. If they chose to stay among the Muslims, they could become members of the Muslim community. If they wished to continue in their faith they had the right to do so and were offered security. The only obligation on them then was to pay *jizyah*, a tax exempting the person from military service and from paying *zakāt*, which the Muslims have to pay – a tax considerably heavier than the *jizyah*. Neither had the option of refusing to pay, but in return the non-Muslims were given the protection of the state. *Jizyah* was not a poll-tax, and it was not charged on the old, or poor people, women or children.[10]

Humanitarian Intervention

Humanitarian intervention is allowed, even advocated in the Qur'an, under the category of defending the oppressed. However it must be done within the restrictions specified in the Qur'an, as we have shown above. In intervening, it is quite permissible to co-operate with non-Muslims, under the proviso:

Co-operate in what is good and pious and do not co-operate in what is sinful and aggression.

5:2

International Co-operation

In the sphere of war and peace, there is nothing in the Qur'an or *ḥadīth* which should cause Muslims to feel unable to sign and act according to the modern international conventions, and there is much in the Qur'an and *ḥadīth* from which modern international law can benefit. The Prophet Muhammad remembered an alliance he witnessed that was contracted between some chiefs of Mecca before his call to prophethood to protect the poor and weak against oppression and said:

> I have witnessed in the house of Ibn Jud'an an alliance which I would not exchange for a herd of red camels, and if it were to be called for now that Islam is here, I would respond readily.[11]

There is nothing in Islam that prevents Muslims from having peaceful, amicable and good relations with other nations when they read and hear regularly the Qur'anic injunction, referring to members of other faiths:

> *God does not forbid you from being kind and equitable to those who have neither made war on you on account of your religion nor driven you from your homes. God loves those who are equitable.*
>
> 60:8

This includes participation in international peace-making and peace-keeping efforts. The rule of arbitration in violent disputes between groups of Muslims, is given in the Qur'an:

> *If two parties of the believers take up arms against one another, make peace between them. If either of them commits aggression against the other, fight against the aggressors until they submit to God's judgement. When they submit, make peace between them in equity and justice. God loves those who act in justice.*
>
> 49:9

This could, in agreement with rules of Islamic jurisprudence, be applied more generally to disputes within the international community. For this reason, Muslims should, and do, participate in the arbitration of disputes, by international bodies such as the United Nations.

Modern international organisations and easy travel should make it easier for different people, in accordance with the teachings of the Qur'an, to 'get to know one another', 'co-operate in what is good' and live in peace. The Qur'an affirms:

There is no virtue in much of their counsels: only in his who enjoins charity, kindness and peace among people ...

4:114

6
Tolerance in Islam

Islam is generally regarded in the West as being anything but tolerant – a religion of the sword and belligerency. The previous chapter shows that this is the result of misinterpretation, and we continue here to examine the Islamic position on tolerance in general. A Muslim may wonder why this subject has assumed so much importance, but reference to European history shows that the history of the Christian West with regard to tolerance, by the admission of Western authors themselves, is shocking. In fact, it is this background that makes people now insist on tolerance and campaign for it to an extent for which the Muslims, with their different background, do not see such a need.

Under the heading 'Tolerance' or 'Toleration', Western history books and encyclopaedias actually recount a long history of *intolerance*, and hesitant movements – only in recent times – of attempts to alleviate it. The Toleration Act of 1689 passed in England, granted to religious dissenters freedom of worship, under certain conditions. Roman Catholics and those who did not believe in the Trinity were not covered by the Act. Political disqualifications were not removed by the Act and dissenters were not allowed to hold public office until the Occasional Conformity Act of 1711. The Catholic Emancipation Act of 1829 came to repeal earlier penal laws, which subjected the Irish Catholics to persecution. Such was the state of intolerance even within Christianity itself, let alone towards non-Christians.

What is Tolerance?

The lexical meaning of tolerance is 'to bear, to endure, to put up with'. In the Encyclopedia Americana we read:

> Toleration, however, has a peculiarly limited signification. It connotes a refraining from prohibition and persecution. Nevertheless it suggests a latent disapproval and it usually refers to a condition in which the freedom which it permits is both limited and conditional. Toleration is not equivalent to religious liberty, and it falls far short of religious equality. It assumes the existence of an authority which might have been coercive, but which, for reasons of its own, is not pushed to extremes ... However lamentable the fact may be, it should not surprise us that greater intolerance has been found amongst the Christian nations than among any other people.[1]

Traditionally, campaigns for tolerance were confined to the sphere of religion in a limited sense. In recent years, however, the meaning and the scope of the concept have become much wider, as we shall see later.

When we come to consider the issue of tolerance in Islam we find a different situation altogether. First of all there was no ready equivalent term in the Arabic language to mean what is traditionally understood in English by 'tolerance'. When Muslims began to talk about this subject as a reaction to its use in English, the word they used in Arabic was *tasāmuḥ*, which has become the current term for 'tolerance'. The root form of this word has two connotations: 'generosity' (*jūd wa karam*) and 'ease' (*tasāhul*).[2] Thus the Muslims in Arabic talk about *tasāmuḥ al-Islām* and *al-tasāmuḥ al-dīni*, in a quite different way from the English usage. Where 'tolerance' indicates a powerful authority, grudgingly 'bearing' or 'putting up with' others who are different, the Arabic term denotes generosity and ease from both sides on a reciprocal basis. The term is always used in the reciprocal form.

In fact, tolerance is born out of the very nature of Islam – which seems to be the only religion that is not named after a race of people, like Judaism and Hinduism, or after any single person like Buddhism or Christianity. 'Islam', the name given to the religion in the Qur'an by God Himself, means 'devotion to God'; 'dedication to God alone', conventionally translated as 'submission to God'. God, in Islam, is not the Lord of the Arabs or the Muslims but the Lord of all human beings and all the worlds, *Rabb al-'ālamīn*, who states in the Qur'an, 'We have honoured the Children of Adam' (17:70) – all the Children of Adam are 'chosen' by God to be honoured.

Islam, moreover, is not an exclusive or novel religion; it is part of the whole history of religion. Its book, the Qur'an, 'continues' and 'confirms' the previous scriptures (12:111), and its Prophet is only one in the long line of prophets Muslims have to believe in. For example, eighteen prophets are mentioned in one place in the Qur'an, and Muhammad is told:

These are the people God has guided. Follow the guidance that has been given to them.

2:136; 6:83–96

The Qur'an declares: 'Muḥammad is but a messenger, before whom other messengers were sent' (3:144) and he never said, 'No man cometh to the Lord except by me.' Christians and the Jews who lived among an overwhelming Muslim majority are referred to in the Qur'an, by using the honorific term *ahl al-kitāb* (the 'People of the Book') not as 'minorities', in the way that other religious groups in the Christian West, are described. The Qur'an does not brand the 'People of the Book' as a whole as unacceptable. It says:

They are not all alike. Of the People of the Book there is a staunch community who recite the revelations of God in the night season, falling prostrate [before Him]. They believe in God and the last day, and enjoin right conduct and forbid indecency, and vie one with another in good works. These are of the righteous. And whatever good they do, they will not be denied the reward thereof.

3:113–5

It does not brand them all as dishonest. It says:

Among the People of the Book there is he who, if you trust him with a weight of treasure, will return it to you. And among them there is he who, if thou trust him with a piece of gold, will not return it to you unless you keep standing over him.

3:75

Similarly, the Qur'an allows Muslims to eat the food of the 'People of the Book' and to marry their women who remain Christians and Jews (5:5). It does not allow Muslims to be carried away by fanciful hopes, but says:

It will not be in accordance with your desires, nor the desires of the People of the Book. He who doeth wrong will have the recompense thereof, and will not find against God any protecting friend or helper. And whoso doeth good works, whether of male or female, and is a believer, such will enter paradise and they will not be wronged [by so much as] the groove in a date stone.

4:123–4

It instructs Muslims not to argue with the 'People of the Book' except in the fairest manner and to say to them:

We believe in what has been revealed to us and in what has been revealed to you. Our Lord and your Lord is one and the same, and to Him we submit ourselves.

29:46

Muslims are instructed to appeal to the 'People of the Book' through what is common between them and Islam.

Say, 'O People of the Book! Come to common terms as between us and you: That we worship none but God; that we associate no partners with him; that we erect not, from among ourselves, Lords and patrons other than God.' If then they turn back, say: 'Bear witness that we submit to God's Will'.

3:64

In the Qur'an, God addresses Muslims and the followers of other religions, saying:

We have ordained a law and assigned a path to each of you. Had God pleased, he could have made you one nation, but it is His wish to prove you by that which He has bestowed upon you. Vie, then, with each other in good works, for to God you shall all be returned, and He shall declare to you what you have disagreed about.

5:48

This command, to leave differences to be settled on the Day of Judgement, is repeated many times in the Qur'an. Even in their relations with polytheists, who stand as the extreme opposite of the fundamental Islamic belief of monotheism, the Muslims are instructed in the Qur'an:

God does not forbid you, to be kind and equitable to those who do not fight you for [your] faith, nor drive you out of your homes: for God loves those who are just.

60:8

Addressing all people, God says:

O mankind! We created you from a single pair of a male and a female, and made you into nations and tribes, that you may know each other. Verily the most honoured of you in the sight of God is the most Righteous of you, and God has full knowledge and is well acquainted [with all things].

49:13

The variety of their colours, tongues, and races are regarded as a sign of God's power and mercy (30:22; 49:13), and as such should lead to closeness, rather than to discrimination or intolerance.

These instructions are not isolated or casual instances in the Qur'an, but are repeated many times and are part of the whole fabric of the message of Islam. On this basis, tolerance has been, from the beginning, a natural, inseparable part of Islam. It did not tolerate non-Muslims grudgingly, but welcomed them to live freely in Muslim society. At the height of Islam's success, the Qur'an set the principle, *lā ikrāha fi'l-dīn*, 'There is no compulsion in religion' (2:256). Here it employs the strongest and most permanent negative form in Arabic, the *lā* of absolute negation, used in the Qur'an for such fundamental negations as: 'There is no god except God', and 'There is no changing the words of God' (47:19; 10:64). We also find the repeated pattern: 'To me is my religion; to you is yours,' (109:6); 'To me is my work, to you is yours' (10:41).

The Qur'an affirms that God has created people to be different, and they will always remain different, not only in their appearance but also in their beliefs (11:118–19) and it is up to each person whether to become a believer or not.

Had your Lord wished, all people on earth would have become believers. Will you [Muhammad] then compel all people to become believers?

10:99

The two key expressions: *wa law shā'a rabbuka* (had your Lord wished) and *fa man shā'a* (whoever wishes to) occur more than twenty times in the Qur'an.[3]

The Qur'an not only 'tolerates' Christians and Jews who live in a Muslim society, but instructs the Prophet:

Say: 'O People of the Book! You have naught of guidance, till you observe the Torah and the Gospel and that which was revealed to you from your Lord'.

5:68

God speaks, saying:

We have revealed the Torah. There is in it guidance and light. By it, the Prophets who have surrendered themselves to God judge the Jews and so do the Rabbis and divines. Those who do not judge in accordance with God's revelation are unbelievers.

5:44

Let the followers of the Gospel judge in accordance with what God has revealed therein. Evil doers are those that do not judge in accordance with God's revelation.

5:47

In accordance with the instructions of the Qur'an, in AD 638 when the Muslims, under the Caliph 'Umar, entered Jerusalem, then called Aeilia, 'Umar made the following covenant with the inhabitants:

In the name of God, the Merciful, the Compassionate! This is the security which Umar, the servant of God, the commander of the faithful, grants to the people of Aeilia. He grants to all, whether sick or sound, security for their lives, their possessions, their churches and their crosses, and for all that concerns their religion. Their churches shall not be changed into dwelling places, nor destroyed, neither shall they nor their appurtenances be in any way diminished, nor the crosses of the inhabitants, nor aught of their possessions, nor shall any constraint be put upon them in the matter of their faith, nor shall any one of them be harmed.[4]

This was not a freak piece of history: it is modelled on what the Prophet said and did, in obedience to the Qur'an, the authority for all Muslims at all times.

Another example of Islamic treatment of non-Muslims is the generosity shown by Saladin in 1188, when he repossessed Jerusalem from the Crusaders. In the first campaign (1096), the Crusaders had ransacked the city and slaughtered a great number of Muslims and Jews. One of the Frankish chronicles records that:

They also ordered that all the corpses of the Saracens should be thrown outside the city because of the fearful stench; for almost the whole city was full of their dead bodies. The Saracens who were still alive dragged the dead ones out in front of the gates, and made piles of them, as big as houses. Such a slaughter of pagans no one has ever seen or heard of; the pyres they made were like pyramids.[5]

When Saladin came, he found the Crusaders defiling the mosque by keeping pigs in it. Even European historians concede that he did not retaliate, but forgave the Crusaders, with the exception of a very few individuals who had been more vicious. He accepted ransom money from some of these and let others who could not pay go free.

Again, in 1492, when the last Muslim king of Granada surrendered the city to the Christian King Ferdinand, with a treaty that stipulated that all Muslims in the city should not be harmed, the Christians ignored the treaty and started the infamous Inquisition. Muslims in their own lands did not take revenge on any Christians living there. Moreover, Jews who were forced to flee from Spain came to the Muslims in North Africa and Turkey to continue enjoying the protection they had always received under Muslim rule in Spain.

Islamic tolerance allows non-Muslims to live according to their customs, even if these are forbidden in Islam. Thus Christians are allowed to breed pigs, eat pork, make and drink alcohol in Muslim countries even though such things are forbidden in Islam and it would not be asking Christians too much to refrain from such practices out of respect for Islam. In Egypt, for example, courts administer to non-Muslims laws of their own religious denominations, which are all incorporated into Egyptian law.

Some people in the West quote, as an example of Muslim intolerance, the fact that in the past they called Jews and Christians *dhimmis* (ignoring the real sense of this term which means 'those who enjoy protection') and the fact that Muslims collected *jizya* tribute from them. The *jizya* was 1 *dīnār* a year for every able-bodied male who could fight in the army – monks were exempted. As non-Muslims they were not obliged to fight for the Muslim armies. This is a liberal attitude, which recognised that it would be unfair to enlist people who do not believe in Islam to fight for the Muslim state, something which their own religion and conscience might not allow them to do. The *jizya* was their contribution to the defence of the Islamic state they lived in. Muslims, on the other hand were obliged to serve in the army, and all Muslims had to pay the much higher *zakāt* tax part of which is spent on defence. When non-Muslims chose to serve in the Muslim army they were exempted from the *jizya*, and when the Muslim state could not defend certain subjects from whom they had collected *jizya*, it returned the *jizya* tax to them giving this as a reason. In return for the *jizya* non-Muslims also enjoyed state social security.[6]

The Muslims charged Christians 1 *dīnār* a year and allowed them to live in Muslim society and practise their religion freely; the Christians, in Jerusalem, Spain and other places, did not charge Muslims 1 *dīnār* a year – instead they wiped them out.

It is a fact that there have always been Christians and Jews living among the Muslims, some even serving as members of the government at the height of the Islamic state; but no Muslims were left, for example, in Spain, Sicily, and other places from which Christians expelled them, and genocide was still practised in Europe in the 20th century.[7]

Within the Muslim world itself, people are aware of the magnanimous nature of Islam as expressed by the Prophet, who called it *ḥanīfiyya samḥa* 'lenient and magnanimous'. There have always been different *madhhabs* or schools of law, which accept each other, enlightened by the statement attributed to the Prophet: 'Differences of opinion in my community are a mercy'. There is nothing in Islamic history similar to what happened between the Protestants and the Catholics, or the conformists and non-conformists in the West.

Leniency marks Islamic teachings, even in strictly legal matters. In the Qur'an, the door is always open for repentance and making amends for major penal offences like premeditated murder, highway robbery, theft and adultery, as well as in all offences that require punishment in this world and the next. Apostasy has no punishment in this world specified in the Qur'an; the penalty is left to the Day of Judgement:

But whoever of you recants and dies as an unbeliever his works shall come to nothing in this world and the world to come. Such people shall be the tenants of Hell.

2:217

If any among you renounce their faith, God will replace them by others who love Him and are loved by Him.

5:54

Those who return to unbelief after God's guidance has been revealed to them, are seduced by Satan and inspired by him.

47:25

In the Bible the situation is different:

If you hear it said about one of the towns the Lord your God is giving you to live in, that wicked men have arisen among you and have led the people of their town astray, saying, 'Let us go and worship other gods' (gods you have not known), then you must enquire, probe and investigate it thoroughly. And if it is true and it has been proved that this detestable thing has been done among you, you must certainly put to the sword all who live in that town. Destroy it completely, both its people and its livestock. Gather all the plunder of the town into the middle of the public square and completely burn the town and all its plunder as a whole burnt offering to the Lord your God. It is to remain a ruin for ever, never to be rebuilt.

DEUTERONOMY: 13:12–16

A man or woman who is proved to be worshipping other gods is to be stoned to death to 'purge the evil from among you'.[8]

The death penalty mentioned in the *ḥadīth* of the Prophet Muhammad was not just for apostasy but for those who commit high treason against the Muslims by joining the enemy at war with them, or who commit other capital crimes against Muslims. The Qur'an itself tells us that a group of 'People of the Book' schemed to enter Islam at the beginning of the day and renounce it at the end of the day so that the Muslims themselves might abandon Islam (3:72).

The Current Meaning of Tolerance

'Tolerance' now refers to tolerating the views, beliefs and practices of others that differ from one's own. This is dictated by the demands of the new spirit of globalisation, pluralism, democracy, campaigns for human rights, non-discrimination laws, freedom of expression, secularisation, and the dwindling influence of religion in the life of the West. In the light of this there has been more emancipation for women, campaigns against discrimination on grounds of ethnicity, class and, more recently sexual orientation, as well as for the protection of minorities. This new sense of tolerance is broadening so fast that there are people now, even in the West, who are worried about the extent of the new spirit of tolerance:

> The redefined notion of tolerance, on the other hand, doesn't merely ask for a respect of differences but often demands acceptance of the beliefs and practices of others.[9]

Against this background, the Islamic revival, which reasserts the role of religion in the Muslim countries appears, to many people in the West, to be intolerant.

Can Islamic teachings be 'tolerant' in this current sense? Can Muslims maintain that Islamic teachings could be reinterpreted to sanction campaigns for sexual freedom, for instance? Can Muslims say that these are matters of personal freedom and religion has no say in them? Such a position, if held by a Muslim, would be untenable. Muslims read in the Qur'an that there are things which God has forbidden and even if individuals cannot live up to that standard, no one has the right to determine as lawful that which God has made unlawful (16:116). Those who deviate from religious norms know they are deviating and know that God forgives those who come back to Him but would not accept from them to claim or campaign for their practices to be accepted as a norm.

Limits to the Concept of Tolerance

Islamic law does not search into the heart or the private behaviour of any person: the Prophet of Islam even recommended that individuals who deviate from religious norms should keep their sins to themselves and ask God for forgiveness but, as Law, Islam protects social order. Thus it ordains enjoining what is good, and forbidding what is wrong. In fact, no religion can be said to be fully 'tolerant' in this respect, nor can any legal system. In this age of political lobbies and campaigns, Islam would not allow campaigning for the decriminalisation of drugs or practices that fundamentally undermine the family system:

Those who love to see scandal spread about among the believers will have a grievous penalty in this life and the life Hereafter: God knows, and ye know not.

24:19

Muslims in non-Muslim Countries

In Western society, where religion is increasingly marginalised, Muslims, within their own community, are under the obligation to maintain the Qur'anic injunctions of ordering what is good and forbidding what is wrong, and acting within the general rule, 'Call to the way of your Lord with wisdom and kindly exhortation' (16:125). They are under the obligation not to dilute their religious teachings in keeping with whatever practices or campaigns appear in the society around them. In their relations with others, the guiding principles for Muslims are that 'there is no compulsion in religion' (2:256), 'to you is your religion and to me mine' (109:6) and 'Whoever will, let him believe and whosoever will not, let him disbelieve' (18:29). Muslims are under a religious obligation not to force their religion or norms on others and they are forbidden to accept norms of 'tolerance' that undermine their religious teachings, which others may attempt to force on them. They are under a religious obligation to co-operate with other people who work to maintain what is good, but not to do what is wrong:

Aid one another in what is good and pious; do not aid one another in what is sinful and aggression.

5:2

A draft report presented to the European Parliament in 1997, entitled 'Fundamentalism: a challenge to the European Judicial System'[10] asserted that:

The model of Western society draws its characteristics from the history of Europe. Some key elements of this are democracy, the rule of law, human rights, separation of church and state. It shows evidence of a great tolerance with regard to ideas, convictions and different modes of life...

Democracy, the rule of law and human rights are all cherished by Muslims. 'The history of Europe' with regard to tolerance has already been discussed. As for respect for human rights, the European country that issued a Declaration of the Rights of Man and the Citizen two centuries ago still denies Muslim girls the right to wear headscarves in school.

If, because of their historical background, some in the West feel that in order to become tolerant, they have to 'separate Church and State', and distance themselves from religion, Muslims do not have to abandon their religious teachings in order to become tolerant: true tolerance is enshrined in the teachings of the Qur'an.

7
Life and Beyond

In the Qur'an life in this world is an inseparable part of a continuum, a unified whole – life, death, life – which gives our life a context and relevance. In this context, the life of the individual is made meaningful and enriched inasmuch as it is full of 'good works'. Life in this world leads to the afterlife, a belief which is fundamental in the Qur'an. The afterlife is not treated in the Qur'an in a separate chapter, or as something on its own, for its own sake, but always in relation to life in this world.

Linguistically it is not possible in the Qur'an to talk about this life without semantic reference to the next since every term used for each is comparative with the other. Thus: *al-'ūlā* and *al-ākhira* (the First and the Last life), *al-dunyā* and *al-ākhira* (the nearer and the further/latter life). Neither has a name specific to itself, or independent of the other. Consequently, the frequency of the terms in the Qur'an is the same, in the case of *dunyā* and *ākhira* – each appears 115 times.[1]

There is a reference, direct or indirect, to one aspect or another of the afterlife on almost every single page of the Qur'an. This follows from the fact that belief in the afterlife is an article of faith which has a bearing on every aspect of the present life and manifests itself in the discussion of the creed, the rituals, the ethics and the laws of Islam. In discussing the afterlife, moreover, the Qur'an addresses both believers and non-believers. The plan of two worlds and the relationship between them has been, from the beginning, part of the divine scheme of things:

It is God Who created you, then He provided sustenance for you, then He will cause you to die, then He will give life back to you.

30:40

It is We Who give life and make to die and to Us is the homecoming.

50:43

He created death and life that He might try you according to which of you is best in works.

67:2

According to the Qur'an, belief in the afterlife, which is an issue fundamental to the mission of Muhammad, was also central to the mission of all prophets before him.[2]

Belief in the afterlife is often referred to in conjunction with belief in God, as in the expression: 'If you believe in God and the Last Day'. Believers are frequently reminded in the Qur'an, 'Be mindful of God and know that you shall meet Him' (2:233) (used in this instance to urge fitting treatment of one's wife in intimate situations). 'To Him is the homecoming/ the return' (36:83; 40:3 and *passim*). As a belief in the afterlife is so fundamental to Islam, it is only right that Muslims should regularly be reminded of it not only throughout the pages of the Qur'an but also in their daily life. Practising Muslims in their five daily prayers repeat their praise of God at least 17 times a day, 'The Master of the Day of Judgement' (1:4). Being inattentive to the afterlife (30:7) or to the prospect of coming to Judgement (32:14) are signs of the unbeliever. All this heightens the believer's sense of responsibility for actions in this life. In fact the principles and details of religion are meant to be seen within the framework of the interdependence of this life and the afterlife and to colour the Muslims' conception of life and the universe and have a bearing on their actions in this life.

The Importance of the Resurrection and Judgement in the Afterlife

Divine wisdom and justice necessitate the resurrection of the dead and judgement in an afterlife:

We have not created the heavens and the earth and all that is between them save in truth. Surely the Hour[3] is coming.

15:85

Did you think that We created you in vain and that you would not be returned to Us? Exalted by God, the King, the True!

23:115–6

It is not in vain that We created the heavens and earth and all that lies between them. That is the fancy of the unbelievers ... Are We to equate those that have faith and do good works with those that corrupt the earth with wickedness? Are We to equate the righteous with the transgressors?

38:27–8

In the Qur'an, as in other scriptures, people are required to labour, doing certain things and refraining from others. Justice requires that labour should be rewarded. Recompense is made, not during the period of labour in this world, but in the afterlife:

What then can make you deny the last Judgement? Is God not the best of judges?

95:7–8

The resurrection is thus:

... a binding promise from God that shall be fulfilled though most people may not know it, so that He may resolve their differences for them.

16:38–9

In the Qur'an, Judgement is so essential to human beings that God has created them with a peculiar, innate permanent judge within themselves, that is 'conscience', the 'reproachful soul'. Indeed this is marked in a chapter entitled *The Resurrection* in which God declares:

I swear by the Day of Resurrection, and by the reproachful soul! Does man think We shall never put his bones together again? Yes indeed: We can remould his very fingers.

75:1–4

The 'reproachful soul' foreshadows the judgement and is here placed side by side, in the oath, with the resurrection that precedes the judgement. In answer to the unbelievers' incredulity that the scattered bones of dead people can be resurrected into new life, God swears that it will be done. Modern interpreters see in the phrase, 'his very fingers', reference to the power of God who moulds our finger prints in a way unique to each individual: He has done it in this life and can do it again in the afterlife.

The Possibility of the Resurrection of the Dead

In addition to the necessity and desirability of the resurrection and afterlife, the Qur'an turns repeatedly to its possibility. During the Meccan period of the Prophet's mission, a great deal of the Qur'an was concerned with the three fundamental beliefs of the Unity of God, the Prophethood of

Muhammad and other prophets before him, and the resurrection and judgement. The resurrection in particular seemed incredible to unbelievers. Indeed much of what one hears today is reminiscent of what unbelievers said at the time of the revelation of the Qur'an. They felt the resurrection to be biologically impossible, asking again and again:

How, after we die and become dust and bones could we be raised again?

56:47

Against this, the Qur'an employs a basic argument which is not difficult to accept rationally, equating two similar feats: the power that can accomplish something once can do it again. From the fact that human beings now exist, it is clear that divine power was not incapable of making them: why should it be assumed that such power will be incapable of doing for a second time what it achieved the first (50:15)? Indeed a second creation is easier than a first one (30:27).

The Qur'an repeatedly reminds people that they were made into human beings from something very small:

Is man not aware that We created him from a little germ? Yet he is flagrantly contentious. He raises an argument and forgets his own creation. He asks: 'Who will give life to rotten bones?' Say: 'He Who first brought them into being will give them life again: He has knowledge of every creation; Who has made for you out of the green tree fire and lo! from it you kindle.'

36:77–80

This last point affirms the ability of a power that generates things from seemingly opposite or different things – a fire from green trees and bodies from bones and dust; just as a full grown man is different from the little germ that was his beginning. If they ask:

'What! When we are lost in the earth shall we be created afresh?'

32:13

The answer comes:

We know all that the earth takes away from them. We have a book which records all things.

50:4

Another rational argument the Qur'an uses to convince disbelievers of the truth of the resurrection is the comparison between the greater act of creation and the lesser act of resurrection:

Has He Who created the heavens and the earth no power to create the like of the unbelievers? That He surely has. He is the All-creator, the All-knowing.

36:81

The Qur'an asserts for those who may not know it:

Certainly the creation of the heavens and the earth is greater than the creation of men, but most men know it not.

40:57

Perhaps when the unbelievers say it is not possible to turn dust into a new creation, what they really think is that it is not possible for human power like their own; but, after all, they have not created themselves or the heavens and the earth (52:35–6). A greater power than their own has created them once and can do so again, and has also created what is greater than them. As the Qur'an argues with the unbelievers, sometimes it even omits the name of the Creator, in order to focus their minds more clearly on the argument itself, saying simply, 'He Who did it first', 'Who created the Heavens', etc. When the Prophet recites Qur'anic verses that confirm the resurrection in the afterlife, the unbelievers of his time challenge him personally:

Bring back to us our fathers, if what you say be true!

The Qur'an directs the Prophet:

Say: 'It is God Who gives you life, then makes you die, then He shall gather you to the Resurrection.'

45:25–6

In discussing the resurrection, moreover, the Qur'an cites phenomena very familiar to human beings to show the power that takes creation through different stages, particularly in the life of people and plants.

People, if you doubt the Resurrection, remember that We first created you from dust, then from a living germ, then from a tiny clinging thing, and then from a half-formed lump of flesh, so that We might manifest to you Our power.

We cause whatever We please to remain in the wombs for an appointed term, and then

We bring you forth as infants, that you may grow up and reach your prime. Some are caused to die young, and some are left to live on to abject old age when all that they once knew they know no more.

You sometimes see the earth dry and barren: but no sooner do We send down rain upon it than it begins to stir and swell, putting forth every kind of radiant bloom. That is because God is Truth: He resurrects the dead and has power over all things.

22:5–6

Indeed the Qur'an uses the very same Arabic verb for 'bringing forth' people from their mothers' wombs (16:78), 'bringing forth' plants from the earth (6:99) and 'bringing forth' people from the earth at the resurrection (30:19).

Not only does the Qur'an present proof of the resurrection, but it turns the argument against those who deny it, pointing out that they themselves have no proof for their own position:

They say: 'There is nothing but our present life; we live and die; nothing but time destroys us.' Of this they have no knowledge; they merely conjecture.

45:24

At the resurrection they will know that what they said was wrong and will regret it.

16:39; 6:31

Beyond this Life

Every soul shall taste of death (3:185)

Death is the gateway to the return to God (6:61–2). Man's body may disintegrate after death but his soul is not the object of annihilation. By death man enters the stage of *barzakh*, an intermediate state between this life and the resurrection (23:100). The Qur'an says little about this stage: it indicates only that the soul will receive reward or punishment (3:169–71; 16:32; 40:45–6; 71:25). Much more is to be found in the traditions of the Prophet.[4] On visiting or passing by a grave or a cemetery, a Muslim greets the dead with the same greeting as for the living: 'Peace be to you!' and adds, 'You are our forerunners and we are following after you, may God forgive us and you!'

At the resurrection the time spent in the grave will appear to men 'as if it were an hour of the day' (10:45). The state of *barzakh* will end at 'the

Hour', the end of the world, and then the resurrection will take place. The time of this 'Hour' is known only to God (7:187). Thus, when asked by one of his followers when it would come, the Prophet directs him to what is more fruitful, answering, 'What have you prepared for it?'

Compared to the little that is said about the state of *barzakh*, there is much in the Qur'an about the end of the world, the resurrection, the Judgement, and the recompense in the final abode.

The Nature of the Resurrection

Will the resurrection and afterlife be only spiritual, or will it be bodily as well? Although some, especially Sufis, hold that it will be only spiritual,[5] and that Qur'anic statements which suggest it is bodily are no more than figures of speech to assist the general reader's comprehension, the general character of Qur'anic statements indicates that it will be bodily and spiritual. As the Muslim philosopher Ibn Rushd (known in the West as Averroes) explains:

> Some Muslims consider that existence in the afterlife is of the same nature as in this life, only there it will be permanent. Others believe that bodily existence there is different from bodily existence here.

As Ibn 'Abbas, the companion of the Prophet, said, this world shares nothing with the afterlife except the names of things. The Qur'an itself indicates that bodily existence in the afterlife will be a 'new' creation, so that our bodies there will not be those we have here (e.g. 56:35, 61). It speaks of the descriptions of Paradise as being likenesses – *mathal* – (e.g. 13:35; 47:15) and the food there 'appears similar' – *mutashābih* – to what it is here (2:25). The Prophet says about Paradise: 'There are in it things that no eye has seen, no ear has heard and what has never occurred to the mind of man.'

As Ibn Rushd points out, this view of the resurrected body as a different, spiritual one, is more appropriate for the educated, who can understand it, since the spiritual existence is permanent and the concept that the soul returns in a new body avoids such complicated arguments as the objection that the worldly body turns into dust, and nourishes plants, which are then eaten by other people, from whose bodies come the bodies of their descendants, and so on.[6] Conversely, Ibn Rushd explains, the representation of existence in the afterlife as being bodily and not merely spiritual, is more suitable for the majority of people, as it is easier to understand and more moving.[7] Figurative representation of spiritual realities may be appropriate only for speculative thinkers, whereas the simpler religious explanations are aimed primarily at the great majority.

Judgement

There are graphic descriptions in the Qur'an of the end of the world, resurrection and judgement.[8] A most important element is the judgement, when 'people will come to be shown their deeds', each facing judgement 'alone'. 'No soul will carry the burden of another'. Each will be confronted with a book of their deeds:

Read your book. Your own soul suffices you this day as a reckoner against you.

14:16

The book shall be laid open, the prophets and witnesses shall be brought in and all shall be judged with fairness, they shall not be wronged. Every soul will be paid in full what it wrought. He knows very well what they do.

39:69–70

Whoever does an atom's weight of good shall see it, and whoever does an atom's weight of evil shall see it also.

99:7–8

Whoever brings good, he will have better than it; and whoever brings evil, those who do evil will be requited for what they did.

28:84

Good deeds can be multiplied as much as seven hundred times (6:160; 2:261). Thus the judgement is vital for, although God is the most merciful (12:64) and His mercy encompasses all things (7:156), without the judgement, divine commandments would make no sense: observation and violation, good and evil deeds would all be the same.

Are We to equate those that have faith and do good works with those that corrupt the earth with wickedness? Are We to equate the righteous with the transgressors?

38:27–8

Exalted be God, the King the Truth.

23:116

Recompense

There is much description in the Qur'an of rewards and punishment. As human beings have bodies, minds and spirits, all of which are gifts from God and as, out of His grace He provided mankind with the means of gratifying all these components in this life, so in the afterlife He will provide means of gratifying them all to 'those who believed and did good works' (7:32). Bodies, as we have noted, will be 'a new creation' and in Paradise will not suffer the shortcomings of worldly bodies. As will be seen in the following chapter, in Paradise, 'No mortal knows what comfort is in store for them as a reward for their labours' (32:17). 'No evil shall visit them' – the Arabic word *sū'* includes whatever is undesirable (39:16; 40:7). There is no tedium there, such as sceptics now invoke as an argument against eternal existence. 'They will live in the land of perfect peace' (6:127). The honour God will confer on them will be their highest reward.[9] An opposite picture is given of punishment, the essence of which is humiliation.[10]

As already pointed out, the Qur'an does not treat the afterlife as something theoretical or in a separate chapter at the end of the book. It is embedded in the text throughout and its effect on the reader is enhanced by the vivid and powerful language of the Arabic text. After a short conjunction like 'when' to indicate the afterlife, it commonly employs the past and present tense as if it had happened and was already here.[11]

There is an obvious interdependence between this life and the afterlife. We have seen how the terms occur with equal frequency in the Qur'an and how linguistically one cannot utter the name of one without semantic reference to the other. Everything in the judgement has to do with action in the world. Dwellers in Paradise or Hell sometimes talk about what they did in this world (52:28; 40:47).

The Afterlife and the Present Life

In the Qur'an, life in this world, through its relation to the afterlife, has much more significance than it would otherwise have. A whole new dimension is given to the lives of those who believe that they will live beyond the grave, and will not be terminated in dust. They are continually reminded of this (at least seventeen times a day, as we have said, for practising Muslims). The life of the individual continues in the two worlds, but through different stages: from the womb to the world, to the grave, to the resurrection, judgement and lasting life in the final abode – the intervening period in the grave will seem 'a mere part of a day' (23:113).

The Qur'an does not disparage the present life; both lives are created by God and

To God belong the last life and the first life.

53:25

He created for you all that the earth contains.

2:29

Eat of what your Lord has given you and render thanks to Him.

7:10; 50:7; 34:15; 7:32

In gathering wealth the faithful are 'seeking the bounty of God'. They are directed to do this after finishing the prayer in which they praise 'the Master of the Day of Judgement' (62:10; 65:17; 73:20). In seeking to attain Paradise, they should always bear in mind the Qur'anic exhortation: 'Do not neglect your share in this world' (28:77).

The Qur'an nonetheless states (as something that earlier scriptures confirm) that the afterlife is 'better and more lasting than this life' (87:17–9). God objects to

... those who do not expect to meet Us and are well pleased with the present life and content themselves with it and who give no heed to Our revelations.

10:7

In Islam a believer, while enjoying what is good in this life, can at the same time be working for the next one. Islam does not recognise a clear-cut distinction between what is worldly and what is religious. The Prophet once mentioned that among the 'good deeds' which one can store up for the afterlife is having sexual intercourse with one's spouse. A companion exclaimed: 'Prophet, but this is something we enjoy, how can we be rewarded for it?' to which he answered: 'If you were to do it unlawfully, would you not be punished for it?' 'Yes.' 'Conversely you will be rewarded for doing it lawfully.'

The Qur'an emphasises that no-one will escape death, the resurrection or judgement, and that the way to salvation in the afterlife is through faith and good works in this life; but 'God does not charge a soul with more than it can bear' (2:286). The length of life given to any person here is limited by its 'appointed term' (*ajal*– a word that is mentioned in the Qur'an some forty times). This is the only chance to work for a good life in the next world (35:37). The urgency is expressed by the frequent use of the expression 'before' (*min qabl an*) death or the Hour comes, for example:

Give of that with which We have provided you before death befalls any of you, and you say: 'Reprieve me my Lord, a while, that I may give in charity and be among the righteous.' But God reprieves no soul when its term expires. God is aware of all your actions.

63:10–1

The Prophet said:

He whose day is no better than the day before it has done himself wrong.

He also said:

When a son of Adam dies his deeds cease, except through three things: a running charity that he founded, useful knowledge he left behind, or a good child who prays for him.

Of the judgement he said:

No person will leave the judgement place before being asked about four things: his life span and how he spent it, his knowledge and what he did with it, his body and in which things he wore it out, and his wealth – from where he collected it and how he spent it.

Life in this world is made more significant by the fact that judgement and recompense in the afterlife are only for 'deeds' done in this one. Good deeds are good for the individual, society, humanity and all the world which God, *Rabb al-'ālamīn* (the Lord of all Worlds), created, appointing man 'a viceroy on earth' (2:30). The Prophet of Islam said: 'If the Hour comes while one of you is holding a palm-seedling, if he can plant it before the Hour overtakes him, he should plant it.' We know that the Hour puts an end to the present order of things, yet the 'good deed' should be done. The Qur'an addresses Muslims and followers of other faiths:

God has ordained a law and a path for each of you. Had God wished it, He could have made you into one nation, but in order to try you in what has come to you, He has made you as you are. So vie with one another in good works, for to God you shall all return and He will declare to you what you have disagreed about.

5:48

Believers are taught in the Qur'an to pray:

Lord, give us good in this life and good in the afterlife.

2:201

8

Paradise in the Qur'an

Paradise, the abode of the righteous in the hereafter, is called, in the Qur'an, *al-janna*, meaning 'the Garden'. It is one of the major themes of the Qur'an, occurring under this name over one hundred times[1] and under other designations, like the *Firdaws*,[2] Home of Peace, and Home of the Righteous and many more. This reflects the fundamental significance of the final judgement and requital in Islamic theology. People are given time in the present world to make real choices for themselves. To allow full requital in the here and now would run counter to this plan (35:45). Whatever recompense may come in this world is not comprehensive, lasting or complete, and is mixed with the imperfections of this world (42:30; 3:165; 87:17). Full, pure and lasting rewards will come about in the phase of judgement. This is a binding promise from God, who does not break promises. As already explained in the previous chapter, the Qur'an thus repeatedly produces arguments for the desirability, necessity and possibility of the resurrection and judgement.

'The Garden' and 'Gardens'

Following the judgement, the righteous are admitted to the *janna*. The basic meaning of *janna* is 'a garden with trees, rivers and fruits'.[3] Another basic element is the shade provided by the numerous luxuriant luscious trees.[4] The garden, with its vitality, abundance and comfort, provides a fitting home for those who 'believe and do good works', especially as it always contrasts in the Qur'an with Hell, the abode of evil-doers.

Janna, in the eschatological sense, occurs in the Qur'an thirty-five times in the singular, in the dual (*jannatān*) twice and in the plural (*jannāt*) sixty-nine times. In the singular it refers to one entity, the entire abode of the righteous, in contrast to Hell as the abode of the wicked. Within this large entity of Paradise, individual believers with their families will have their own private *jannas*. The multiplicity of reward, seen here in the use of the plural form, is an example of one of the features of Qur'anic style by which descriptions of rewards give the impression of unlimited plenty. The dual of *janna* occurs in a context where the pious are surrounded by two gardens, on the left and on the right – a privilege contrasting sharply with the torment of the evildoers, who roam between fire and boiling water.[5] Usually, more descriptive details recur with the dual and plural (where the righteous reside) than with the singular of *janna*, the whole realm of Paradise, where the references are more general. Compare:

... they will be in Jannat and in happiness, rejoicing in the bliss which their Lord has bestowed on them ... eat and drink! ... seated upon couches ...

52:17–28

... receive the glad tidings of (al-Janna) which you were promised!

41:30

With the exception of very few cases, particularly the final short *sūras*, every *sūra* in the Qur'an has something to say about *janna* in varying degrees of detail. In dealing with such a vital belief as the judgement and the consequences of human life and actions, the Qur'an does not isolate the discussion of rewards in one comprehensive chapter, which would have been limited, less likely to excite the imagination and less likely to be read, heard or remembered by some people. As it is, in their reading or hearing the Qur'an in daily life and prayer, Muslims are regularly reminded of the consequences of their actions and of their destiny in the more lasting life in the Hereafter. The distribution of the material varies in length between one *sūra* and another, sometimes very short (e.g. 85, 89, 101) and sometimes much longer (e.g. 55, 56, 76), but even when it is very concise the material recalls and evokes the more extended descriptions. This is brought out particularly in Qur'an commentaries which apply the two principles: *al-Qur'ān yufassir ba'ḍuh ba'ḍa* 'different parts of the Qur'an explain each other' and *yuḥmal al-muṭlaq 'ala-muqayyad* – 'unqualified statements should be interpreted in the light of qualified ones'.

Entering the Garden

Understandably, *janna* is a very special place and it is a great distinction to be admitted through its gates (39:73). 'Entering' is clearly so important that the word is used in different derivations fifty-seven times: e.g. 'Enter among My servants', 'Enter My *janna*', 'Enter in peace and security' (89:29–30; 15:46); 'God will cause those who believe and do good works to enter the Gardens beneath which rivers flow', or 'Assuredly He will cause them to enter – an entry that is well-pleasing to them' (22:14, 59). Such a public welcome enhances the honour conferred on them in front of all.

Protection

Obviously, an important aspect of defining the rewards in Paradise relates to the contrast the Qur'an normally shows in adjacent verses between Paradise and Hell. The true picture of Paradise can be more fully appreciated in the light of the contrasting picture of Hell:

Which is better, this [Hell] or the Garden of Immortality which the righteous have been promised?

25:15

Not equal are the heirs of the Fire and the heirs of the Garden.

59:20

Hell is 'an evil dwelling and an evil resting place', while Paradise is 'a blessed dwelling and a blessed resting-place' (25:66–76). Naturally the most important thing in rewards is first to be protected from Hell and its torment. *Wiqāya* (protection, preservation) occurs twelve times in this context.

The dwellers in Paradise rejoice in what their Lord has given them and He has protected them from the torment of Hell-Fire.

52:18

The Qur'an does not just describe the state of the righteous in Paradise, but frequently makes them express their state and feelings directly:

Praise be to God who has put grief away from us. Toil cannot touch us nor can weariness affect us.

34:34–5

God has been gracious to us and preserved us from the torment of the breath of Fire.

52:27

Even in the world the believers have been praying:

Lord give us good in this world and good in the Hereafter and protect us from Hell-Fire.
2:201

Protection from Hell is their first reward, but within *janna* itself, the righteous are further protected from everything that might spoil their joy.

Evil shall not touch them, nor shall they grieve.
39:61

No fear shall be on them, neither shall they sorrow.
10:62

Protection from *ḥazan* (grief) is repeated fourteen times and the number is about the same for *khawf* (fear). Unlike those in Hell, they will suffer no shame (66:8), no malice will spoil their friendship (15:47).

In it they will hear no idle talk nor any lying.
78:35

They will not hear the even the slightest sounds of Hell.
21:102

No discomfort or ill health will result from eating and drinking there. The drink is pure. It neither dulls their senses nor causes intoxication (37:47); it causes no headaches (56:19); it is 'a cup wherein there is neither vanity nor cause of sin' (52:23).

Unlike this world, where everything good is doomed to end, those in Paradise will not taste death (44:56). Their gifts will have no end (38:54). The fruits will be unending and unforbidden (56:32). It is an abode of eternity (35:35). In it they will abide for ever (98:8). The importance of this sense of security and peace in Paradise is borne out by the fact that it is repeated over forty times. It is further emphasised by confirmation that the blessed will not be expelled from it (15:48), nor will they desire to move away from it (18:108).

The Physical Picture

The physical picture one gets from Qur'anic references to *janna* is that it is vast, 'as wide as are the heavens and the earth' (3:133; 57:21). Its inhabitants can move freely and settle wherever they wish (39:74). It is lofty (69:22;

88:10), 'underneath which rivers flow'. This is an essential feature occurring no less than thirty-six times. Rivers in the Garden are always in the plural (*anhār*) and always flow (*tajrī*), which suggests sparkling, cooling and enlivening sounds. There are running springs and fountains (nine times) of fragrant drinking water (76:5, 18). The trees give plentiful, spreading shade (4:57; 56:30). The temperate climate is unspoiled by harshness of sun or cold (76:13). An important element in the garden is fruit (twelve times) – plentiful, unforbidden, never ending, its clusters are within easy reach (56:22–3; 69:23).

In these pleasing surroundings stand 'goodly dwellings' (9:72) with 'lofty chambers above and rivers flowing beneath' (39:20). There are detailed descriptions of these goodly dwellings (e.g. 55:52–72; 56:15–34; 88:13–16) – raised couches upholstered in brocade, goblets placed ready, cushions arranged and carpets outspread. We see the dwellers in pleasant company: 'They shall enter the garden of Eden, together with the righteous among their parents, their spouses and descendants' (13:23; 52:20–1) adorned in green silk. They sit on couches in a relaxed manner, engaged in pleasant conversation, recalling happy memories, absorbed in rejoicing; their faces shining, laughing and joyous (80:38–9) – the effect of life in the hereafter on faces is particularly pronounced in the Qur'an.[6] They will be attended by servants of immortal youth, who, to the beholders' eyes, will seem like sprinkled pearls, offering to them pure drinks, flesh of birds, and fruits of their own choice; they will have whatever they call for (36:57; 52:22–5; 56:18–21; 76:15–19).

Proper Perspective

The popular conception of Paradise in the Qur'an (based perhaps on an exaggeration of this physical picture) is that it is the abode of sensual pleasure[7] par excellence; but examination of actual descriptions in the Qur'an gives quite a different picture.

It will be seen in the following discussion that: (i) the inhabitants of *janna* are not seen to indulge in sensual pleasures; (ii) material rewards are seen to be symbolic of honouring; (iii) material rewards are actually outnumbered by moral and spiritual rewards; (iv) material rewards are also outranked by these non-material ones.

Although food is provided, throughout the Qur'an the dwellers in Paradise are not usually seen actually eating. Four items of food are mentioned: flesh of fowl twice, fruits twelve times, and pure honey and milk once. They are invited to 'eat and drink' but this invitation is made only three times out of the twenty-seven where this expression is used in the Qur'an; the rest of the references are to do with this world. In any case, eating and drinking in the Garden is not for the protection of life or health, as God has given the inhabitants bodies that do not deteriorate.[8] The meat and fruit available in Paradise (described as being 'of what they choose' and 'of what they desire' (56:20–1) are offered as a token of honour (37:42).

There are more references to drinking but the inhabitants are still not seen actually drinking:

And their Lord gave them to drink a drink most pure: This is a reward for you, your endeavour is thanked.

76:21,22

This is a high honour indeed: the Lord Himself gives them a drink and they are told by God (or the angel) that their endeavours are thanked. Intoxicants are mentioned by name only once (47:15) and drinks there do not lead to headiness or sin (37:47; 52:23).

The luxurious couches, cushions, carpets, cups and plates 'which they themselves have measured to their liking' (76:16); the servants, the green silken robes and the ornaments they will wear (with which there is nothing inherently wrong by human standards) are all tokens of the honour given them by their Lord (76:22). As Muhammad Abdallah Diraz has rightly asked:

Why should some people insist at all costs on removing any material element from happiness in the afterlife? Does the order and beauty in nature harm the order and beauty in the soul? ... There is no doubt that when a wise person knows their smaller value he will not seek them for their own sake, but he will not reject them either when they are provided. Is it right that we should reject a friendly hand extended to give us a present or place an ornament on our chest? The material value of such things is smaller than their symbolic meaning which indicates satisfaction that we cannot reject in the face of the presenter without injury to the sense of good taste.[9]

The Qur'an repeats (seventeen times) that the righteous will dwell in *jannāt al-na'īm. Na'īm* has been rendered by some translators as 'pleasure' or 'delight'. This is rather restrictive to the wider meaning of *ni'ma* (from which *na'īm* is derived) as used in the Qur'an: favouring humanity with religion, prophethood, grace, blessing, causing unity after disunity, freedom, prosperity, cleanliness (among others) – all are said in the Qur'an to be *ni'ma* from God.[10] *Na'īm* should be interpreted in the light of the full picture of *janna*; superficial, ill-founded interpretation of *ni'ma* as 'pleasure' contributes to the distorted popular picture of Paradise in the Qur'an.

Another aspect of *janna* which contributes to the popular image of physical pleasure is the '*houris*'. Part of God's blessing on the righteous is that they will be joined in Paradise with the righteous of their parents, spouses (*azwāj*) and offspring (13:23).[11] This is in stark contrast to the dwellers of Hell who will suffer loneliness. The *azwāj* (mentioned seven times) are described as being 'made pure' (2:25; 3:15; 4:57)[12] and four times as being *hūr* – i.e. of wide, brilliantly black and white eyes. Beauty of the eyes is part of the beauty of faces, and the dwellers in Paradise delight in looking at each other's faces. *Al-Janna* is not the home of 'believing men' only but also of 'believing women'. This is made clear in such passages as 3:195; 4:124, 176; 9:72; 16:97; 33:35 and 48:5. The believing women of this world will be *hur* there, as the Prophet explains in his *ḥadīth*. The *hur* will be lustrous in colour, like rubies and pearls (55:58; 56:23). First they are described as being of modest gaze, then as having beautiful eyes (37:48). They are described once as being *kawā'ib* and mutually affectionate (78:33), and twice as being of similar age to their companions (78:33; 56:37). Many translators render *kawa'ib* as 'of swelling breasts'. Pickthall gives 'maiden' which is the correct rendering: in the *ḥadīth*, as Ibn Manzur explains in *Lisān al-'Arab*, *kawā'ib* refers to young girls when their breasts are beginning to appear (*al-ka'āb: al-mar'a ḥīna yabdū thadyuhā li'l-nuhūd*), so the description actually refers to the young age rather than emphasising swelling breasts. They have been created anew and made virgin (56:35–6).

In fact physical description of women is limited. There is no overt mention in the Qur'an of sex taking place between spouses in *janna*, although the relationship is lawful between spouses and the Qur'an does not shy away from mentioning it in the context of this world: for example, in explaining what is permissible during the nights of the fast, it says, 'You may lie with your spouses and eat and drink' (2:187); but in Paradise, even though at times the inhabitants are invited to 'eat and drink', there is no overt mention of relations with spouses and no similar permission is given. The mutual love between spouses in the Garden (56:37–8) epitomises the most fulfilling aspect of the relationship between spouses as expressed in the Qur'an:

And of His signs is that He created for you, of yourselves, spouses that you might repose in them; and He has ordained between you love and mercy.

30:21

People in Paradise are never seen lying down or sleeping. Seven times they are said to be *muttaki'in.* Translators render this as 'reclining', which is incorrect as this is the colloquial meaning and not the one used in the Qur'an. As Ibn Manzur observed: '*al-muttaki'* in Arabic is anyone who sits on something (like a couch or a chair), firmly seated; the common people know the *muttaki'* only as someone who is reclining on his side.' The dwellers in Paradise are thus shown in the Qur'an sitting and talking to each other.

The most frequently recurring physical characteristic of *janna* is that rivers run beneath it or beneath the dwellings (thirty-four times, and four times beneath the inhabitants).[13] Water in *janna* is not seen stagnant, as in a tank, lake or reservoir, but flowing and gushing in rivers or springs (55:50, 66; 88:12). It is always beneath so it does not fall on the inhabitants or soak them. They can also look down on it and derive the delight one experiences in gazing from above on running water. This emphasis on the living qualities of water in Paradise (which in any case is not surprising in a garden) has to be seen in the light of the importance of water in the Qur'an in general.[14] God declares:

We made from water every living thing.

21:30

And you see the earth barren and lifeless, but when We send down water upon it, it thrills and swells and puts forth every joyous kind of growth.

22:5

Do you not see that God sends down water from the sky and then the earth becomes green on the morrow?

22:63

The cleansing quality of 'pure water' is also clearly emphasised in the Qur'an, but some verses also indicate moral and spiritual effects of water beyond the physical cleansing.

He sent down water from the sky to purify you thereby and to remove from you the stain of Satan and to strengthen your hearts.

8:11

One cannot ignore the juxtaposition of water with moral qualities in Paradise, in such verses as:

We removed from their hearts any rancour; beneath them rivers flow and they said 'Praise be to God Who has guided us to this.'

7:43

In the garden is no idle talk; there is a gushing fountain.

88:11–12

Clearly they delight in contemplating such beauties. They praise God for them and are freed from anger and idle talk.

In none of the numerous passages on *al-janna* throughout the Qur'an do we get a full picture. What we have, even in the longer passages, is like a photographic snapshot of a scene. These snapshots appear to be taken on arrival after the judgement, of which this reward is the outcome.[15] All the scenes are of groups (not individuals or couples) sitting (not lying down or reclining) on couches lined up (56:15) in 'lounges'. The furnishings provided are clearly for gatherings:

... *facing each other.*

15:47

They advance upon each other, asking each other questions.

52:25

... *their faces being shining, laughing and joyous.*

80:38–9[16]

We have removed all rancour that may be in their breasts; in brotherhood, face to face they sit on couches raised.

15:47

Contrary to what might be expected according to the popular picture, on examining the utterances of the inhabitants of *janna* they are never heard to say, 'How delicious this food or drink is!' or 'How beautiful this damsel is! How luxurious the furniture, garments or ornaments or rivers or trees or fruits!' These are examples of what they actually do say:

Their call therein is, 'Glory be to You, O God,' Their greeting: 'Peace' and their call ends: 'Praise belongs to God, the Lord of all being.'

10:10

We have found that which our Lord promised us to be the Truth.

7:44

Praise be to God who has put grief away from us. Surely our Lord is All-Forgiving, All-Thankful, who of His bounty has made us to dwell in the abode of everlasting life, wherein no weariness assails us nor fatigue.

35:34

Praise be to God Who has fulfilled His promise to us.

39:74

God was gracious to us and guarded us against the torment of the burning wind; we used to pray to Him. He is the All-Benign, the All-Compassionate.

53:27–8

In fact, the examination of Qur'anic material reveals that the number of references to spiritual and moral rewards in *janna* exceed those to material rewards:[17]

For them are glad tidings.

10:64

No fear, no grief, no shame.

10:62; 66:8

They will hear no idle, sinful or lying talk.

56:25; 78:35

They will have great bounty from God.

33:47

God will thank them.

2:158; 76:22

They are the prosperous.

2:5

Their rewards will be according to the best of their deeds and more.

16:97; 10:26

He will increase their rewards many times over.

2:245

He will admit them by the gate of honour; by a gate that is well-pleasing to them.

4:31; 22:59

On their way to Paradise their light will be seen 'shining forth before them and on their right hands' (57:12). On their arrival the angels will greet them (39:73); when they are settled the angels will go and visit them (13:22). They will be in good company 'with those whom God has blessed, Prophets, the just, martyrs, the righteous: good companions they!' (4:69).

Within individual examples; the order of importance is made clear. Thus the inhabitants of *janna* are 'brought nearer to God' first and 'in Gardens of bliss' (56:10–11) afterwards. God first commands, 'Enter among My servants!' and then 'Enter My *janna*!' (89:29–30). The spouses are 'kept pure' first, then 'wide-eyed' (37:48); 'good' first, then 'comely' (55:70).

'And Greater Still ...'

Furthermore, spiritual rewards are clearly designated as the most important ones. The blessed will have 'a sure footing with their Lord' (10:2):

Their greeting when they meet Him is 'Peace!' and He has prepared a generous reward for them.

33:44

He will bring them nearer.

56:11

Their faces will be radiant; gazing upon their Lord.

75:22–3

They will be in a sure abode in the presence of a King Omnipotent.

54:55

God is well pleased with them and they are well pleased with Him.

98:8

God has promised the believers, men and women, gardens underneath which rivers flow, forever therein to dwell, and goodly dwelling places in the Garden of Eden; and greater, God's good pleasure; that is the supreme triumph.

9:72

This theme, of God's pleasure, which is greater than anything else, occurs no less than twelve times.

'Allocation Most Fitting'

Ibn Rushd (Averroes) observed that the allocation of physical and spiritual rewards in Islam is most fitting. The physical rewards appeal more to the understanding of the majority and are a greater incitement to them to gain the advantages in the abode of rewards, while the spiritual illustrations would appeal to the minority.[18] The fact that the popular picture has exaggerated the material enjoyments of the Garden goes only to confirm this observation. But in *janna* people will have whatever they individually or collectively wish, desire, or call for (16:24; 36:57; 42:22; 50:35; 52:22).

Style

The style in which *janna* is presented in the Qur'an is thus appropriate to addressing people of varying tastes, at different times and places. Everything in *janna* is understandably very special. Nouns are normally qualified: 'a *janna* as broad as the heavens and earth'; there is water which is not staled by time; milk, the taste of which does not alter, drink that will not give rise to headiness or lead to sin; flesh of fowl which the blessed desire; fruits of their own choice, unending and undenied; spouses kept pure, of similar age with mutual love. Life there is *rāḍiya*, pleasing, contented; the faces of the inhabitants are jocund, laughing and rejoicing at glad tidings.

They will enter through an entrance that will please them; there will be plenty of shade (*ẓill ẓalīl*) and flowing springs; they will live in goodly dwellings. The intensive forms of the adjectives are frequently employed, for example *al-fawz al-'aẓīm* (the supreme triumph) and *al-faḍl al-kabīr* (the great bounty). The order of merit is maintained: God's pleasure is the greatest bliss of all (9:72). The frequent use of *mā* (whatever), which has a universal application (*min alfāẓ al-'umūm*) provides for individuals *mā yashā'ūn* – whatever they wish, *mā yadd'ūn* – whatever they call for *mā yashtahūn* – whatever they desire.

The frequent use of the plural – *jannāt* and *anhār* – helps maintain the scale. The attribution of provision to God in the plural of majesty ensures a very special privilege e.g. *adkhalnāhum* (We made them enter), *amdadnāhum* (We provided them) and *zawwajnāhum* (We joined/paired them); when provision is attributed to Him in the singular it is given in the form of *rabbuhum* (their Sustainer) (e.g. 2:63; 3:169; 42:22; 45:30; 68:34; 76:21) or in the form of 'My Servants' (21:105; 89:29). On the other hand, the use of the passive form of the verb, which is noticeably frequent, gives finality of action effective in its contexts: the Garden which the righteous 'were promised' 'has been prepared' and 'brought near to them'; they were 'made to enter and inherit it'; were 'made happy' in it. In passive structures the active subject is deleted; but the deletion of the object can also be very effective: *'ala'l-arā'iki yanzurūn* ... (upon couches, gazing ...)' (83:23) – the object of 'gazing' is left to the imagination.

We have noticed that the Qur'an presents 'scenes' of gatherings in *janna*. The scenes as presented in this style in Arabic give the impression of the present. Most of the translators into English provide a future auxiliary, 'will', taking the view that we are now in the present life and in these scenes the Qur'an is talking about the hereafter. They are also governed by the stricter rules of tense in English grammar. This practice, however, weakens the effect inherent in the Arabic style. The Qur'an in fact brings the future into the present, or takes the present to the time when people are in *janna*. This is facilitated in Arabic by an introduction in the preceding verses (not necessarily immediately preceding) of a phrase like 'on that day' to announce a scene in *janna* after which we find the present tense and 'today' (which is admissible in Arabic grammar and style), thus:

The inhabitants of janna today are busy in their rejoicing.

36:55 *see also* 23:101; 43:68; 57:12

where the verb is in the present tense. In such cases as:

The angels enter upon them from every gate: 'Peace be to you because you persevered'.

13:23–4

Translators insert 'saying' between the two sentences; the Arabic text does not, which creates immediacy and dramatic effect.[19] Reading through a number of these 'scenes' in the Arabic will show the reader the extent to which the present tense is used. The past tense in the Arabic text is also used as if events had already taken place: 'We gave them …', 'We provided them …'. In the following example the pattern of Arabic tenses is retained to give an idea of the effect, although English scholars and translators seem bewildered by the apparently illogical shift of tense/pronoun:[20]

Those who were duteous to their Lord were led in companies to the Garden. When they drew near, and its gates were opened, and keepers said to them: 'Peace be to you, well you have fared, enter it to dwell for ever,' they said, 'Praise be to God who fulfilled His promise to us and gave us this land to inherit, that we may dwell in the Garden wherever we please.' How excellent is the reward of the righteous. And you see the angels circling around the Throne, proclaiming the praise of their Lord; and justly the issue had been decided between them, and it was proclaimed: 'Praise be to God, the Lord of All Being.'

39:73–5

The picture is full of lively, vibrant actions – happening now or already having happened.

The Real Nature of Reward in *Janna*

> It is inevitable that rewards [in *janna*] should be made in a kind which is pleasing (and torment be made in a kind painful) and that its nature cannot be apprehended except by giving a standard or gauge for it of what human senses have experienced.[21]

Thus commented the tenth-century Muslim philosopher, al-'Amiri (d.381/992). We have already seen how material objects in *janna*, are named in the Qur'an to give some idea of what will be there, but even these objects are different from what we know in this world: pure water which time does not corrupt, milk, the taste of which never alters, food and drink which one never gets bored of, which is always enjoyable and always healthy, trees whose shade and fruit are eternal. In the Hereafter, people themselves will be created as 'a new creation' in forms 'which you do not know' (56:35,61).

'The earth shall be changed to other than the earth and the heavens also shall be changed' (14:48). It is not surprising that Ibn 'Abbas, the Prophet's cousin and an authoritative commentator on the Qur'an, observed: 'There is nothing in this world which it shares with what is in *janna* except the names of things.'[22]

The Qur'an clearly states that the descriptions that are given of *janna* are given as *mathal* (13:35; 47:15) which the translators have rendered as 'parable, 'similitude' or 'likeness' – in other words, specific representations of things that belong to this world but are used to refer to the next. Numerous *mathals* are employed in the Qur'an:

Such mathals We propound for mankind so that they may reflect.

59:21

Full knowledge of the real nature of the rewards of the righteous, the Qur'an says, 'is kept hidden', it has not been given to any human. The same verbal form is used in Arabic to negate such knowledge – *lā ta'lamu* – applies to the present and to the future: *fa-lā ta'lamu nafsun mā 'ukhfiya lahum min qurrati a'yunin.* (No soul knows what joy is laid up for them secretly as a reward for what they were doing.)

9
The Face, Divine and Human, in the Qur'an

The face is the vital and most quintessential part of a person. Biologically, in addition to the forehead, cheeks and chin, it contains the eyes, the nose, the mouth and the ears.[1] This means that the senses of sight, hearing, smell and taste are sited in the face, together with the biological functions of breathing and feeding and the social function of verbal communication. The face, moreover, plays a most prominent role in non-verbal signalling. Facial expressions supplement and support speech: emotions like happiness, fear, anger, surprise and interpersonal attitudes such as liking/dislike, or inferiority/superiority, are shown on the face.[2] Such organs and functions are effectively gathered in one prominent place at the front of the body. Consequently the face is probably the area most noticed, instantly recognised and the one that identifies a person. Because of the importance and attention given to the face people take special care to clean and beautify their faces.

The face gives a person an identity and affects what others think of his or her personality: 'We categorise one another in terms of personality. There are many different features of the face which affect impressions of personality.'[3] The face of a person also means his/her presence. A person is present above all by virtue of his face, we deal with him mainly through the face, as he 'faces' us, we say in Arabic: 'Never show your face around here again!' His face stands for what he projects himself to be. Thus, we talk of *dhu'l-wajhayn*, the 'two-faced' person. 'Facing' means being active, confronting a situation and dealing with it, as well as taking a specific orientation, direction or course. In Arabic also face, orientation and direction have the same root (w-j-h): *wajh* (face), *wijha* (direction), *ittijāh*, *jiha* (orientation, direction). As we shall see in the Qur'an, you 'set your face to', means that you 'take', or 'adhere to' a course; to 'surrender one's face to God' means to follow His teachings wholeheartedly, and go in the direction He ordains.

Because of the vital functions of the face as the frontier of the senses and as it stands for the identity and presence of a person, the word in Arabic also stands for his dignity: you honour someone's face, and you act *li-wajhallāh* (i.e. for the sake of God, in honour of the Face of God). Accordingly, to save someone's dignity you may take a face-saving measure; conversely, a person can lose face, in Arabic *arāq mā' wajhih* – literally 'spilt out the water of his face', i.e. sold his honour. Because of the prominence and dignity of the face, *wahj* (face) / *wajīh* in Arabic means the chief or the dignitary of a community. When the angels told Mary that God was giving her the good news that she would have a son, the Messiah, they said he would be *wajīh* – illustrious in this world and the next; one of those brought near to God (3:45).

By turning your face to someone, you show respect and attention; by turning your face away from them you ignore them. *Aqbal 'alayhi bi-wajhih* (turned to him with his face, i.e. gave him his full attention, welcoming him). Joseph's brothers plotted against him so that their 'father's face might be free for them' i.e. they would have no rival in his care and attention (Q.12:9). On the other hand, we say in Arabic: *ashāḥ 'anhu bi-wajhih* (he turned his face away from him disdainfully); *ughrub 'an wajhi!* (get away from my face!); *shamakh bi-anfih* (turned his nose up arrogantly) and such and such will be done *raghm anfih* (in spite of him, literally with his nose rubbed in the dust).

In *ḥadīth* we find numerous references to the face, particularly as a reflector of the emotions. The Prophet's face is described in detail[4] and we find such observations as: 'he came with good news showing on his face', 'his face gleamed with joy'; a new convert said to the Prophet: 'your face was the face I hated most; now it is the one I love most'. The Prophet himself is clearly shown to have been keenly observant of, and to have commented on emotions and attitudes that showed on the faces of his Companions. We find frequent reference to this, as for instance: 'He saw in my face what was on my mind' and 'He said: "Sa'd's face shows that he has some news"'.[5]

The Qur'an contains numerous references to the Face of God and the faces of men which we will study here in this order. We shall see how this theme is connected to the Islamic creed, worship, ethics, rituals, daily life and civilisation. The treatment of this theme will, in addition throw some light on the language and style of the Qur'an.

The Face of God

The Face of God is referred to in the Qur'an twelve times. References to the fact that 'He speaks/says ...' occur many times; reference to someone or something being 'under His eye' occur five times; His being *samī'* (All-Hearing) occurs over forty times and *baṣīr* (All-Seeing) again over forty times. The faces of the faithful will also have the joy of gazing at Him in the hereafter. This frequency highlights the significance of this subject and, as will be seen later, throws light on a very important feature of Qur'anic style.

Expressions that establish such attributes to God or state that He will be seen by the believers in the Hereafter became a subject of controversies amongst theologians who were engaged in discussion of 'the religion of *tawḥīd*'. Those expressions may suggest anthropomorphism, *tūhim al-tashbīh.* Three standpoints were recognised: (i) Those who denied the attributes of God *nafy al-ṣifāt* on the basis that they would detract from His unity. This is the view of the Mu'tazilites whose stand has been branded by their opponents as that of *ta'ṭīl.* (ii) The stand of the anthropomorphists[6] which became known as *tashbīh/tajsīm.* (iii) The view of those who took the middle course represented by *ahl al-ḥadīth* (those who base their view on *ḥadīth*) and the Ash'arites. The second stand was dismissed by both Mu'tazilite and Sunnite theologians whose views continued to have followers and gave rise to vigorous discussion in successive generations, and it is their view that we will consider here. However, before we deal with verses that speak specifically about the face of God, let us first cite this verse which governs the views of these theologians, and which is usually cited in dismissing the view of the Anthropomorphists.[7]

There is nothing like Him; He is the All-Hearing, the All-Seeing.

42:11

This verse sums up the issues that occupy a great deal of discussion in Islamic theological works. 'There is nothing like Him' sets up God as Unique and apart from all created things. 'He is neither a substance (*jawhar*), a composite body (*jism*), nor an accident (*'araḍ*), no place contains Him, nor does He exist in time, He is the First, with nothing before Him, the Last, with nothing that can be said to come after Him'. This is the belief of the 'Followers of the Truth' *ahl al-ḥaqq* (as opposed to *ahl al-tashbīh* the Anthropomorphists), expressed by Sayf al-Din al-Amidi (d.631/1233) in the chapter on 'Negation of Anthropomorphism', *ibṭāl al-tashbīh,* in his book *Ghāyat al-marām fi-'ilm al-kalām.*[8] *Jism, jawhar* and *'araḍ* are three divisions of things brought into being by the Originator, they are *muḥdathāt,* and He is not and cannot be like them.[9]

On the other hand the 'All-Hearing, the All-seeing' are two attributes that may suggest anthropomorphism. The Mu'tazilites deny the attributes, *ṣifāt,* and say that they are nothing other than His essence, and that *al-Samī'* and *al-Baṣīr* are names of God like *al-Raḥmān* and *al-Raḥīm.*[10] The Ash'arites affirm the *ṣifāt,* and unlike the Anthropomorphists, they remain within the bounds set by 'There is nothing like Him,' and say His attributes are fitting for Him alone, and not like those of His creatures: His hearing is not like theirs and His seeing is not like theirs.[11]

As regards expressions involving the face of God, here, again, we find (apart from the anthropomorphists who held it to be a physical face) the Mu'tazilites held that 'the face of God' means God Himself, that it is common in Arabic to use 'the face' and mean the person.[12] On the other hand, the Ash'arites maintained that He does have a face, that His Face is an attribute pertaining to His essence *ṣifat dhāt.*[13] Building on the principle of *tanzīh/mukhalafatuhu li'l-ḥawādith* 'that nothing which is applied to a created being should be ascribed to God in the same sense',[14] the Ash'arites consider that – unlike the Mu'tazilites – they have not compromised the meaning of Qur'anic expression, while at the same time, unlike the *mushabbiha,* they have not conceded to the danger of anthropomorphism.[15] Al-Asha'ri summed up the view of *ahl al-ḥadīth* who state on this point: 'We say nothing on the subject except what God Almighty said and what the Prophet (peace be upon him) said. Thus we say: He does have a face, without specifying how.'[16]

Similarly, Ibn 'Abd al-Barr, having summed up the views of the *ahl al-sunna* in general, who believed in the divine attributes without specifying how, and those of the Jahmites, the Mu'tazilites and the Kharijites who denied the attributes, concluded that the truth lay with those who adhere to what has been uttered in the Qur'an and the *sunna* of the Prophet.[17]

The first verse we come across in the Qur'an that talks about the Face of God is:

To God belongs the east and the west; wherever you turn, there is the Face of God.

2:115

According to one opinion this verse was revealed on the occasion of changing the *qibla* (prayer direction) from Jerusalem to Mecca. According to another opinion, it was revealed when some companions reported to the Prophet that they had been on a journey and could not establish the *qibla* at night and realised in the morning that they were praying in the wrong direction; the verse came to reassure them and still applies to those who cannot establish the *qibla* and to travellers when praying.[18]

The Mu'tazilites explain away 'the face' here as 'the direction which He ordained and chose'.[19] We also find that Razi spent a great deal of time in attempting to explain away 'face' concluding that it means: His *qibla*, or mercy or blessing or the way to His reward or pleasure. However, the Qur'an uses *qibla*, not *wajh* for the direction of prayer (2:143–44). 'Mercy, blessings, way to' would seem forced here; surely the view of those who 'accept the Qur'anic expression without specifying how' is more convincing. Moreover, the Prophet said in a *ḥadīth* 'God puts His Face in front of the face of His servant at prayer'.[20] In another *ḥadīth* he said: 'God turns His Face towards a worshipper at prayer as long as he does not turn his face away; if he does so, God turns His Face away from him.'[21] He also recommended that one recite at the beginning of the prayer: 'I have turned my face to Him Who has created the heavens and the earth as one of pure faith and I am not of the idolaters' (6:79). It is difficult to accept here that what is meant by 'to Him' is merely the direction He chose.

In Arabic someone at prayer is also said to be 'in front of God'. 'Wherever you turn, there is the Face of God' is a very powerful statement as it is, showing the significance of the experience of prayer. The 'Face' certainly has more effect on the believer than 'direction'. We can say metaphorically or without specifying how that the Qur'an employs the word 'face', but linguistically it must be conceded that the metaphor has an effect and its impact must not be overlooked. How can we sacrifice the beautiful expression of 'the eye of God' reminding Moses that when he was a baby 'I shed on you love from Me so you may be brought up before My eye' (20:39); or, talking about Noah and his Ark, sailing away 'under Our eyes' (54:14); or saying to Muhammad, at times of hardship, 'wait patiently for the judgement of thy Lord: surely you are before our eyes' (52:48)? Awareness of being face to face with God may partly explain the Prophet's statement that in prayer was the delight of his heart, and when the time for prayer came, he would ask Bilal to make the *adhān* for it, saying: 'Give us comfort, Bilal, with it!' In addition, standing before God five times daily with such an awareness is more likely to give prayer the significance the Qur'an attaches to it.

The Prophet, unlike the theologians, did not hesitate to talk of the 'Face of God'. At the height of his persecution in Mecca, he prayed: 'If You are not angry with me I care not about anything else. I take refuge in the light of Your Face that dispels the darkness and puts in order the affairs of this world and of the next world ... '[22]

Although 'Wherever you turn there is the Face of God' came in the context of prayer, it is still a general statement and reminds those who recall it that God is watching them. This is reinforced by other Qur'anic verses:

He is the All-hearing, the All-seeing.

42:11

He is with you wherever you are: God sees all that you do.

57:4

Verses about the Face of God are connected to the sense of *taqwā* which is the mark of true believers and the essence of their awareness of the presence of God. In the same way it is connected to the state of *iḥsān* which the Prophet explained as 'to worship God as though you are seeing Him, for if you do not see Him, He sees you'. The numerous verses that talk about God as *samīʿ* (All-Hearing) and *baṣīr* (All-Seeing), give the impression of His Face being everywhere and are, as we said, connected to the sense of *taqwā* and *iḥsān.*

His Face is 'everywhere' and at 'all times' while all else perishes in time:

Call not upon another god with God; there is no god but He. All things perish, except His Face; His is the judgement and to Him you shall return.

28:88

It is remarkable that although the meaning is definitely that everything shall perish except God Himself, we have instead 'except His Face', which impresses upon the consciousness of the listener the effect of His majestic face watching over things that have perished, and for this He is the only One worthy of being worshipped. Similarly we read:

All that dwells upon the earth is perishing, yet there remains the face of your Lord with its Majesty and Bestowal of Honour: Which, then of your Lord's bounties do you deny?

55:26–28

Another group of eight verses in the Qur'an talk about doing something 'for the Face of God' or 'desiring the Face of God': 2:72; 6:52; 13:22; 18:28; 30:38–9; 76:9 and 92:20. The statement that the believer is doing something for the sake of His Face or desiring His Face, rather than any other gain, has a powerful effect in encouraging him to do the required act.

It is not surprising that this idea of desiring His Face should occur as an encouragement to do something thought to be particularly difficult. An example is the giving of wealth to the needy rather than making money by exploiting their needs:

Give their due to the next of kin, to the helpless and the traveller in need; that is best for those who desire God's Face – such are they who will prosper. What you give in usury that it may increase on other people's wealth increases not with God; but what you give in charity desiring God's Face shall be repaid to you manifold.

30:38–39

Though [the righteous] hold it dear, they give food to the needy, the orphan, the captive: 'We feed you only for the Face of God, we seek of you neither recompense nor thanks'

76:9

Such people, who fear 'a frowning' day at the Judgement will be spared the evil and God will recompense them, making their faces 'radiant' in the hereafter when there shall be 'radiant faces gazing at their Lord' (72:22–23). The Prophet teaches the believer to pray to God to 'grant me the joy of looking at your Glorious Face'.[23] Thus those who do good deeds in this world 'for the Face of God', will be radiant in the next life and they will have the joy of looking at the Face of their Lord.

It may be observed that while 'for/desiring the Face of God' occurs in the Qur'an in connection with charity, it also occurs as an incentive to patience/enduring with fortitude:

Those who endure with fortitude desiring the Face of their Lord, attend to their prayer and give alms in private and in public and ward off evil with good shall have a blissful end.

13:22

The Prophet is asked:

Restrain yourself together with those who pray to their Lord morning and evening desiring His Face. Do not turn your eyes away from them desiring the adornment of the present life, nor obey him whose heart We have made heedless of Our remembrance; who follows his lust and gives a loose rein to his desires.

18:28

The joy of seeing the Face of God in the next life is an extra reward:

For those who do good is the best reward and much more.

10:26

This 'more' has been interpreted as seeing God.[24] The guilty transgressors who deny the day of judgement now will be barred in the hereafter from seeing their Lord (83:15). Seeing God is an issue which traditionally had a place in theological works with the Mu'tazilites denying *ru'yat Allāh* (seeing God) since seeing something implies that it is a body, in a place and a special direction. Faced with such Qur'anic references (75:22–23) they attempted to interpret them in such a way as to avoid seeing God. In the case of verses 75:22–23 cited above, they say the believers will look at the reward of their Lord (not at Him), an argument powerfully refuted by the Ash'arites and their followers.[25] In fact the task before the Mu'tazilites was not as easy as they seemed to make it; it is not merely a matter of one or two verses about the Face of God and seeing God, but also of many verses about the hand of God, His Throne and many acts of God as in 48:10; 2:255; 10:3; 39:67; 2:245; 89:22 and 5:64. Sayyid Qutb (d. 1965) rightly points out that arguments were raised about such examples whenever polemics became a favourite occupation, whereas in fact they only follow a pattern of expression common throughout the Qur'an: *taṣwīr* (representation, imagery), which aims at explaining abstract ideas and bringing them nearer to our understanding. It is a consistent pattern that employs concrete imagery and personification. *Tawḥīd* (the belief in the Oneness of God) necessitates complete negation of anthropomorphism; the fact that the Qur'an does not deviate even in this area from its normal patterns of expression is clear evidence that *taṣwīr* is the basic rule of Qur'anic expression.[26]

We have seen how important the face is in the human experience and how powerful the impact of 'the Face of God' is in the Qur'an. Qur'anic expressions are surely meant to have their effect on the mind and soul of the reader/listener; the Qur'an is revealed as guidance for people at large, not as a subject for polemics among scholastic theologians. The effect of its expressions are surely not meant to be denied by philosophers or Mu'tazilite polemicists. The *ahl al-ḥadīth* Ash'arite position is more convincing in accepting the expression 'Face of God' as it is, believing that His Face is one of his *ṣifāt* (attributes) and accepting the expressions 'His Hand' 'He holds' and so on – not cancelling them but merely saying '*bilā kayf*' (without specifying how) and understanding them to have meanings fitting for His Glory. In any case, what is said about the Face of God in the Qur'an is all-fitting for

His Glory. 'Wherever you turn, there is the Face of God'; it abides for ever when all else has perished with Its Majesty and Bestowal of Honour; He is All-Seeing, All-Hearing; seeing His Face is the ultimate desire and bliss for the faithful. Unlike the human face in the Qur'an there is no mention in connection with the Face of God, of feeding, breathing, cleaning, change reflecting emotions, as we shall see below:

There is nothing like Him; He is the All-Hearing the All-Seeing.

42:11

The Human Face

The Qur'an abounds with references to the human face in this world and in the next, dealing with such aspects as the grace of God in shaping the face; its vital organs; cleaning the face; the face in worship; as showing the orientation of the character; as reflecting the emotional state; and moral teaching connected with the face. In the hereafter the human face figures prominently as reflecting the emotional and physical state and as showing that the good have been honoured and evil-doers abased. We shall deal with these aspects in this order.

In numerous verses the Qur'an reminds men of the grace of God in shaping them, and providing them with the vital human organs.

He fashioned you into comely shape.

64:3

He created you, then fashioned, then proportioned you.

82:6

It is He Who has brought you into being and given you hearing and sight and hearts; little thanks you show!'

67:23

Say: 'Who provides for you from heaven and earth, who possesses sight and hearing?'

10:31

Do but consider: if God took away your hearing and your sight, and set a seal upon your hearts, could any but God restore them to you?

6:47

Some were told that He could:

... obliterate their faces and turn them backward.

4:47

Have We not given man two eyes, a tongue and two lips, and shown him the two paths?

90:8–9

He created man and taught him how to communicate.

55:3–4

In his prayer, the Prophet used to recite: 'My face has prostrated before Him who created it, shaped it and opened up its hearing and sight; blessed be God, the best of creators!'[27] In this *ḥadīth* we notice that the ears are mentioned as part of the face. Those who obstinately reject the truth when it is repeated to them, and close their eyes, ears and hearts to it are said in the Qur'an metaphorically to have become deaf, dumb and blind (2:18, 171) or deaf, dumb, in darkness (6:39); their hearts have been sealed and on their ears and eyes there is a covering (2:7); about them the Prophet was told:

You cannot make the dead hear you, nor can you make the deaf hear your call when they turn their back and pay no heed.

27:80

Guidance is seeing and following the right path:

Who is more rightly guided: he that goes groping on his face, or he that walks upright upon a straight path?

67:22

Later we shall consider further how reminding men of God's grace in creating and shaping their faces is connected with moral teachings in the Qur'an.

The Islamic ritual of ablution demands of Muslims that they wash their faces a number of times daily when they attend to prayer. This ensures a regime of cleaning and refreshing the face peculiar to Muslims. The believers are told that by enjoining ablution, God 'seeks to purify you, and to perfect His favour to you, so that you may give thanks' (5:6). Purifying oneself in ablution is said by the Prophet to be '*shaṭr al-imān*' (half of faith).[28] In this regime, he recommended rinsing the mouth, cleaning the nose and ears, three times preferably. Moreover using the toothbrush (*siwāk*) is very highly recommended with the daily prayer, or more often as the Prophet did and said: it purifies the mouth and pleases the Lord – in fact one of his last acts on his death-bed was to brush his teeth with the *siwāk*. In addition, the effect of ablution will, according to the Prophet, show on the face on the day of resurrection. On that day the Prophet's followers will be called *al-ghurr al-muḥajjalūn*, (those having whiteness on their foreheads, their wrists and on their ankles) from the effect of performing the ablution.[29]

As observed earlier, a believer in prayer faces God. He is recommended to recite: 'I have turned my face to Him Who created the heaven and the earth as one of pure faith, and I am not one of the idolaters.' All Muslims turn in one direction at prayer, the *qibla*: 'Wherever you be, turn your faces to it' (2:144). In congregation each row of worshippers should be straight, with no gaps between individuals. When the Prophet saw a man out of line he said to the congregation: 'you should be in straight lines or else God will make your faces go in different directions'.[30] A Muslim bows down and prostrates his face – the centre of his pride and dignity – before God. We have mentioned earlier the statement which the Prophet recited and recommended the believers to recite in the state of prostration, this position being reserved solely for Him 'Who created the face, shaped it, and opened up its hearing and sight', just as the face is turned 'to Him Who created the heavens and the earth'. The spiritual orientation of the Muslim is defined in the Qur'an:

Set your face to the religion as one of pure faith'; 'Set your face to the true faith before there comes a day which may not be put off against the will of God.

30:30, 43

'Surrendering one's face to God' is the surest sign of *tawḥīd* and of taking the right course:

Who has a better religion than he who surrenders his face to God, does what is right, and follows the faith of Abraham whom God took for a friend?

4:125

It is, moreover, the safest stand:

Whosoever surrenders his face to God, being a doer of good, has verily grasped the firm hand-hold. To God shall all things return.

31:22

Qur'anic teachings about ablution promote personal hygiene and have implications in helping to maintain a social atmosphere of health and cleanliness. There are other Qur'anic teachings relating to moral attitudes in connection with the face or some of its organs. The faces of those who tell lies about God will be seen on the day of Resurrection as 'darkened' (39:60). There are repeated references to the grace of God in granting people sight and hearing which, if He were to take away, none could restore. There are traditional prayers said individually or by a leader of a congregation to protect their hearing and sight: 'Grant that we enjoy them as long as you keep us alive!' The gifts of His grace have moral implications:

Do not follow what you do not know; the hearing, the sight, the heart – all of these shall be questioned.

17:36

He knows the furtive eye, and what the bosoms conceal.

40:19

The tongue is a gift; believers should speak the truth, 'words straight to the point' (33:70). Those who defame honourable women will be cursed in this world and in the hereafter, and punished on a day when 'their tongues, hands and feet will testify against them as to what they used to do' (24:24).

Believing men and believing women should restrain their eyes from temptation and guard their chastity: that is purer for them' (24:30–1). Similarly, the face of the believer should not be used to show an improper attitude:

Do not turn your cheek away from men in scorn: God does not love the arrogant and the boastful.

31:18–19; 4:36; 57:23

Conversely, the Prophet said, 'to smile in your brother's face is a meritorious act.'

The pious are described as 'ready to prostrate and praise their Lord' (32:15); they 'seek bounty from God and His acceptance; their mark is on their faces, the trace of prostration' (48:29). The guilty who disdain to prostrate themselves in this world when they are safe and sound will, on the Day of Resurrection, be told to prostrate, but they will not be able to, they will stand with eyes downcast, thoroughly humbled (68:42–43).

We have seen earlier how the face reflects personal emotions and interpersonal attitudes. The following two examples from the Qur'an illustrate this.

First, commenting on the pre-Islamic attitude of some fathers to the birth of daughters rather than sons it says:

When one of them receives news of the birth of a female his face darkens and he is filled with gloom. On account of the bad news he hides himself from men: should he put up with the shame or bury her in the earth? How ill they judge!

16:58–59; 43:17

Second, the reaction of the unbelievers on hearing the Qur'an is described thus:

When Our revelations are recited to them in all their clarity, you will note denial in the faces of the unbelievers. They all but assault those who recite Our revelations to them ...
22:72

In both examples the face is mentioned first as mirroring the emotion or attitude, followed by another expression of emotion – 'full of gloom' – and attitude – 'they all but assault'.

It should be noted, however, that, compared to the *ḥadīth*, where there are numerous examples of the features as a vehicle for emotions and attitudes, the Qur'an has very few examples of this particular type relating to this world, but many (I have counted nearly forty) relating to the Hereafter. The explanation lies in two things. First, the difference in material and style between the Qur'an and the *ḥadīth*: by its nature much of the *ḥadīth* material is informal and conversational, with a listener perhaps contributing to the discourse with comments and various details at the time, saying, for example: 'As he said this his face reflected his joy or displeasure...'. The Qur'an, on the other hand, is communicated from a higher level, is formal and with no scope for the recipient of the revelation or the listener to comment. Second, treatment of the human features in the Qur'an relating to this world centres on showing the grace of God in creating and shaping the face and its vital organs – teachings related to physical instructions and moral implications rather than showing emotions and attitudes on faces. The situation is reversed in the Hereafter: there is less scope there for talking about creating faces and their organs for life in this world, and no scope for religious instruction. The Hereafter is the abode of requital not instruction, honouring or abasing the person. The face – which is the proudest and most visible vehicle for expression of non-verbal communication – shows the effects of this most vividly.

The Human Face in the Hereafter

Have you heard the story of the Enveloper?
Faces on that day downcast,
Labouring, toilworn
Scorched by burning fire,
Watered at a boiling fountain,

No food for them but cactus thorn
Neither nourishing nor releasing from hunger.
Faces on that day joyful
Glad for their effort past,
In a sublime garden
Hearing there no babble;
Therein a running fountain
Therein high couches ...

88: 1–13

What is remarkable here is that in giving the news of the Day of Judgement/story of the Enveloper, the Qur'an goes straight to the faces of the damned, then the blessed, as if between them they sum up the whole story. It now speaks to people of the result of their life here in the abode of requital. Showing the psychological effect of that requital is evidently very important and will readily appear on the face, the true mirror of the soul – the time being over for repressing or concealing emotions or thoughts.

On that day, neither dust nor ignominy shall overcast the faces of the blessed.

10:26

Their faces are described as 'shining', 'laughing, rejoicing at good news' (80:38–39); they will be joyful, well pleased with their past effort (88:8–9); 'radiant, gazing at their Lord' (75:22–23).

In their faces you shall mark the glow of bliss.

83:24

Those whose faces will become bright shall abide forever in God's mercy.

3:106

Out of the many examples that deal with the face in the Hereafter in the Qur'an there are two instances that mention two types of people whose faces will turn dark, *is wadda/muswadd* (for which English translators inconsistently give 'darkened' or 'blackened'):[31]

On the Day of Resurrection you shall see their faces darkening, those who lied about God.

39:60

Those whose faces have turned dark will be asked: 'Did you disbelieve after your profession of faith? Taste the torment because you have disbelieved.'

3:106

There are two other verses in the Qur'an dealing with one class of people whose faces turned dark in this world: pre-Islamic Arab men, when told that a daughter rather than a son was born to them (16:58; 43:17).

It should be noted that the verb form used in the Qur'anic verses just cited signifies 'becoming or turning' a particular colour (form IX in Arabic grammar books), so what we have is a new colour or degree of it. It is clear from classical Arabic dictionaries and modern usage that to describe someone's face as darkened (*iswadda*) is a figure of speech 'expressive of grief or sorrow or displeasure, occasioned by fear'[32] as in the case of the 'fathers of daughters'. In this world people are never referred to in the Qur'an as having a specific colour (white, yellow, dark, black). Rather, human beings in their totality are described as having a diversity of tongues and colours, which is one of the signs of God for men of knowledge (30:22). There is one other example in the Qur'an that mentions the colours of human beings as an example of the diversity in creation, in this case along with the colours of fruits, mountains, beasts and cattle, again as a sign of God, the pondering of which should lead learned men to regard Him with veneration and awe (35:27–28).

To continue with the discussion on the faces of the guilty, in contrast with the shining, radiant, joyful faces of the blessed who will rejoice, these are described as covered with dust, overspread with darkness (80:40–41); they will be grieved (67:27); with downcast eyes, disgrace covering them, (70:44); 'the guilty will hang their heads before their Lord' (32:12). The evildoers will be mustered to Hell upon their faces, deaf, dumb, and blind (17:97) – the proudest part of their bodies will be humiliated; when they closed their eyes and ears and refused to speak out in worship, they were said in the world to have become metaphorically deaf, dumb and blind, and so they will be on the day of judgement. Hot water will scald their faces (18:29), and flames will scorch them (23:104). The exposure of the face, the proudest, and most publicly visible, part of their body, to such treatment is an additional torment (44:48–49). In this world people are so protective of their faces from any harm; in the hereafter the evildoers will not be able to guard their faces against chastisement (39:24). Those who consume the wealth of people unjustly, debar them from the path of God and hoard gold and silver and do not spend it in God's cause, their treasure will be heated up in the fire of Hell and their foreheads, sides and backs will be branded with them (9:34).

Man has been equipped with such gifts as the eyes, the tongue, the lips, the hands, the feet and has been 'shown the two paths' (90:10) of good and evil; it is his responsibility to see that his organs are means of his salvation rather than of his damnation. In the Hereafter the tongues of the guilty will testify against them (24:24). Their eyes, their ears and their very skins will testify to their misdeeds; they will ask their skins: 'Why did you testify against us?' The answer will be tormenting: 'You did not hide yourselves so that your eyes, and ears and skins could not be made to testify against you; you thought that God did not know much of what you do. It was the thought you entertained about your Lord that ruined you' (41:21–23).

The faces of the damned will be seen 'darkened ..., but God will deliver the righteous to their place of salvation' (39:60–61), 'Those that surrender their faces to God and do good works shall be rewarded by their Lord; no fear shall come to them, nor shall they grieve,' (2:112). The pious person who spends of his wealth in charity 'for the face of his Lord the Most High, shall surely be content' (92:20–21), and

The Face of your Lord shall remain, Glorious, Bestowing Honour.

55:27

10

Adam and Eve in the Qur'an and the Bible

In Judaism, Christianity and Islam, Adam and Eve are the first human couple and foreparents of the human race, it is in the Bible, and the Qur'an, where accounts of their creation and lives appear. There is much in common between these accounts. They explain that Adam and Eve and the human race were created by God, sinned in the Garden, saw their nakedness, and then came out of the Garden, with enmity between Satan/the Serpent on the one hand, and the humans on the other, to live on earth. But the Bible and the Qu'ran differ in their approach, the amount and type of information that they provide, and the objectives of the stories. These have consequences and bearings on the status of men and women, on the concept of God and the moral standing of human beings in this world and in their destiny beyond it.

Summary of the Texts

The Bible gives two different accounts of the creation of Man in the Book of Genesis, the first in 1:26–31 and the second, considered to be older in 2:7–5:5. Adam is also referred to in the New Testament writings of St. Paul (1 Corinthians 15:22, 45–47; Romans 5) to explain the nature and scope of Christ's redemption of human beings.

The first Biblical account

In the first Biblical account, God decided to make man 'in Our own image, after Our likeness'. His purpose was that man would rule over the fish and birds and animals, and God blessed him to multiply. It is noted that God admired His creation: when God created each thing before man, we have the phrase 'God saw that it was good'. This is not repeated immediately after the creation of Adam, on the sixth day, but we do have the final statement that 'God saw everything he had made: it was very good'. It is also interesting that in this first account, God named every creation that He had made, terminology being very important from the beginning.

The second Biblical account

In the second Biblical account we find much more detail about Adam and Eve. God made man 'of the dust of the ground' and breathed into his nostril the breath of life, planted a garden East of Eden and placed man there. The Lord God made to grow every tree that was pleasant; the Tree of Life in the midst of the garden and the Tree of Knowledge of Good and Evil (there is a digression to mention the four rivers outside the Garden). The Lord took the man and put him into the garden 'to dress it and to keep it', and commanded him:

> Of every tree thou mayst freely eat, but of the Tree of Knowledge of Good and Evil thou shalt not eat, for in the day that thou eatest thereof, thou shalt surely die.
>
> GENESIS 2:16–17

In the second account, it is not good that the man should be alone: so God created a helpmeet for him, woman. The Lord created every beast of the field, and every bird of the air after the creation of Adam, and brought them to Adam to see what he would call them, and Adam 'gave names to every cattle, and to the fowl of the air', but still Adam could not find a 'helpmeet for him'. God caused Adam to sleep, and took one of his ribs and closed up the flesh in its place, and of the rib He made a woman and brought her to Adam. Adam said: 'This is now bone of my bone and flesh of my flesh: she shall be called woman.'

The serpent, which was subtle, asked the woman, whether God had forbidden them to eat from every tree of the garden. She replied, that they could eat, but that God had said: 'Of the tree which is in the midst of the garden ye may not eat, neither shall ye touch it, lest ye die.' The serpent tells her that they will not die, but on the contrary, if they eat it their eyes will be opened and they will be 'as gods, knowing good and evil'. So the woman ate of the tree (it is not clear which tree) and gave her husband 'and he did eat'. They became aware of their nakedness and, when they heard the sound of God, walking in the Garden, they hid. The penalty was for the serpent to crawl on its belly and eat dust to the end of its life, and enmity would be put between the offspring of the woman and the serpent. The penalty for the woman was that her pains would be multiplied in conception: 'in sorrow shalt thou bring forth children, and thy desire shall be to thy husband and he shall rule over thee.' As to Adam, he was told:

> Because thou hast harkened unto the voice of thy woman and hast eaten of the tree, cursed is the ground for thy sake. In sorrow shalt thou eat of it all the days of thy life. Thorns also and thistles shall it bring forth to thee. In the sweat of thy face shalt thou eat bread, till thou returnest to the ground, for out of it wast thou taken, for dust thou art and to dust shalt return.
>
> GENESIS 3:17–19

And then Adam called his wife's name 'Eve' (Eve means life – the mother of all living).

> The Lord said that man has become like one of us, knowing good and evil and that he might stretch his hand and eat from the tree of life and live for ever. Therefore the Lord God expelled him from the garden to work on the earth from which he was taken.
>
> GENESIS 3:23–4

Adam knew Eve and she conceived and bore Cain. It is interesting that this 'knowledge' came only after they left the Garden.[1] Then he knew her again and she bore Abel, and then Cain eventually killed Abel, and knew his woman who conceived his son Hanuk. Adam again knew his woman and she gave birth to Shith. Adam lived until he was 930, and following that there are lists of how long his children lived etc.

In the Qur'an

The Qur'an, on the other hand, does not give a chronological account in the first chapter, but uses scenes from the story of Adam and Eve, distributed in different parts, and used for moral purposes within specific contexts. The creation of Eve is not linked to the narrative about the creation of Adam, but it is mentioned in separate sections of the Qur'an, and used for different purposes.[2] They vary in length, some over a page long, others only a few lines. The first scene occurs in 2:30–39, the second in 5:27–31, the third in 7:11–27, then 15:27–48, 17:61–64, 18:50, 20:116–126, 38:71–85. There are some other verses that refer to individual scenes: 14:22–23,

36:60–64. There are references to Adam and Eve in 4:1, 49:13 as the parents of all human beings, and also in 7:189 being created as the first married couple. I will give here a summary of some of the more important scenes, put together to form a continuous narrative.

In the first scene, readers are asked to remember the story:

... when your Lord said to the angels: I am placing on the earth on a khalifah [viceregent]. [The Angels] replied 'Would you put there one who will do evil and shed blood when we have long sung your praises and sanctified your name?' He said, 'I know what you do not know.' He taught Adam the names of all things and then set them before the angels saying, 'Tell Me the names of these if what you say be true.' They replied, 'Glory be to You. We have no knowledge except what you have given us. You alone are all-knowing, the wise.' So He said to Adam 'Tell them the names of these,' and when he told them the names, God said: 'Did I not tell you that I know the hidden things in the Heavens in the Earth and all that you hide and all that you reveal?' And when We said to the angels, prostrate yourselves before Adam, they all prostrated themselves, but Iblis did not. In his pride, he refused and became an unbeliever.

2:30–34

In another scene Iblis (Satan) is asked:

'Why did you not prostrate yourself?' 'I am better than Adam' he replied. 'You created me of fire and him of clay.' God said, 'Begone from Paradise, this is no place for your contemptuous pride. Away with you. Henceforth you shall be humble.' Iblis replied, 'Reprieve me till the day of Resurrection.' 'You are reprieved,' said He. Iblis said, 'Because you have thrown me out/caused me to be thrown out, I will waylay your servants as they walk on your straight path, and spring upon them from the front and from the rear, from the right and from the left. Then you shall find the greater part of them ungrateful.' 'Begone,' said God, 'A despicable outcast you shall henceforth be. With those that shall follow you, I shall fill the pit of Hell.'

7:12–18

In a further scene (7:19–27), God speaks:

We said to Adam, 'Dwell with your wife in the Garden, and eat of any fruit tree you please, but do not approach this tree, or you shall both be wrongdoers.' But Satan tempted them, so that he might reveal to them their nakedness. He said, 'Your Lord has forbidden you to approach this tree only to prevent you from becoming angels or immortals.' Then he swore to them that he would give them friendly counsel. Thus he cunningly seduced them and when they had eaten of the tree their shame became visible to them, and they began to put on themselves some of the leaves of the Garden. Their Lord called them both, saying: 'Did I not forbid you to approach that tree, and did I not warn you that Satan was your sworn enemy?' They replied, 'Lord we have wronged our souls. Pardon us and have mercy on us or we shall surely be among the lost.'

7:23

... his Lord relented towards him. He is the Forgiving One, the Merciful

2:37

He said, 'Go out, one of you a foe unto the other. There will be on earth a habitation and provision for a while. There you shall live and there you shall die, and thence shall you be brought forth. O Children of Adam! Let not Satan seduce you as he caused your first parents to go forth from the garden, and removed from them their clothing, that he might manifest their shame to them. He and his tribe see you from whence you see them not.'

7:27

Returning to the first scene (2:38–9), after sending them out of the garden, God tells them:

'Go out of it, all of you. When guidance comes to you from me, whoever follows the guidance shall have nothing to fear or to grieve them, but those that deny and reject our revelation shall be the heirs of Hell and there they shall abide forever.'

2:38–9

Form and Language

The Biblical account is clearly in the form of a historical narrative. It occurs in the first book of the Bible in the story of the Creation. The language is chronological and historiographical and the events of Adam's life are detailed, from his date of birth (on the sixth day) to the end (he died at the age of 930 years). However, there are no details after the fall except in relation to knowing his wife and producing his offspring. In the period before the fall, the second account in the Bible gives much more detail than the Qur'an, in the mode of a factual history. We have times, locations and descriptions of places, things and persons. This makes it difficult to assume that the story was meant from the beginning to be symbolic, and for numerous generations, up to Darwin, people would have treated it as historical fact. The presence of so many details gives rise to questions in the modern mind. For instance, does the serpent eat dust throughout its life? Was Eve created from Adam's rib? How did he know that she was 'flesh of his flesh', and was to be 'mother of all living'? Can the pains of pregnancy and birth now be taken to be a punishment for women?

The first account is more impressive in language, particularly in drawing attention to the profusion of God's creation and grace in blessing His creation is so that they multiply, and does not contain such problematic details as those in the second account. Muslims, used to the Qur'anic ways, find nothing difficult to accept in the first account. In fact they would find the language thrilling.

Although Adam and Eve are mentioned in many parts of the Qur'an, in different scenes, the language of the Qur'an makes it clear that these are not given as history in the same way as in the Bible. A scene normally begins with *wa idh* – '(remember) when', the omitted verb being understood as is a common feature in the Qur'an. This shows that it is mentioned rather for the lessons to be drawn from it and used in the context of the given chapters. The Qur'an gives far fewer physical details. There is no serpent, rib or special punishment of Eve. In the Qur'anic version, even such details as God forming Adam with His own hands and the number of days in which He created Heaven and Earth have to be understood, on the instructions of the Qur'an itself, symbolically because elsewhere in the Qur'an we are told that there is 'nothing like God' (42:11; 5:103; 112:3), and that 'a day with God is like 50,000 days of yours' (70:4). Because of the declared figurative nature of the language and the lack of detail in the Qur'an, Darwin's theories of evolution did not have the same effect on the Muslims as they had in the West.

In the Bible the story refers to God in the third person whereas, in the Qur'an, God is the narrator, speaking in the first person, normally the plural of majesty, which gives the language a grand style, undiminished by physical details such as the nostrils in the following example. Compare:

When I breathed into him of My spirit …

QUR'AN 38:72

with

God breathed the breath of life into his nostrils …

GENESIS 2:7

The Qur'an is briefer and more inclusive, attributing Adam's knowledge to God's teaching. In the Qur'an, God taught Adam the names of all things; in the Bible animals, birds and sea creatures were brought before Adam and he gave them names.

The narrative tone and detail in the Bible story, on the other hand, puts it in a literary genre of its own, and makes it enjoyable as literature, appealing even to non-believers. The cunning of the serpent; God calling Adam who was hiding; God's admiration of what he had created, saying that it was good, and giving it a name; His making two shirts of skin for Adam and Eve and dressing them after the fall; details about the profusion of plants, animals and birds, breathing into Adam's nostril, all appeal on a human scale and make the account particularly endearing. However, these very details cause difficulty to some on the theological level and make many people, even Christians, in our times regard the story as no more than literature.

The Cause of the Fall

In the Bible, Adam lived in the Garden happily in obedience to the commandments. All his troubles started when the woman appeared. Although she was aware of the commandment, she was confused about which tree was which, saying they were forbidden to eat from the tree in the middle because, if they ate its fruit they would die, whereas the one in the middle was earlier stated to be the Tree of Life. Eve appears gullible, easily deluded by the serpent's cunning. Not only did she disobey, but she made sure that Adam shared the disobedience and also ate the fruit. Neither of them had the strength of character to take responsibility. She said, 'It is the snake that made me do it,' and Adam said, 'It is the woman you placed with me that made me eat.' Although we might now regard Eve's curiosity with more indulgence, in the Bible she is clearly condemned for her part in the Fall.

In the Qur'an, Adam and Eve were admitted to the Garden at the same time, and both were warned against eating the fruit of one tree, the nature of which is not specified. We do not have here the problem of why God should forbid Adam and Eve from eating from the tree of the knowledge of good and evil, and why he should punish them for such knowledge. Does it mean that without knowledge they would remain in a state of innocence? In the Qur'an, it is clear that, from the beginning, man was meant to live on earth and even to have both the moral capacity to judge between good and evil and the freedom to choose between them, so that his success or failure are of his own making (2:30 and 76:3, 90:10 and 91:8–10).

In the Qur'an, Satan deceived Adam and Eve together and in fact it is clearly said that Adam had forgotten God's commandment and lacked resolve (20:115). Whereas in the Bible Adam is told, 'Because you have listened to the voice of thy wife, and eaten of the tree ...', in the Qur'an Eve was not the cause of the fall, nor was there any serpent. In the Bible, Satan's temptation consists of a promise of immortality and God-like knowledge; to this the Qur'an adds promise of everlasting sovereignty, but in the Qur'an people are warned that Satan himself will admit, on the Day of Judgement, that his promise was false. He will say to those who followed him:

'True was the promise which God made you. I too made you a promise but did not keep it, yet I had no power over you. I called you, and you answered me. Do not blame me, but blame yourselves. I cannot help you, nor can you help me.'

14:22

The Punishment

In the Bible Adam was warned: 'But of the Tree of the Knowledge of Good and Evil, thou shalt not eat of it: for in the day that thou eatest thereof, thou shalt surely die' (2:17). After Adam and Eve eat the fruit, however, there is no more mention of dying, unless we understand 'die' in the sense of 'become mortal'. Both Adam and Eve had this punishment. In addition, Eve had the double punishment of the pains of pregnancy and desiring her husband who would rule over her. Adam was to earn his living with the sweat of his brow. The earth was cursed (clearly for the mistake of the humans!). Thistles and thorns are shown here to be part of the curse of God.

Genesis 3:17–18 shows the punishments to be for eating of the forbidden Tree of the Knowledge of Good and Evil. In verses 22–3, the expulsion was not the result of any disobedience, but a precaution on the part of God lest man might become immortal:

Lest he put forth his hand and take also of the Tree of Life and eat, and live forever: therefore the Lord God sent him forth to till the ground from whence he was taken, so he drove out the man.

3:22–23

The serpent was punished by having to crawl on his belly and eat dust.

In the Qur'an, Adam and his wife were warned that if they ate from the tree they would be wrongdoers, and that if they listened to Satan, he would cause them to be deprived of the Garden (2:35; 20:117).[3] The plan from the beginning was that they would live on earth (2:30) and we know that Satan had challenged God saying that he would do his best to mislead the humans. Placing Adam and Eve in the garden gave them their first experience of coping with this challenge. After they failed the test, they had to leave the garden but Adam and Eve both repented and were forgiven by God (2:37; 7:23). Their repentance was fully accepted in the Qur'an – nothing further was needed – and Adam indeed was then chosen to be the first prophet to receive guidance from God (3:33), and is counted among all the other prophets of Islam.

In the Christian theology, Adam and Eve sinned and were punished themselves and in their offspring. In Christian theology this original sin persisted in the Children of Adam to be remedied only by the Crucifixion of Jesus. In the Qur'an, Adam's sin, like anyone else's, is a personal liability and can only be redeemed by personal repentance:

No soul shall bear another's burden, and each man shall be judged by his own labours, and his labours shall be scrutinised and he shall be fully requited for them.

53:38–41

In the Bible, neither Adam nor Eve repented, nor were they rehabilitated in the Old Testament.

In the Qur'an, the pains which women suffer in pregnancy and childbirth, are cited many times in order to demand that kindness and gratitude be shown to mothers (e.g. 31:14–15; 46:15–18). When a woman protested to the Prophet Muhammad that, 'Men go to war and have great reward for that, what do women have?' he answered, 'When a woman is pregnant, she has the reward of someone who spends the whole night praying and the whole day fasting, and when contractions strike her, nobody knows how much reward God gives her for having to go through all this, and when she delivers her child, for every suck it draws from her, she gets the reward of keeping a soul alive.' According to the Prophet Muhammad, a woman who dies in childbirth is a martyr. There is no mention in the Qur'anic account that any of this is a punishment, nor that she will desire her husband and that he will rule over her. Mortality is not said to be a punishment, the earth was not punished, and Eve was not punished.

The Character and Status of Adam and Eve

In the Bible man was formed in the image of God. Eve was created to be Adam's 'helpmeet' and he was placed in Paradise before her. She was created from one of his ribs and God gave Adam his name, but not Eve. The Bible keeps referring to Eve as 'his woman'. It was Adam who first defined her by gender as 'woman' (2:23) then gave her the personal name of Eve after she had caused ruin (3:20). She was made to desire him and have him rule over her.

In the Qur'an, we are not told that Eve is created from the rib of Adam, but people are told that God created them all from 'one soul' and from it God created its mate, and that through them 'He bestrewed the earth with countless men and women' (4:1). 'From it' is an ambiguous expression in Arabic which has resulted in two interpretations, each of which has supporting arguments: one takes it to mean 'part of' that soul, without any specification as to which part exactly; the other interpretation takes it to mean 'of the same kind'.

The purpose of creating the mate is that they should find repose in each other (7:189; 30:21) and, in fact, the need for comfort is mutual (2:187). Eve is not given a personal name but, in the Qur'an, only Prophets have names, as a rule, and the only woman named is Mary because of the miraculous birth of Jesus.[4] In the Qur'anic account of Adam, Eve is referred to as 'your spouse'.

In the Qur'an Adam is given great honour. God states: 'I have created man with my own hand, and breathed into Him of my own spirit.' God made Adam his viceroy on earth and taught him the names of all things, and by this knowledge he was placed above the angels. In the Bible things were brought before Adam to see what he would call them, and these were land animals and the birds of the sky. In the Qur'an, God accepted Adam's repentance and made him a prophet. He also honoured his children (17:70). In nearly every citation of the story in the Qur'an, it is mentioned that the angels were made to bow down to him.

Consequences of the Story: Male–female relations

In the second Biblical account, Adam lived in Paradise on his own for some time. Unlike the first account, in the second animals and birds were created after Adam, because God said it was not good that he had no 'helpmeet'. Eve came after that, as the animals and birds were not enough but, in spite of God's good intentions, her arrival resulted in trouble for him, and he was punished because he listened to her and ate of the tree. In the Qur'an, we get the impression, from the succession of verbs and the conjunction 'and' that Eve was created soon after Adam:

It is He who created you of a single soul, and of it He created its mate, so that they may find repose.

7:189

They were placed in Paradise together (2:35 and many other instances). They clearly did give each other repose and neither was the cause of ruin for the other. In Islam, repose comes through marriage, and marriage is the way of the Prophet of Islam. He said, 'Whoever shuns my way does not belong to me'.[5] Celibacy and monasticism, far from being recommended, are described in the Qur'an as a human invention which could not be properly maintained (57:27). Likewise, the Prophet Muhammad, also denounced those who choose not to marry. He himself is an example to the Muslims in marriage. Indeed marriage is reckoned to be so good that men are even permitted to marry more than one wife, and both men and women are encouraged to remarry if they lose their spouse. Woman was not the cause of ruin in the first Garden and, in the Qur'an, the company of women will be part of the reward in the final Garden – Paradise.[6] Muslims, nurtured in this culture, would consider Paradise without a spouse to be a dismal, desolate place, and no doubt if the Biblical Adam had not been given a 'helpmeet' he would have agreed! The 'repose' which is considered in the Qur'an to be the objective of creating spouses, is shown in Qur'anic teaching in the first Garden, in this world, and in the final Paradise – in short, always: man and woman cannot live without each other, otherwise they become unsettled, and worse.

The Employment of the Story in the Qur'an

Whereas the Bible leaves the reader to draw moral teachings from the story, which is used only at the beginning of the book, the Qur'an employs it regularly in support of its teachings on beliefs and conduct, making the connections clear.

First, it is used as a proof of the power of God, as compared with human beings. It is one of God's signs that he was able to create human beings from dust and multiply them in this way:

And of His signs is this: He created you of dust, and behold! You human beings ranging widely in the world.

And of His signs is this: He created for you spouses of your own kind, that ye might find repose in them, and He ordained between you love and mercy. Lo! Herein indeed are signs for those who reflect.

30:20–1

Second, the 'creation from dust' is regularly used to demonstrate that He Who could create the first person from dust could raise the dead from the dust. This is used at least six times in the Qur'an as an argument for the Resurrection, which is one of the fundamental beliefs in Islam.[7] Whereas in the Bible Adam is told, after the expulsion from Paradise, 'You are made of dust, and to dust you will return' (3:18), the Qur'an says, in the same situation:

From it We created you, to it we return you, and from it we will resurrect you.

20:55

Third, in spite of being created out of dust, Adam in the Qur'an had the spirit of God breathed into him and was taught the names of all things. God ordered the angels to bow down to him, because Adam knew more than them and was thus superior. This confirms the status of knowledge, much stressed in the Qur'an. 'It is those who know that are most aware of God' (35:28), and 'God raises the status of those who know' (58:11).

Fourth, in the Qur'an the fact that Adam, like Jesus, was created without a father is used as an argument against those who used the virgin birth of Jesus to support their belief in his divine status (3:59). If Jesus were allowed divine status, this would compromise the most fundamental belief in Islam, which is the Oneness of God.

Fifth, creation of all human beings from one male and one female is used in the Qur'an to support moral teachings, for instance, to stress that human beings are one family, in the context of dissuading them from injustice to the poor and weak (4:1). It is used to eliminate any sense of superiority, whether of class, tribe or race (49:13).

Sixth, the connection of human beings with the earth is much stressed in the Qur'an. The repetition of the fact that we are created from earth strongly suggests this affinity with earth, and our responsibility towards it and dependence on it.

Seventh, Satan's refusal to admit Adam's superiority, and his challenge that he will do everything he can to mislead people, are frequently used to warn the Children of Adam that Satan and his invisible hosts will tempt them and cause their ruin, just as he caused their parents to be deprived of the Garden. The Qur'an tells its readers that, on the Day of Judgement, God will question the Children of Adam:

'Have I not commanded you to serve Me, not Satan, as he has misled many generations, and now he and his followers will be cast into Hell?'

36:62–4

When in Hell, the Qur'an tells us that Satan will remind those who followed him:

God has given you his true promise, but I have promised and did not fulfil. I had no power over you, I only called you and you followed me. Don't blame me, rather blame yourself. I cannot help you now, nor can you help me.

14:22

Eighth, Adam and Eve repent in the Qur'an and their repentance is accepted. In the Qur'an, God taught Adam the way to repent:

And Adam received some words from His Lord [of revelation] and He relented towards him; lo, He is the relenting, the Merciful.

2:37

In fact the prayer they use in their repentance was repeated by Moses after he murdered an Egyptian (28:16), and his repentance was accepted. Another prophet, Dhu'nnūn (21:87–8), also used a similar formula, which the Prophet Muhammad recommended to the Muslims. This is encouraging and optimistic, as the door of repentance is always open to believers, prior to the point of their death. There is a promise from God that He will accept it. Indeed, in 22:70, God promises: 'Those who repent and do good deeds, He will change their bad deeds into good ones.' This path of repentance open to Adam is open to anyone; in the Bible Adam and Eve erred and were punished, with a punishment which applies to all the following generations. Christianity has its collective remedy in the Crucifixion of Jesus Christ.

The pedagogical function of the story in the Qur'an

The repetition of scenes from the story throughout the Qur'an makes it much more effective than if it were left at the beginning of Chapter 1, as in the Bible. God also calls on Muslims to read the Qur'an, learn it, and listen intently to it when it is recited. These stories are read daily in prayers and, in many Arab countries, listened to as recitations of the Qur'an on the radio and television, so that Muslims hear the whole book regularly from the beginning to the end. This keeps the story and its morals and lessons alive and effective in the minds of the believers.

The Concept of God

God's power over all creation is common to both scriptures, and so is His grace in providing for Adam and Eve and their descendants. His plan appears more consistent in the Qur'an. From the beginning He intends that Adam and Eve will live on earth, knowing that they will cause trouble. He has warned them what harm Satan will bring to them, given them their first experience of this in the Garden, and yet taught them how to repent and come back to Him. This lesson is put before their descendants as a warning against Satan, and the way is made clear to all those who follow the guidance, to return to the Garden. Those who follow Satan, however, will end up deprived of the second Garden, as their parents were of the first (7:27; 14:22; 36:60–4). The result of the mistake of Adam and Eve for themselves and all their offspring is more punitive and final in the Old Testament story than in the Qur'an.

There are more physical details about God in the Bible. He is heard 'walking' in Paradise and He blows life 'into the nostril' of Adam, afterwards extracting a rib and filling its place with flesh. He also 'planted the Garden Eastward in Eden, and there he put the man whom He had formed' (2:8). Such details enabled Christian artists to conceive an anthropomorphic picture of Him, and to make Him appear in numerous genres, from mystery plays to films. In Christianity, he is even incarnate in Christ ('the Second Adam'). In the Qur'an, this is not the case and no such representation is permitted or seen in Muslim cultural history.

The Qur'an gives us the supreme example of God's liberal method of government. Satan is represented in opposition to God, yet he is given full freedom of expression and action to the end of the world. Satan says:

'Do you see this being whom you have exalted above me? If you give me respite till the Day of Resurrection, I will take control of all but a few of his descendants.'

17:62

God said:

'Go. Hell is your reward and the reward of those who follow you. An ample reward it shall be. Rouse with your voice whomever you are able; muster against them all your forces; be their partner in their riches and in their offspring; promise them what you will. Satan promises them only to deceive them, but over my true servants you shall have no power.'

17:63–4

This is just one example, but there are others. God knew that Adam was going to cause mischief on the earth and shed blood, and yet He created him, to the amazement of the angels. He gave humans the freedom to choose, err, and repent if they wish. This says much about freedom and maturity of character. Humans are allowed to act and make their own mistakes, suffering only 'part of' the consequences (30:41) in order to show them the error of their ways and allow them to learn God's better ones. God does not make anyone suffer for the fault of anyone else.

Readers used to the Qur'anic story may find it difficult to understand why God should forbid Adam and Eve to eat or come near the Tree of the Knowledge of Good and Evil, and then punish them when they have this knowledge, or why He should expel them, seemingly as a precaution against their eating of the Tree of Life and becoming 'like one of us' in immortality, rather than because they had gained the knowledge of good and evil. Such readers may wonder why God did not take such a precaution with guarding the Tree of Knowledge, which also made man 'like one of us in knowledge'?

Both scriptures, however, give us an explanation of the beginnings and destiny of the human race, of the purpose of God on Earth and His grace. They have inspired and will continue to inspire countless generations of people.

11

The Story of Joseph in the Qur'an and the Bible

Introduction

Joseph's story in the Qur'an has been approached by many non-Muslim writers[1] who were content to list which items have been missed out from the Biblical story and which added, maintaining that these had their origins in biblical or other Jewish sources. Our treatment here concentrates on the texts of the story in the Qur'an and the Old Testament, attempting to identify the differing functions and preoccupations of the two accounts in their respective contexts, to show how this difference affects the choice of material and the treatment given to it. This chapter concludes that readers, both Muslims and non-Muslims, should approach the two versions with this difference in mind in order to appreciate the message and qualities of each.

The Story and its Functions

Thus We relate to you, Muhammad, stories of the apostles to strengthen your heart.

QUR'AN 11:120

In their stories there is a moral for people of understanding.

QUR'AN 12:111

Haste ye, and go up to my father and say unto him, Thus saith thy son Joseph, God hath made me lord of all Egypt: come down unto me, tarry not: And thou shalt dwell in the land of Goshen and thou shalt be near unto me, thou, and thy children, and thy children's children, and thy flocks and thy herds, and all that thou hast.

GENESIS 45:9–10

The story of Joseph is common to both the Old Testament (Genesis 37–50) and the Qur'an (*Sūrat Yūsuf*: Chapter 12). In the Old Testament, outside Genesis, Joseph receives scant attention;[2] in the Qur'an Yusuf is mentioned only twice outside Chapter 12 – in 6:84 and 40:34. Therefore the discussion here concentrates on the story as related in Genesis and *Sūrat Yūsuf*. On reading the two texts it becomes clear that the main events of the story are the same in each and the results of these events are the same, but the function of the story differs, and therefore the tone, the timespan, the characterisation and the artistic forms are also different in each.

The Genesis story is part of a history; it continues the story of the patriarchs of the family of Abraham and follows the story of Esau and the early story of Jacob, taking its place 'in the concatenation of events that led to the migration of the Israelites to Egypt, their enslavement and redemption'.[3] We shall see how this national historical aspect – although it is not the only function of the Genesis narrative – colours the biblical version and makes it different from that of the Qur'an. In the Qur'an the story is not part of a continuous relation of history. It does not follow on from *Sūra* 11; it ends before the end of *Sūra* 12 and it does not continue in *Sūra* 13. Like other similar stories in the Qur'an it is *min anbā' al-ruṣūl* – namely stories of the apostles to strengthen the Prophet and the believers and give them guidance.

Sūrat Yūsuf consists of 111 verses. Verses 1–2 are about the revelation of the Qur'an and the importance of understanding it. In verse 3 God speaks in the first person plural: 'We relate to you the best of stories in revealing the Qur'an to you ...'. Verses 4–6 are an introduction to the story of Joseph, giving a preview of what is to follow. In verse 4 Joseph relates his dream to his father. In verses 5 and 6 Jacob warns Joseph against telling his dream to his brothers lest they plot against him and interprets it as foretelling a great future for Joseph and the house of Jacob. Verses 7–101 relate the stages of the story, which ends in the Qur'an with the arrival of the whole of Jacob's family in Egypt, fulfilling the dream with which the story began. (Genesis, by contrast, goes on to see Jacob die seventeen years after his arrival in Egypt and later shows Joseph at the age of 110.) Verse 102 in the Qur'an is an immediate comment on the story, stating that it is a revelation to the Prophet Muhammad of things previously unknown (to him and his people),[4] and verses 103–111 are a general comment on the prophets' call and the unbelievers' response, confirming that a good future lies ahead for prophets – a lesson to be learned from their stories in the Qur'an.

Joseph's Dream(s) and his Brothers' Plot Against Him

The introductory verses in the *sūra* describe the dream, which is in fact a preview of the story, forecasting its outcome in symbolic manner. Joseph says to his father:

Father, I dreamed of eleven stars and the sun and the moon, I saw them prostrate themselves before me.' 'My son,' he replied, 'relate nothing of this dream to your brothers lest they plot evil against you: Satan is the sworn enemy of man. So will your Lord choose you, teach you to interpret dreams and perfect His blessing upon you and on the House of Jacob as He perfected it formerly on your fathers Abraham and Isaac; surely your Lord is all-knowing and wise.

12:4–6

The essence of Joseph's story is that the evil act committed against him turns out eventually to his advantage and through him to the advantage of Jacob and his wife, as well as all his children, who will need Joseph and benefit from his elevated position in Egypt. All this is contained in the dream of stars, sun and moon, to which the Qur'an goes directly, leaving out the other dream about sheaves given in Genesis, in which only the brothers are involved.

Introducing a long story like that of Joseph with an introduction of this kind – it has been described as a summary – is one of the techniques of storytelling in the Qur'an, employed for instance in Chapter 18:9–12.[5] Since a main objective of telling the story in the Qur'an is to strengthen the hearts of the believers, right at the beginning we are given a forecast of eventual good, presented in a brief symbolic form which leaves the whole story still to be told. In the Qur'an Jacob is a prophet who can interpret the dream, as we have seen. Realising its significance and clearly aware of the brothers' jealousy and ill feeling towards Joseph, he addresses him lovingly (using the diminutive *bunayya* to denote endearment and tender age) advising him not to tell his brothers about it. Naturally he is pleased to read in the dream that Joseph will be chosen as a prophet and that God will perfect His blessing upon him (and on Jacob's house) as He did with his fathers

Abraham and Isaac before him. It is a joy for Jacob to see the line of prophethood continue in his family, and good education to tell young Joseph that he descends from such a line so that his beliefs and conduct may befit his ancestry. We shall see Joseph refer to this later when in prison in Egypt.

The Genesis version begins differently, as a continuation of the story of Jacob. It is announced at the beginning of Chapter 37 that his descendants will be listed. The stages of the story are gone through at greater length, in chapters 37, 39–50, than in the Qur'an. Whereas the Qur'an ends the story with the arrival of Jacob's family in Egypt, fulfilling the dream, Genesis continues, as already mentioned. From the beginning the story gives the impression of containing a strong element of the chronicle:

And Jacob dwelt in the land wherein his father was a stranger, in the land of Canaan. These are the generations of Jacob. Joseph, being seventeen years old was feeding the flock with his brethren; and the lad was with the sons of Bilhah, and with the sons of Zilpah, his father's wives: and Joseph brought unto his father their evil report. Now Israel loved Joseph more than all his children, because he was the son of his old age: and he made him a coat of many colours. And when his brethren saw that their father loved him more than all his brethren, they hated him, and could not speak peaceably unto him.

GENESIS 37:1–4,

This specifies Joseph's age and exactly which brothers – identified by their mothers, his father's wives – he was with while feeding the flock. Specification of exact names and precise times, locations and quantities is a prominent feature in Genesis but is absent in the Qur'an, which concentrates on the bold outline of events and the lessons to be drawn from them (a point to which we will return later).

Joseph then tells his brothers of his dream that they were binding sheaves in a field when their sheaves gathered around and bowed low before him, and there is another dream which he relates to his father and brothers, that the sun, moon and eleven stars bowed down to him.

And he told it to his father and to his brethren: and his father rebuked him, and said unto him, What is this dream that thou hast dreamed? Shall I and thy mother and thy brethren indeed come to bow down ourselves to thee to the earth?

GENESIS 37:10

Jacob here takes the patriarchal attitude, rebuking his favourite son for not conducting himself properly towards his parents and older brothers even in a dream. He is clearly not an interpreter of dreams; indeed he implies that Joseph should not even have dreamed the second dream, and in fact we find no further reference to it in the story later on. In the Qur'an Jacob's reaction is to rejoice in perceiving a blessing coming to his son, seeing that God will 'perfect His favour upon him' (and the whole house of Jacob) as He perfected it on his fathers Isaac and Abraham.

In the Qur'an, after the introductory dream and its interpretation, the story begins, giving the reasons for the brothers' hatred of Joseph and their plan to dispose of him:

They said [to each other], 'Joseph and his brother are dearer to our father than ourselves, though we are many. Truly our father is in manifest error. Kill Joseph or cast him away in some far-off land so that your father's face may be free for you and thereafter you may be righteous men.' One of them said: 'Do not kill Joseph; if you must, rather cast him into a dark pit. Some caravan will take him up.' They said to their father: 'Why do you not trust us with Joseph? Surely we wish him well. Send him with us tomorrow, that he may play and enjoy himself. We will take good care of him.' He replied: 'It would much grieve me to let him go with you; for I fear lest the wolf should eat him when you are off your guard.' They said: 'If the wolf could eat him despite our number, then we should surely be lost!'

12:7–15

Genesis gives three reasons for the brothers' hatred of Joseph. First, he reported their misdeeds to their father. Second, Jacob showed obvious favouritism to him, making him a 'coat of many colours' (a beautiful detail) – a favouritism for which he has been taken to task by some rabbis.[6] This second reason is the only one given in the Qur'an, but Jacob is not said directly to have shown favouritism; rather it was the brothers who conceived it so. Third, Joseph's dreams showed him as the object of his brothers' adoration.

In the Qur'an Jacob is shown to be more aware of the brothers' attitude to Joseph, and advises him not to tell them his dream. In spite of the terrible harm the brothers are about to do to Joseph, Jacob is pictured in Genesis as having no suspicion of their ill-feeling: it is even he who takes the initiative of sending his beloved boy to see whether the band of ten men and the flock are all right. In the Qur'an, the suggestion that Joseph should join them comes from the brothers, and Jacob only reluctantly agrees.

Genesis gives much detail in tracing Joseph's movements on his way to his brothers. Failing at first to find them, he meets a man who asks him 'Who are you looking for?' He answers 'My brothers,' and the man tells him, 'I heard them say "Let us go to Dothan".' So Joseph goes to Dothan (Genesis 37:15–17).

The brothers sat down to eat bread; and they lifted up their eyes and looked, and, behold, a company of Ishmaelites came from Gilead with their camels bearing spicery and balm and myrrh, going to carry it down to Egypt.

GENESIS 37:15–25

This is a very full report, of the kind that might perhaps be useful for a detective investigating every available detail surrounding the crime (we nevertheless find no explanation for the absence of Reuben at the crucial moment of Joseph's sale), or to students of history and ancient trade. The Qur'an has a different aim:

And when they took him with them, they resolved to cast him into a dark pit. We revealed to him Our will, saying: 'You shall tell them of all this when they will not know.' At nightfall they returned weeping to their father. They said: 'We went off to compete together, and left Joseph with our packs. The wolf devoured him. But you will not believe us, though we speak the truth.' And they showed him their brother's shirt, stained with false blood.
'No!' he cried. 'Your souls have tempted you to evil. Sweet patience! God alone can help me bear the loss you speak of.'

12:18

In the Qur'an, as we have said, Jacob is a prophet. He always speaks of God and patience, trusts in Him and seeks His assistance. With Joseph, too, God figures prominently, protecting and aiding him, speaking in the first person plural of His revelation to Joseph in the pit, reassuring him; protecting him, then teaching him to interpret dreams, when he is sold into Egypt (12:21), and later elevating him (12:56). In Genesis, on the other hand, it has been observed that: 'Most striking and, in fact, unique, is the secularistic complexion of the narrative. There are no miraculous or supernatural elements, no divine revelations are experienced by Joseph.'[7]

In the Qur'an the brothers' report to their father betrays their pretence; Jacob does not appear convinced by the wolf story, perspicaciously seeing that the stained shirt is not torn. This is important for the development of the Qur'anic story, as Jacob the prophet never loses faith that the grace of God may one day bring Joseph back (12:84–87). In Genesis the brothers' report to their father is cool and detached and Jacob himself volunteers the explanation of the wolf, believing that Joseph is gone for ever:

And they took Joseph's coat, and killed a kid of the goats, and dipped the coat in the blood; and they sent the coat of many colours, and they brought it to their father; and said, This have we found; know now whether it be thy son's coat or no. And he knew it, and said, It is my son's coat; an evil beast hath devoured him; Joseph is without doubt rent in pieces. And Jacob rent his clothes,[8] and put sackcloth upon his loins, and mourned for his son many days.

GENESIS 37:31–34

This is followed in Genesis by Chapter 38 – thirty verses which have nothing to do with the story of Joseph, but which talk about Judah who had sexual intercourse for payment with Tamar, his daughter-in-law, who pretended to be a harlot and became pregnant by him. The chapter ends with an account full of vivid and interesting details about how the babies were received by the midwife and named. Here again we have an example of difference in style between the Qur'an and the Bible. The Qur'an would not give such details as those given in Genesis 38; such a deed would also be accompanied in the Qur'an by an explicit condemnation.

Joseph in Egypt

The story resumes in Genesis Chapter 39 with Joseph being sold into Egypt; unlike the Qur'an, which merely speaks of the Egyptian who 'bought him' or the 'noble' (12:21, 30), in Genesis the buyer is identified as 'Potiphar, an officer of Pharaoh, Captain of the Guard, an Egyptian', the Arabic Bible saying 'one of Pharaoh's eunuchs'.[9] The Qur'anic version shows tenderness towards Joseph, who is pictured as a likeable person. We feel the cry of jubilation of the man who finds him: 'Rejoice, here is a boy!' and in Potiphar's saying to his wife 'Be kind to him. He may prove useful to us, or we may adopt him as our son.' Then God speaks: 'Thus We established Joseph in the land and taught him to interpret dreams' (a fitting introduction to what will happen in prison). 'God has full powers over His affairs, though most men do not know' – again a fitting comment on the situation and how the story will develop: the very ordeal of slavery inflicted on Joseph by his brothers is destined by divine providence to lead to his elevation – 'And when he reached maturity, We bestowed on him wisdom and knowledge. Thus do We reward the righteous' (12:21–22). In Genesis we read:

And the Lord was with Joseph and he was a prosperous man ... his master saw that the Lord was with him and made all that he did to prosper in his hand ... and he had made him overseer.

GENESIS 39:3–4

In contrast to the Qur'an, where reference to God's care of Joseph is constant in all situations, this is one of very few occasions where such reference is made in Genesis. In the Qur'an, moreover, God's grace, which has been shown to Joseph, is made more general at the end of the verse: 'Thus do We reward the righteous.'

Joseph, however, was destined to go through another ordeal as a result of Potiphar's wife's attempts to seduce him. Faced with her repeated attempts, the Qur'an tells us that he would have succumbed were it not for the fact that he 'saw the proof of his Lord. So was it that We might turn away from him evil and abomination; he was one of our devoted servants' (12:24). Joseph's loyalty to his master is clear in both scriptures. Non-Muslim writers[10] have observed with surprise, and considered it an embellishment added by Muhammad, that in the Qur'an Joseph's shirt (which was torn as he tried to escape from her) was torn from behind – proof that she had not protected herself from Joseph, but rather that she had tried to get hold of him when he was fleeing (12:25–26). In Genesis, however,

> She caught him by his garment, saying, 'Lie with me': and he left his garment in her hand, and fled.
>
> GENESIS 39:12

As this stands, either he slipped himself out of his garment, or she stripped it off him – either way, he just left it with her and fled. Genesis gives a more detailed account of the deception of Potiphar's wife, and the wicked allegation to her husband, which prompts him to throw Joseph into prison. The Qur'an relates that certain women in the city mocked the noble's wife for soliciting her slave-boy, at which she invites them to a meal, and presents Joseph to them; they are so enraptured by his beauty that they cut their fingers with their knives. She threatens Joseph with imprisonment if he does not give in to her. He prays: 'Lord, prison is dearer to me than what they call me to. Shield me from their cunning or I shall yield to them and lapse into folly.' His Lord answers his prayer and wards off their wiles from him. Nevertheless, they thought it right to jail him for a time (12:30–35).

'And I will Teach You to Interpret Dreams'

In the Qur'an when Joseph is asked by the two prisoners to interpret their dream because they can see he is a 'good' man, he replies that he can interpret since:

'My Lord has taught me for I have left the faith of those that disbelieve in God and deny the life to come. I follow the faith of my fathers Abraham, Isaac, and Jacob. It is not for us to worship anything beside God. That [comes] of the grace of God to us and to mankind, yet most men do not give thanks. Fellow prisoners, are sundry gods better, or God the One, the Omnipotent? ... Judgement rests only with God; He has commanded you to worship none but Him. That is the true faith, yet most men do not know it.*

12:37–40

*This teaching is mentioned four times, in verses 6, 21, 37 and 101.

Jacob the prophet foresaw in Joseph's dream that he would be chosen as a prophet to follow in the footsteps of his forefathers (12:6). We now see the fulfilment of this. Joseph's statement here echoes what is said by Abraham and Isaac elsewhere in the Qur'an.[11] The difference in emphasis between the Qur'an and the Old Testament may be illuminated by comparing this long Qur'anic statement with the brief one in Genesis, which on other occasions gives lengthy statements and a wealth of detail. When the prisoners say they have had dreams and there was no interpreter, the Joseph in Genesis replies: 'Do not interpretations belong to God? Tell me them' (40:8).

Pharaoh's two dreams and request for interpretation are expressed in the Qur'an in two and a half lines in Arabic and are retold to Joseph, with the request for interpretation again occupying two and a half lines (12:43–46); the cup-bearer's suggestion that he was the one to interpret is one line; yet the statements are very clear as they stand. In Genesis this part of the story takes a full 32 verses (41:1–32). This is an example of the remarkable brevity of the Qur'anic style with which we will deal later. The dreams are the same and, apart from the fact that the Qur'an adds a year of abundance which Joseph the prophet could see coming after the lean ones, the interpretation is the same, as is the suggested solution, but there is a difference in the order of events.

Joseph, a prophet wrongly imprisoned, considers it important to be first declared innocent of the accusation made by Potiphar's wife – she confesses her misdeeds and declares his truthfulness (12:50–53). Joseph then goes to meet Pharaoh (the Qur'an speaks of him as 'the king'). Genesis, unlike the Qur'an, gives a wealth of colourful detail, not omitting to mention that Joseph shaved and changed his clothes before appearing in front of Pharaoh (Genesis 41:14).

After his appointment 'over the storehouses of the land', we have the comment in the Qur'an, with God speaking in the divine plural:

Thus We established Joseph in the land to dwell there where he wishes. We bestow Our mercy on whom We will and We waste not the reward of those who do good. The reward of the hereafter is better for those who believe and are righteous.

12:56–57

Again, God appears on every occasion and the aid he gives to Joseph is universalised as attainable by anybody who follows the course described here. The lessons are there and the way is open throughout the *sūra.* Genesis, on the other hand, delights in listing the profuse honours conferred on Joseph and how powerful he has become, how he 'gathered corn as the sand of the sea, very much, until he left numbering' (41:49) with an abundance of vivid personal and environmental detail.

It is interesting to note at this point that there is a consistent tendency in Genesis to put Joseph in charge of everything wherever he goes after he is sold to Potiphar. Thus we find that Potiphar

... made him overseer over his house, and all that he had he put into his hand ... And he left all that he had in Joseph's hand; and he knew not aught he had, save the bread which he did eat.

GENESIS 39:4,6

Likewise, when he is in prison, 'the keeper of the prison committed to Joseph's hand all the prisoners that were in the prison ... and looked not to anything that was under his hand' (39:22–23). Then, when he meets Pharaoh, Pharaoh says to him, 'I have set thee over all the land of Egypt ... and he made him to ride in the second chariot and they cried before him "Bow the knee": and he made him ruler over all the land of Egypt ... and said to him: without thee shall no man lift up his hand or foot in all the land of Egypt' (Genesis:41–44). There is no such emphasis in the Qur'an.

Joseph in Charge of the Storehouses

Now all countries came into Egypt to Joseph for to buy corn: because that the famine was so sore in all lands. Jacob saw there was corn in Egypt and said unto his sons, Why do ye look one upon another? ... I have heard there is corn in Egypt: get ye down thither and buy for us from thence, that we may live and not die.

GENESIS 41:57; 42, 1–2

The two scriptures agree in reporting that when the brothers come before Joseph, he recognises them but does not declare himself, and asks them to bring the youngest brother for him to see; but Genesis shows him as appearing rough, accusing them of spying and keeping Simeon in prison as security for their return with Benjamin (42:16–24). In the Qur'an Joseph does not use this stratagem but generous treatment and persuasion instead (12:59–60). This is in keeping with the general picture of the Qur'anic Joseph as a pleasant, gentle and kind man *min al-muḥsinīn*, different from the picture given in Genesis later of Joseph distributing corn in Egypt and the price he exacts for it. Nevertheless, from the time he sees his brothers until the reconciliation, Genesis presents very touching situations on the personal level. Faced with the accusation of spying, the brothers are shown to remember and recognise their guilt in regard to the young Joseph; they see their present predicament as divine retribution and Reuben reminds them of his plea 'not to sin against the child'. When Joseph (whom they think does not understand their tongue) hears this, '... he turned himself about from them and wept' (Genesis 42:24).

Both texts (Qur'an 12:63–66 and Genesis 42:39–43:14) show the brothers pleading hard with Jacob to send Benjamin. In the Qur'an he makes them promise in the name of God to bring him back, and when they do, he says 'God is the witness of what we say.' He advises them when in Egypt not to enter through one gate together, but as a prophet he comments:

'I cannot save you from anything against the will of God. Judgement is His alone. In Him I put my trust. In Him let all put their trust.'

12:67

In Genesis, characteristically, he asks them to take a present to 'the man (i.e. Joseph): a little balm, and a little honey, spices and myrrh, nuts and almonds' (43:11) (What a lovely present from this old man!).

In the Qur'an, when they meet Joseph he embraces his brother and says, 'I am your brother. Do not grieve at what they did' (Q. 12:69). In Genesis this declaration comes later: Joseph first asks his steward to take them to the house and prepare for lunch. In Genesis, Joseph speaks to Benjamin:

'God be gracious unto thee, my son.' And Joseph made haste, for his bowels did yearn for his brother: and he sought where to weep.

GENESIS 43:30

When they sat for the meal:

He took and sent messes unto them from before him: but Benjamin's mess was five times so much as any of theirs. And they drank and were merry with him.

GENESIS 43:34

Both texts speak of the placing of the goblet in Benjamin's bag as a device to keep him in Egypt, and both mention the brothers' plea to Joseph (when the goblet is found and Benjamin is ordered to be detained) to let him go back to his old father and take one of them into bondage instead, 'as we see you are a good, kind man' (Qur'an 12:78–80; Genesis 43:18–34). In Genesis, the apprehension of these strangers in the house of a high official in a foreign land is touchingly expressed in their fear that the man may seize their asses and make them slaves, as punishment for the 'theft' of the goblet. They submissively explain they have brought it back and 'the man' reassures them that they are safe. We also have the very moving speech of Judah before Joseph, repeating material that has been said before but which is therefore all the more effective in this situation, since the intention is to bind Joseph and make him see that the brothers' present predicament is the result of his own earlier instructions:

> ... 'When I come to thy servant my father, and the lad be not with us; seeing that his life is bound up in the lad's life ... when he seeth that the lad is not with us he will die and thy servants shall bring down the gray hairs of thy servant our father with sorrow to the grave... Let thy servant abide instead of the lad, a bondsman to my Lord, and let the lad go up with his brethren' ... Joseph could not restrain himself and wept aloud and the Egyptians and house of Pharaoh heard.'
>
> GENESIS 44:31–34

At this point Joseph declares himself to his brothers and reconciliation takes place.

In the Qur'an the reconciliation is delayed. The brothers go back to Jacob without Benjamin and the eldest brother. As a prophet, Jacob never loses faith in God's grace, saying:

> *God may bring them all to me. He alone is all-knowing and wise.*
>
> 12:83
>
> *And He turned away from them and cried: 'Alas for Joseph! His eyes went white with grief... His sons complained: In God's name, will you not cease to think of Joseph until you ruin your health and die? He replied: 'I complain to God for my sorrow and sadness. God has made known to me things that you know not. Go, my sons, and seek news of Joseph and his brother. Do not despair of God's spirit. None but unbelievers despair of God's spirit.'*
>
> 12:84–87

When they go back to Joseph more distressed than before, and ask him to be charitable with them he replies: 'God rewards the charitable. Do you know what you did to Joseph and his brothers when you were ignorant?' Thus the revelation made to the young Joseph in the pit – 'You shall tell them of this when they will not know you (12:15) is fulfilled here. He declares himself and reconciliation takes place (12:88–92). He asks them:

Take this shirt of mine, throw it on my father's face he will recover his sight. Then return to me with all your people.

12:93

Jacob could smell the scent of Joseph (in the shirt) from a distance.

Joseph's shirt figures three times in the Qur'anic chapter: first stained with blood, to grieve Jacob, then used as evidence of Joseph's innocence with Potiphar's wife, and now as evidence he is still alive; placed on Jacob's face, it brings about recovery of his sight, whereas in Genesis God tells Jacob in a dream to go to Egypt, saying: 'Joseph shall put his hand upon thine eyes' (46:4).

'He Will Perfect His Favour to You and to the House of Jacob'

With such faith and expectation, the Jacob of the Qur'an has no apprehension about going to Egypt. In Genesis, where he is convinced from the beginning that Joseph has been devoured by a wolf, when they tell him Joseph is alive in Egypt his 'heart fainted, for he believed them not' (45:26). Genesis gives details of the carriages Pharaoh orders to be sent to carry Jacob and his household to Egypt, how they come with all their cattle, and then provides a full list of all their names totalling the number of people Jacob brought into Egypt as 70 (46:8–27) – we will return to this point later.

'This is the Interpretation of My Old Dream'

In the Qur'an Joseph embraces his parents, saying:

Welcome to Egypt, safe, God willing! He raised his parents on the dais and they all bowed down to him and he said to his father: This is the interpretation of my old dream: my Lord has fulfilled it. He has been gracious to me. He has released me from prison, and brought you out of the desert after Satan had stirred up strife between me and my brothers. My Lord is subtle in disposing what He wills. He alone is the all-knowing and wise.

12:100

The Qur'an here speaks of the parents and brothers bowing down to Joseph, fulfilling his dream of seeing eleven stars, the sun and the moon bowing to him. In Genesis only ten brothers bow to Joseph when they first come to buy corn (Genesis. 42:7) leaving the rest of the dream unfulfilled.

In the Qur'an, after telling his father of the fulfilment of the dream, Joseph prays in his supreme moment:

Lord, you have given me authority, taught me to interpret dreams, Creator of the heavens and the earth, you are my protector in this world and in the hereafter, make me die in true submission [to you] and join me with the righteous.

12:101

In the Qur'anic story, the first thing Jacob says of the dream when Joseph speaks to him about it in the beginning is:

So will your Lord choose you, teach you to interpret dreams and perfect his blessing on you and on the house of Jacob...

12:6

Joseph's last statement now echoes these words and completes this cycle; the story does not go any further in the Qur'an. In his last words, Joseph is a true prophet in Abraham's line. The picture given later in Genesis, however, of Joseph having bought all the people's silver, then their cattle, then their land, then their bodies in exchange for bread (47:13–22), does not fit with the picture given in the Qur'an. In the latter, with the arrival of Joseph's family in Egypt all has ended well and he prays that the end of his life, when it comes, will be in true submission to God and that He may bring him together in the hereafter with the righteous. These last words of Joseph's, which end his story in the Qur'an, also differ from the last words at the end of the story in Genesis.

So Joseph died, being an hundred and ten years old, and they embalmed him, and he was put in a coffin in Egypt.

GENESIS 50:26

In Genesis, from the beginning of the story to the time when all the family join Joseph in Egypt, the one single time Jacob talks about God or refers to Him is at the peak of his anxiety and helplessness; sending his sons to Egypt the second time, with Benjamin as required, he says:

God Almighty give you mercy before the man, that he may send away your other brother and Benjamin. If I be bereaved of my children, I am bereaved.

GENESIS 43:14

In the Qur'an, on the other hand, Jacob constantly speaks of God; the Qur'anic Jacob is a prophet, a descendant of the great prophet Abraham. For both Jacob and Joseph in the Qur'an, all hope and trust is placed in God (e.g. 12:6, 18, 21, 24, 38, 56, 64, 67, 83, 98, 101).

Two Functions: Two Styles

The story of Joseph in the Qur'an is unquestionably that of a Prophet *min anba' al-ruṣūl*.[12] The only personal names mentioned in it are those of four prophets: Abraham, Isaac, Jacob and Joseph. The article on *Yūsuf* in the *Encyclopaedia of Islam* states: 'The *Yūsuf sūra* is strikingly uncertain and hesitating in that it mentions no one by name except Ya'qub and *Yūsuf* and gives no numbers or time. The only references are to one of the brothers or at best the eldest of the brothers, a king, a noble, his wife, a witness.'[13]

The evidence cited as showing 'uncertainty' and 'hesitation' shows a lack of grasp of the Qur'anic style, particularly in connection with personal names. By this logic we would have to believe that the Qur'an and the Prophet were uncertain about, for instance, the name of the Prophet's closest friend and father-in-law (Abu Bakr), who is spoken of twice without his name being mentioned, reference, at best, being made to 'his companion' in the cave.[14] After the name of God, those of Prophets are the most important names in the Qur'an. Muhammad is mentioned by name only five times, and the Qur'an does not begin with or contain a biography or genealogy of him. Apart from prophets and angels, Satan and some idols, the only names mentioned are Mary, for obvious reasons, Zayd (33:37), for reasons of legislation and the nickname Abu Lahab (the Father of Flames) (111:1), for reasons of condemnation. If we bear this in mind, it becomes clear that the Qur'an conveys its message without reference to personal names. For the Qur'an it was not important to specify that Joseph was sold to Potiphar; what is important is that this boy in his affliction reached (by the Grace of God who is 'subtle in disposing His will') a safe refuge in the household of an important person who looked after him well, that it was this very household that later led to another ordeal in prison, and that this in turn led to his meeting and being elevated by the king or pharaoh. (It is true that Genesis does not give the name of the pharaoh but it gives the name of everybody else.)

In Genesis the picture is different because the function of the text is different. Clearly the story there is part of Jewish history. In Chapter 46 we have the names of seventy persons who migrated to Egypt 'all the souls of the house of Jacob which came to Egypt were three score and ten.' (47:27)

The historiographical nature of the text here even prompts a grand total to be given at the end of the list. It matters very much to Jewish readers to know the names of their ancestors – whereas to Muslim readers knowing these names is not necessary or, if it is, they can be sought in history textbooks, not in the revealed text of the Qur'an.[15] In connection with revelation, on the other hand, it matters very much to Muslims to know the names of Abraham, Isaac, Jacob, Joseph, etc., because being Muslim means believing in these prophets: 'We make no distinction between one and another of His apostles' (2:285).

The moral of the story is quite undiminished by the fact that it follows the regular pattern of the Qur'an as regards personal names. Thus, it is not a matter of 'uncertainty' about names as is suggested in the *Encyclopaedia of Islam*.[16]

The story of Joseph is told in the Qur'an in 100 verses, 10 pages in Arabic; in Genesis it contains more than 450 verses and takes up 26 pages of the Arabic Bible. The difference in size is due partly to the longer timespan in Genesis, but mainly to the differing styles and functions of the two texts. Genesis talks about Joseph's marriage after meeting Pharaoh and the subsequent birth of two children whose names will be included in the long list of Jacob's offspring in Egypt because this is part of Jewish history. The Qur'an, on the other hand, concentrates on the major issue of the famine and its results which were part of the fulfilment of Joseph's old dream. Joseph's marriage and the exact names of his children are not part of this. Genesis also uses more narrative. It obviously delights in including a wealth of personal and local detail, and long lists of names; and within the style of narrative it sometimes includes long statements repeated verbatim (e.g. Pharaoh's long statement of his dream, repeated again before Joseph; compare also 42:29–35 with the earlier part of the chapter.)

The Qur'an uses a different technique for telling the story, which has been called 'dramatic'. The story falls into 28 scenes[17] structured on movement and dialogue; what little narrative there is serves mainly to introduce the characters by 'he said', written as one word in Arabic and followed by the direct speech of the character. I counted seventy-five occurrences of 'he/they said' in the 100 Arabic verses of the story. Thus in verses 8–10 we see the brothers conferring to decide how to dispose of Joseph; in verses 11–13 they attempt to persuade the father to let him go with them; in 16–

18 they go back to Jacob with the stained shirt ... and so on in quick succession. As in a play the curtain falls and rises between scenes with gaps left in time and action because they can be filled in from the remaining text – in the Arabic *Sūrat Yūsuf*, despite the gaps between the scenes, the whole text is clearly understood.[18] Thus at verse 35 the decision is taken to send Joseph to prison; in verse 36 two young men who went to prison with him are already telling him their dreams. In masterly, concise style, both dreams are told in all clarity in a total of two lines. We observed earlier how Pharaoh's dream and request for interpretation were told in two and a half lines, then reported to Joseph in the same amount of space, whereas in Genesis (in the Arabic version), they take up nine times as many lines.

This technique, which relies on scenes (with gaps in between) and dialogue, is sufficient for the purpose of the story in the Qur'an and is by no means unique to the story of Joseph.[19] Naturally this 'gap' technique does not allow the detailed narrative or genealogies found in Genesis. In the Qur'an (verse 69) the brothers come to Joseph with Benjamin as requested, Joseph embraces him, declares himself to him, and reassures him – all succinctly put in one-and-a-half lines. Immediately after this, in verse 70, they are already provided with the corn they came to buy, the goblet is placed in Benjamin's bag and the cry has gone out: 'Travellers, you are thieves' – again, all in less than two lines. This technique serves a different intention to the leisurely, circumstantial narrative in Genesis where the course of the meal is described, together with the seating arrangements, an explanation is given of why the Egyptians will not sit with Hebrews, and Joseph is seen portioning food out from before him and sending it to his brothers, giving Benjamin five times as much as any of the rest!

It is truly remarkable that with all the gaps and great economy of style in the Qur'an, the story is very clear in Arabic and does not require anything from outside the Qur'an in order to be appreciated and its message fully understood. With all the varieties of scenes and dialogue, the story gives a special flavour to the afflictions of Jacob and Joseph – which none of the translators of the Qur'an into English could capture. To an Arab reader the existing translations of *Sūrat Yūsuf* (and of the whole of the Qur'an) are very disappointing.

In the Qur'anic version, the story is structured very tightly, the scenes being bound together in between the introductory 'summary' (12:4–6) and the final restatement by Joseph (12:100). This structure is reinforced by certain expressions and comments that keep recurring to describe how Joseph is being taught, the knowledge and wisdom of God and His grace made universal, Jacob's and Joseph's patience, their abhorrence of injustice, their truthfulness, and Joseph's being good (*min al-muhsinin*) (e.g. vv.6, 18, 19, 21–22, 27, 34, 37, 40, 46, 51, 55, 67–68, 77, 81–83, 86, 96, 101).

Compared to the style of the story in the Qur'an as described above, with its scenes following each other in quick succession, it has been suggested of the style in Genesis, that:

> Of all the Genesis narratives, those about Joseph are the longest, and most detailed. They are not a collection of isolated and fragmentary incidents, but a continuous biography, novelistic in complexion, the artistic creation of a consummate storyteller even though it may have utilised variant traditions.[20]

Gerhard von Rad also observed that 'the Joseph narrative [in the Bible] is a novel through and through'.[21] Part of this technique is the copiousness of detail we have seen in Genesis.[22]

It was noted earlier that the Joseph story in Genesis forms part of the national history of the Jews. This appears to have affected the emphasis and the selection of the material. 'The biblical narrative is probably intended to emphasise the great indebtedness of the crown to Joseph and hence the base ingratitude of the later Pharaoh 'who did not know Joseph' (Exodus 1:8).'[23] Naturally the story of Joseph is also important to the Jews from the religious point of view because it forms part of sacred history: it is part of the process that culminates in the giving of the Torah to Moses.[24] The sacred history of the Old Testament is important also to the Christian because it prepares for the ministry of Jesus. Nevertheless, in addition to the general movement of history in which God's purpose is fulfilled, it seems that such an accumulation of detail also signifies the intention to record the national history as such. This is evidenced by the giving of the names of every one of the seventy individuals who went into Egypt taking their cattle and their goods with them, as well as details of customs and daily life, in the Joseph story. 'National history' and the 'novelistic ... artistic creation of a consummate storyteller'[25] have been perceived as important aspects of the Genesis story. In the Qur'an, on the other hand, the story of Joseph is 'one of the stories of the apostles', told 'to strengthen your heart ... an admonition and a reminder to the believers, and a moral to men of understanding,' (12:111).

It strengthened the Prophet Muhammad's heart, coming, it has been suggested, at the height of his difficulties and the persecution of the Muslim community in Mecca between 'the year of grief' in which the Prophet lost his wife and uncle and the *hijra* (the migration to Medina). It remains in the Qur'an 'a moral to men of understanding', especially as the protection and aid of God to Joseph has, as we said, been generalised in such comments as 'Thus We reward those who do good' (12:22, 56) and Joseph, commenting on the belief in the One God which he held following his fathers Abraham, Isaac and Jacob: 'Such is the grace that God has bestowed on us and on mankind (12:38). The function of a revealed text in Islam is not to give national history; Muslims are not used to this, and the Qur'an does not contain a history of Muhammad's tribe. Nor is it the function of a revealed text in Islam to be like a 'novel through and through'.[26] Naturally, a revealed text may utilise historical information and literary style, as the Qur'an does, but as a means to a religious end. The end in *Sūrat Yūsuf* is different from that in Genesis.

In the Qur'an both Jacob and Joseph are prophets, their stories are 'for guidance' (12:111) and prophets are models to be followed (33:21). In Genesis, Jacob is not presented as a prophet. Accordingly, the picture given of him does not meet this criterion: here is a father who obviously favours one child, takes the initiative in sending him away to those who would harm him, readily offers an explanation for his disappearance – that a wolf has eaten him – even though the shirt is not torn, then tears his own garment in uncontrolled grief, and up to the time the whole family is reunited in Egypt mentions the name of God only once. This last is, in fact, surprising in a man of his advanced age, who would be expected to refer to God more often – a man, moreover, who was the grandson of Abraham and the son of Isaac. The Qur'anic Jacob certainly fulfils the function of guidance.

Joseph's religious side is also far more emphasised in the Qur'an than any other aspect of his personality. He is a prophet whose story offers permanent universal guidance to believers. Although he is also guided by God in Genesis, other aspects of his character and of the whole story gain clear prominence. He appears also as a pleasant, handsome, gifted and able Hebrew economist who played an important role in the history of his nation.

'For Men of Understanding'

The different functions of the story in the two scriptures require different approaches to understanding them. Muslims who approach Genesis in the light of their experience of the Qur'an will quickly begin to feel that something very important is missing and may find the national chronicling an intrusion; this is liable to interfere with their response to it as a great story recounted in a delightful style. Likewise, non-Muslims who are accustomed to Genesis may find, if they approach the Qur'an with similar expectations, that it fails to provide what they are looking for, and may even find the didactic spirit in *Sūrat Yūsuf* an intrusion,[27] which may interfere with their appreciation of this version of the story which has greatly inspired and given guidance and delight to Muslims throughout the ages.

Nevertheless, when all is told – when each story has run its course in its own style with its own preoccupations – readers of all faiths can see from both texts how God supported young Joseph when his brothers plotted against him, and can read what he said to his brothers:

Ye thought evil against me; but God meant it unto good to bring to pass as it is this day, to save much people alive

GENESIS 50:20,

and what he said to his father when they all met in Egypt:

This is the interpretation of my old dream: my Lord has fulfilled it. He has been gracious to me. He has released me from prison, and brought you out of the desert after Satan has stirred up strife between me and my brothers. My Lord is subtle in disposing what He wills. He alone is the all-knowing and wise.

Lord, you have given me authority, taught me to interpret dreams, Creator of the heavens and the earth, you are my protector in this world and in the hereafter, make me die in true submission (to you) and join me with the righteous.

12:100–101

Indeed, in the story of Joseph there will always be 'a moral for men of understanding'.

12

The Qur'an Explains Itself: The *Sūrat al-Raḥmān*

This chapter argues that a most relevant and fruitful approach to understanding the text of the Qur'an is by means of two key concepts developed by Muslim scholars in the Classical period: context and internal relationships. The importance of context (*maqām*) was recognised and formulated for the study of the text of the Qur'an by Muslim linguists whose work in this respect anticipated by many centuries modern linguistic thinking about the crucial importance of context in understanding discourse. Internal relationships were encapsulated in the dictum: *al-Qur'ān yufassir ba'ḍuhu ba'ḍa* (some parts of the Qur'an explain others) – in modern linguistic terms 'intertextuality' – which, given the structure of Qur'anic material, was argued to provide the most correct method of understanding the Qur'an.

In this chapter one complete *sūra* of the Qur'an, no. 55, *al-Raḥmān* is examined in the light of context and internal relationships. It will be demonstrated that commentators who lost sight of these two concepts, or did not pay due regard to them, made erroneous assumptions, gave inadequate explanations, or arrived at conclusions which proved to have been without foundation and which will be shown to contradict the spirit of the *sūra*.

This chapter also examines the views of some Western authors, Richard Bell and John Wansbrough (with reference also to Julius Wellhausen) about *Sūrat al-Raḥmān* and various verses and sections within it, the views of some who found the whole *sūra* 'an imitation' of Psalm 136, and of others who held that material was added to the *sūra* at one stage or another and that there was juxtaposition of variant traditions or paraphrasing of versions which may have had a liturgical or exegetical origin. It has also been suggested that the 'four gardens' in this *sūra* are in fact two, and that the dual – even in these two – was perhaps understood merely as singular. In addition, it has been suggested that the refrain in this *sūra* served the function of a litany although it was not clear to some why the refrain was introduced after some verses and not others.

As will be seen in the course of the discussion, studying the *sūra* in the light of context and internal relationships explains away such difficulties and removes any reasonable need for such conjectures. Moreover, the approach adopted in this chapter reveals inadequacies (and errors) even in some well-known English translations of certain verses in this *sūra*. It will also explain the structure of this *sūra* more clearly than has been shown hitherto, and make, it is hoped, what will prove to be a useful contribution to the appreciation and exegesis of *Sūrat al-Raḥmān*.

Context and Internal Relationships

As explained in Chapter 1, the Qur'an was the starting point of numerous branches of Arabic and Islamic studies. In his *Itqān*, Suyuti dedicates a chapter to *al-'ulūm al-mustanbaṭa min al-Qur'ān*[1] in which he quotes from the commentary of al-Mursi a passage listing various sciences based on the Qur'an and developed to serve it, and to serve Islamic studies in general: branches such as phonetics, grammar, *uṣūl, fiqh, tafsīr, balāgha* ... and others.

Balāgha was undoubtedly one of the most important subjects for Qur'anic exegesis, and began and developed around the central question of the appreciation of the style of the Qur'an and its *i'jāz* in particular, as witnessed by such titles as *Dalā'il al-i'jāz* of 'Abd al-Qahir al-Jurjani.

The importance of *balāgha*, especially *'ilm al-ma'ānī* and *'ilm al-bayān* for *tafsīr* in general is universally recognised and the attention paid to it by such commentators as Zamakhshari and Razi, gives their work particular distinction.

One of the important contributions of scholars of *Balāgha* was their recognition of the concept of *maqām* (the context of the situation) and its role in determining the utterance and providing the criterion for judging it. A central issue in *'ilm al-ma'ānī* is *muṭābaqat al-kalām li-muqtaḍa'l-ḥāl*[2] (the conformity of the utterance to the requirements of the situation).

Al-Khatib al-Qazwini explains:

> The context that demands the definition, generalisation, pre-positioning of part of a discourse, and inclusion (of particular words) differs from the context that demands the indefinite, specification, post-position and omission; the context of

separation differs from that of joining; the situation that requires conciseness differs from that requiring expansiveness. Discourse with an intelligent person differs from discourse with an obtuse one. Each word with its companion is suited to a particular context. A high standard of beauty and acceptability of speech depends on its appropriateness to the situation and vice versa.

Tammam Hassan points out that when scholars of *balāgha* recognised the concept of *maqām*, they were a thousand years ahead of their time, since the recognition of *maqām* and *maqāl* as two separate bases for the analysis of meaning has been arrived at only recently as a result of modern linguistic thinking. When they said *li-kull maqām maqāl* and *li-kull kalima maʻ ṣāḥibatihā maqām* they hit on two remarkable statements that could equally apply to the study of other languages. When Malinowski coined his famous term 'the context of the situation' he had no knowledge of this work.[3]

Scholars of *uṣūl al-fiqh* have recognised the importance of the notions of *maqām* and *maqāl* for the study of the Qur'an. In his *Muwafaqāt* Shatibi states:

The science of *maʻānī* [meaning] and *bayān* [factual and figurative expression] by which the *iʻjaz* [unimutability] of the Qur'an is recognised, revolves around knowing the requirements of the situation during the discourse from the point of view of the discourse itself, the discursant, the discursee or all of them together; for the same statement can be understood in different ways in relation to two different addressees or more. A question with one and the same form can imply other meanings, such as agreement, scolding etc. Likewise an imperative can have the meaning of permission, threat, incapacity/impossibility ...[4]

The other key tool of Qur'anic exegesis is the internal relationships between material in different parts of the Qur'an, expressed by Qur'anic scholars as: *al-Qur'ān yufassir baʻḍuhu baʻḍa.*

Utilisation of such relationships is considered by Ibn Taymiya to be the most correct method (*aṣaḥḥ al-ṭuruq*) of *tafsīr* – exegesis.[5] He explains: 'What is given in a general way in one place is explained in detail in another place. What is given briefly in one place is expanded in another.' Shaṭibi states that many Qur'anic verses/passages can only be properly understood in the light of explanations provided in other verses or *sūras.*[6]

Certain themes have been treated in more than one place in the Qur'an, including, for instance, God's power and grace, the hereafter, stories of earlier prophets, etc. The conciseness or expansion in one place or another depends on *muqtaḍa'l-ḥāl* (what the situation requires). Commenting on stories of earlier prophets, Shaṭibi again remarked that their purpose was to strengthen the Prophet in the face of various forms of denial and obstinacy from his opponents at different times. The form of the story would echo a situation similar to that which the Prophet was facing.

The particular form of the narrative varies according to the situation while all of it is true, factual, with no doubt about its being correct.[7]

Suyuti mentions a feature of Qur'anic style that further illustrates the internal relationships of Qur'anic passages, namely: *al-iqtiṣāṣ,* where a single word in one verse is expanded and clarified in another. Examples were given, such as the following

wa lawlā ni'matu rabbī la-kuntu min'l-muḥḍarīn
[Were it not for the favour of my Lord, I too would have been brought]

37:57

with reference to:

ulāi'ika fi'l-'adhābi muḥḍarūn
[those who will be brought to punishment]

34:38

and:

yawma'l-tanādi
[the day of calling out]

40:32

with reference to:

wa-nādā aṣḥābu'l-jannati aṣḥāba'l-nāri
[and the people of paradise will call out to the people of the fire]

7:44

Readers of the Qur'an recognise this feature clearly. Take for example a verse from the *Fātiḥa,* that practising Muslims recite many times daily: *ṣirāṭ al-ladhīna an'amta 'alayhim* the path of those you have blessed (1:7) and how it is clarified with reference to *al-ladhīna an'ama-llāhu 'alayhim min'l-nabiyyīna wa'l-ṣiddīqīna wa'l-shuhadā'i wa'l-ṣāliḥīna* those whom God has blessed: the prophet, the truthful, the martyrs and the righteous (4:69). More examples will be met in the discussion of *Sūrat al-Raḥmān.*

The importance of context in determining the meaning of any discourse, Qur'an or otherwise, is now established beyond doubt. The style of the Qur'an being self-referential, the importance of internal relationships in understanding the text of the Qur'an cannot be seriously challenged. Context, with the expression it demands, and intertextuality both focus our attention on the Qur'anic text itself which must surely take priority over any other approach to understanding and explaining the Qur'an. A study of *Sūrat al-Raḥmān* in the light of context and internal relationships will, it is hoped, show the benefit of this approach.

Al-Raḥmān

The title of this *sūra* is *al-Raḥmān*, for which most translators give 'The Merciful'. Arberry gives 'The All-Merciful'; Pickthall and Muhammad 'Ali give 'The Beneficent', while Yusuf Ali gives '(God) Most Gracious'.

Those who choose 'The Merciful' have clearly observed the lexical general meaning of the root word *raḥma* (mercy) while those who opted for 'The Beneficent/Bounteous/Gracious' apparently observe the manifestations of mercy in the root meaning, manifestations they saw listed in this *sūra*. We may adopt the Merciful as a translation of *al-Raḥmān*, along with most translators but in the sense of the One who extends His mercy in the form of the bounties listed in the following verses. The choice of this meaning for *al-Raḥmān* is borne out by the context of this *sūra*.

The *sūra* consists of 78 short verses beginning with the name *al-Raḥmān* and ending with: 'Blessed is the name of your Lord, the Lord of Glory and Bestower of Honour', containing three sections:

1. Verses 1–30 deal with bounties in this world. v.13 challenges the addressees (men and *jinn*) – 'Which, then, of your Lord's bounties do you deny?' – repeated afterwards as a refrain.
2. Verses 31–45 contain a challenge for the addressees to escape the judgement – the guilty will not be able to escape the punishment whose existence they had denied.
3. Verses 46–77 deal with bounties in the rewards of two classes of believers.

Section I: God's Bounties in This World

al-Raḥmān 'allama al-Qur'ān [The Merciful taught the Qur'ān]

VV.1–2

This *sūra* is unique in the Qur'an in that it begins with one of the names of God, *al-Raḥmān* standing as it is, as one separate verse which, it will be seen, summarises the *sūra* and governs the following material both by its signification and its sound. It has been noted that when the name of God occurs in the Qur'an as a subject followed by a predicate verb as in *al-Raḥmān* such an order signifies restriction in the sense of 'It is He Who did such and such'.[8] In our *sūra* we have a series of predicate verbs following each other without conjunction, in the main all dependent on the word *al-Raḥmān*, the sense being: it is *al-Raḥmān* who taught the Qur'an, who created man and taught him how to communicate, who ... who ... etc. Since it is through the Qur'an that we are told about God and all the manifestations of His mercy and beneficence, teaching the Qur'an comes as the first predicate of *al-Raḥmān* stressing also the priority and more lasting effect of spiritual benefit.[9] His beneficence in teaching the Qur'an is so important that it was pointed out in the first verses of the book to be revealed:

'Read! And your Lord is the Most Generous, who taught ...'

96:3–4

as well as on other occasions such as:

'He taught you what you did not know before: God's bounty to you is ever great.'

4:113

Since the context of our *sūra* relates to His bounty 'taught the Qur'an' is used rather than the normal 'sent it down' which is used scores of times elsewhere, so the context here governs the choice of vocabulary.

The effect of *al-Raḥmān* on the meaning of the following material is further emphasised by the effect of its sound, since, standing as a separate verse ending in a long *alif* and *nūn*, it sets the pattern for the *fāṣila* or rhyme at the ends of the following verses which consist mainly of *–ān*, and on a few occasions of *–ām*, which does not alter the pattern much since 'n' and 'm' are both nasal voiced resonant sounds. (vv.1–6 are transliterated to indicate this effect.[10] This results in a pleasing resonance in Arabic that enhances the effect produced by the enumeration of God's bounties. The uniform sound in the close succession of rhymes helps transfer the effect of *Raḥmān* to *Qur'ān* to *bayān, biḥusbān, yasjudān,* etc. Since the Qur'an, *bayān* etc. are manifestations of the mercy of *al-Raḥmān*, the rhyme helps to build the cumulative effect of *raḥma* and maintains it throughout, with even the challenge to deny the obvious benefits (itself in the same rhyme) not cancelling (if not enhancing) the beneficent order established by *al-Raḥmān* in the first line.

Khalaqa'l-insān. 'Allamahu'l-bayān

[He created man and taught him how to communicate]

vv.3–4

Creating man and teaching him *bayān* are two of the manifestations of the bounty of *Raḥmān. Bayān* is the ability to express oneself and to understand the expression of others:

It is He who has brought you into being, and given you ears, eyes and hearts: little thanks you show.

67:23

Have We not given him two eyes, a tongue, and two lips?

90:8–9

The Qur'an describes itself as being *mubīn* – clarifying its teachings so that they are easy to understand.

al-shamsu wa'l-qamaru biḥusbān
[The sun and the moon pursue their calculated course]

v.5

The statement is expanded to show the benefits of the sun and the moon and the exact way they follow their course in such verses as (10:5) (6:96) and (36:40), in the intertextual way explained earlier.

wa'l-najmu wa'l-shajaru yasjudān
The plants and the trees submit [to God's purpose for them]

v.6

Najm in this context means plants that have no stem/trunk as opposed to those that have. Both submit to God in following the course He created them for, as believers submit in prayer,[11] as we see in greater detail in 22:18. Many commentators, referring to the above verse, give for *najm* the alternative meaning of 'stars' and most English translations follow this. However, what we have in vv.5–6 is a contrast between two celestial objects: the sun and the moon, then two earthly ones: trees and stemless plants. The context here dictates the meaning 'plants'.

It is clear from the first two verses and throughout that our *sūra* is built on dualism: 'God the Gracious taught the Qur'an; created man and taught him how to communicate; the sun and the moon pursue their calculated course ... ' etc.

Contrast and dualism are the obvious feature throughout. The context of this *sūra* clearly requires the enumeration of the bounties *ālā'* of *al-Raḥmān* that surround the addressees (dual: men and *jinn*) on both sides, and above and below, so that they are challenged to deny any of them. This context will be seen to govern the choice of material as well as the meanings of words and expressions.

There is one further point about verses 5 and 6. The change of structure in these two sentences, singling out the four items they contain to make them subjects rather than objects of verbs, suggests that, in addition to their being examples of God's bounties, they are placed at this early stage in the *sūra* as a model of submission to God (c.f. 22:18) for the addressees, who may deny the bounties.

And the heavens He has uplifted and set up the Balance
that you might not transgress in the Balance
Weigh with justice and skimp not in the Balance.
And Earth – he set it down for [His] creatures
Therein fruits, and palm-trees with sheathed clusters
Husked grain, and fragrant plants.

VV.7–12

Here we have the manifestation of His grace in the way He keeps the heavens up and the earth stable – the duality and contrast being maintained. The heavens are raised high so that they do not fall on His creatures, c.f. 13:2; 21:32; 22:65. 'Uplifted the heavens', rather than 'created them' which is usual, suits the context. He raised them high but did not cut the addressees off from them, sending down from them the scripture and the balance (42:17).

The Qur'an having already been mentioned (v.2), only the Balance is mentioned here, between heaven and Earth: even before the Earth is mentioned, the Balance is set up. The passage stresses the importance of keeping just balance with no excess or deficiency, a fitting introduction to the repeated question to follow – 'Which of your Lord's bounties will you deny?' – since justice demands that the addressees recognise (without skimping) the bounties of the Merciful with which He surrounds them from every direction. Skimping in the balance elsewhere in the Qur'an has a concrete significance; in this context it carries the additional, metaphorical meaning of due recognition for God's bounties.

Bell makes the unexplained and unsubstantiated claim:[12] 'That you may not transgress ... skimp not in the Balance are later insertions.' However, the equivalent of 'that you might not ...' can be observed in combination with *mīzān* in Q. 57:25 where it cannot be assumed to be a later insertion, and the emphatic repetition with *mīzān* is also observed in such instances as 11:84–85; 26:181–83; 83:1–3.

The repetition of the word *al-mīzān* is particularly effective in this context, coming soon after *biḥusbān* (perfectly calculated courses) to reinforce the sense of exactitude and balance in God's creation, and in the ordered structure of this *sūra*, heightening the demand for just dealing. In this context, the verb *waḍa'a* (set up) is used with *al-mīzān* rather than *anzala* (brought down), as in 42:17, to emphasise the significance of the balance here and, using the same verb (*waḍa'a*) with *al-'arḍ* highlights the crucial importance of maintaining the balance on Earth.

The Merciful keeps the sky from falling down on His creatures and makes the earth stable underneath them. One is made to appreciate the significance of the condensed statement here by reference to such expanded versions as in:

If We will, We can make the earth swallow them or cause fragments of the sky to fall upon them.

34:9

and:

He set firm mountains upon the earth lest it quake with you.

16:15

Al-'anām (the creatures) for whom He set the Earth up are men and *jinn* and other creatures that move on it. Bell translates v.10 as: 'The earth He has set up for the cattle' and says in a footnote 'or all living creatures'. His preferred version is contradicted by the other Qur'anic references just cited, and gives no sense of the fruits, palm-trees and fragrant plants. In the contents of the earth we have the balance of fruits and palm-trees, grain and fragrant plants (*rayhān*). Some commentators take *rayhān* as grains that men eat as opposed to the husk eaten by animals, but this would make it redundant (grain having already been mentioned) and would disturb the balance. The luxury in fragrant plants is counterbalanced later by that in pearls.

Dhāt al-akmām (sheathed) and *dhu'l-'aṣf* (with grains) are two nicely balanced details showing the fruits of palm and corn still in the stage of promise, still dependent on the grace of God to bring them to fruition, which again suits the context.

Men and *jinn*, included among the 'creatures' in v.10 and mentioned in v.14, have been shown the bounties of God and the manifestations of His mercy and beneficence surrounding them from above, below and on either side.

They are now addressed in the dual with the challenging question:

Fa-bi'ayyi ālā'i rabbikumā tukadhdhibān?
[Which, then, of your Lord's bounties do you deny?]

v.13

The change here, *iltifāt*, from 'His' third person pronoun to the noun 'your Lord' is significant, and since *rabb* is related to *rabba* (to bring up, care for), His lordship is caring lordship. The 'Which, then ...?' coming after the surrounding benefits is a cornering challenge, and makes any denial futile, 'your caring Lord' showing its folly and ingratitude.

Such a challenge to deny the obvious blessings and signs of God is referred to in other places in the Qur'an, c.f. 53:55; 40:81; 16:83; 14:34; 56:83; 6:2. In our *sūra* the challenge to men and *jinn* is made thirty-one times, which has given rise to much speculation, largely far-fetched and missing the point. Razi (and others) sought the explanation in the value of the specific numbers of 3 and 10 etc., stating, among other things, that the number with 'bounty' is ten times that with 'punishment' mentioned in the preceding *sūra*, (c.f. 'He that does a good deed shall be repaid tenfold' (6:160). Bell observed that the refrain occurred 'first at v.12, then at intervals of two verses, and then from v.23 onwards at intervals of one, except at 43–44 which should probably form one verse'. He further suggests that the refrain might have been added later, 'when also the eschatological portion from 31 onwards may have been composed'.[13] Bell does not support his suggestion that the material was at one time used without the refrain. Comparison with other instances of challenge cited above shows that the enumeration of bounties could not have been left without a comment like the refrain. As for his comment on the frequency and location of the refrain, our analysis of the context and structure of this *sūra* will, it is hoped, explain why the refrain occurs thirty-one times, why it could not have started earlier, or occurred more times than it does, whether at the end or in the body of the text. Commenting on the refrain, Wansbrough states:

Structurally, it produces the effect of a litany, and its similarity to *ki le-'olam hasdo,* which performs the same function in Psalm 136 has been noted. I should like here to insist upon the term litany rather than refrain. The role of the latter in the Qur'an and elsewhere, is that of concluding formula, which does not adequately describe employment of the device in this passage.[14]

Reference to Psalm 136 will be discussed later. Wansbrough rightly observes that the function of the refrain in the Qur'an is that of a concluding formula but does not agree that this adequately describes the employment of the device in our *sūra*. Our analysis will show that the question ('Which then ...' etc.) is used as exactly that – a concluding formula. As regards litany, this means either: '(1) a form of public prayer, usually penitential, consisting of a series of petitions, in which the clergy leads and the public respond. It may be used as part of a service or by itself, in the latter case often in procession, or (2) (transf.) A form of supplication representing a litany.'[15] Even in a vague sense, then, a litany is quite alien to the Qur'an and the way it is recited in Islamic ritual prayer. There, if a person (an *imām* in prayer or otherwise) reads aloud, all others have to listen attentively, and there is no leader/response form:

When the Qur'ān is recited, listen to it and be silent so that mercy may be shown to you.
7:204

In our *sūra*, contrary to Wansbrough's and Bell's perception, after the first instance the formula always marks the end of a pair. We have here a series of paired bounties surrounding the addressees geographically – above, below, east, west – or qualitatively – fresh and salt water, the ships that float and move over the water etc. Even in the punishment of the guilty later on the pairing structure is maintained. Only when a pair is completed do we have the concluding refrain: 'Which then of your Lord's bounties do you deny?'

It is introduced for the first time just before the addressees – men and *jinn* – hitherto referred to in the word *al-'anām*, make a clear appearance.

He created man of sounding clay, like the potter's,
And created the jinn of smokeless fire,
Which, then, of your Lord's bounties do you deny?

vv.14–16

The statement is so condensed here that the bounties may not be apparent. Comparison with other instances in the Qur'an clarifies the process of creation. In these other instances, both humans and *jinn* are reminded of their origin, and how God, in his bounty developed them into what they now are, human rather than clay and *jinn* rather than fire (32:7–9; 95:4;

36:77; 16:78; 38:76). Were it not for His bounty, they would not have arrived at their present state, nor would the sky have been kept aloft, nor the earth remain stable; the two types of water would not have been kept distinct from each other, nor would the ships have floated and sailed. This reveals a further duality: origin and present state.

Lord of the two easts
And Lord of the two wests
Which, then, of your Lord's bounties do you deny?

VV.17–18

The reference here is to the two extreme points where the sun rises in the winter and the summer; and where it sets in the winter and in the summer (rather than where the sun rises and sets and the moon rises and sets as suggested by some commentators). This shows His grace in the variation of seasons and of the length of the day and night. The selection of the extreme points brings them nearer to the realisation of His mercy in not making the night time, nor the day time, perpetual for them, as explained in 28:71–73. Verse 17 is so condensed by the structure and the demands of the context that its full significance can only be appreciated by comparison with 28:71–3; 73:9 (Lord of the East and West) and 70:40–41 (Lord of the Easts and Wests) which show how the selection and forms of the material serve the context and are determined by it.

So far God's bounties have been shown on land; the following passage deals with water:

He let forth the two seas that meet one another,
Between them is a barrier they do not overpass,
Which, then, of your Lord's bounties do you deny?

VV.19–21

Fresh and salt water, in rivers and seas, meet but do not overrun each other. Unlike in the preceding passage, the end of the first verse does not complete a pair of bounties, so the refrain comes after the second verse: running waters that meet but are kept distinct, as will be explained below.

From them come forth pearls of two kinds
Large ones, and small, brilliant ones,
Which, then, of your Lord's bounties do you deny?

VV.22–23

This is the second of the three cycles of bounties related to the sea. Translators, perhaps with one or two exceptions, translate the second kind (*marjān*) as 'coral', while the majority of commentators explain that it denotes small pearls which are much more brilliant. This is supported by an author on gems who cited verses of Imru' al-Qays.[16] Some commentators give the alternative of 'red beads', and some modern ones (S. Qutb, for instance) talk of coral. We shall see at v.58 that reference to other instances in the Qur'an confirm the meaning we have opted for. In 16:14 and 35:12 the fish that come from the seas also appear, whereas in our *sūra* they are not mentioned: the given pairs are complete without them – another example of how the selection of material suits the context.

Many commentators have experienced a problem with v.22. According to their knowledge, pearls come only from salt water whereas the verse states that they come from both salt and fresh water. An early writer who faced the problem was Abu 'Ubayda (d.210/825) in his *Majāz al-Qur'ān.*[17] He insisted that pearls come only *min aḥadihimā* from one, i.e. salt water, not both (*minhumā*) and explains the Qur'anic expression 'both of them' as being analogous to the expression: 'I ate bread and milk', applying 'ate' to drinking milk as well as to eating bread when in fact it refers only to one. His suggestion that pearls come from 'one' of them only is refuted by Qur'anic usage elsewhere. *Minhumā* was not a freak or a 'slip of the tongue' in the Qur'an and Abu 'Ubayda's attempt to explain it away does not advance his assertion. If we compare Qur'an 35:12, for instance, we have an explicit statement confirming that pearls come *min kullin* from each of the two kinds of water. Indeed Abu 'Ubayda dealt with this verse (II. p. 153) but, faced with the fact that it goes against his assertion about *aḥadihimā*, he passed it over without comment. Doubt has been expressed about Abu 'Ubayda's ability to read the Qur'an without making mistakes.[18] Wansbrough comments on Abu 'Ubayda's statement: '*yakhruju minhumā [min aḥadihimā]*' could not seriously be interpreted as figurative usage or even stylistic option. 'Its presence can only be justified by a principle of inclusion, which took account of passages requiring textual emendation'.[19]

Ibn Qutayba faced the same problem with 55:22, but cited with it 35:12. He still insisted that pearls came only from salt water and even claimed that Abu Dhu'ayb al-Hudhali was wrong in a verse he composed, in thinking, probably after Qur'anic usage, that pearls exist in fresh water.[20] Believing that pearls came only from salt water and trying to justify the Qur'anic statement, commentators suggested, for instance, that pearls came from places where sea and fresh water meet, as in Shatt al-'Arab or that mussels lived in the sea but came up and opened their mouths to receive raindrops which then went into the making of pearls![21] However, Razi's first and preferred interpretation was to accept 'the manifest meaning of the Word of God' (i.e. pearls come from both waters), 'which is more worthy of being followed than the word of some men whose word cannot be trusted. And who knows that pearls do not come from fresh water? And supposing divers did find them or bring them out only from sea water, this does not necessarily mean that they don't exist somewhere else'. Razi would perhaps have been pleased to know what we know today about freshwater pearls:

> Freshwater mussels in the temperate zone of the Northern Hemisphere have produced pearls of great value ... Pearling is still a carefully fostered industry in central Europe, and the forest streams of Bavaria, in particular, are the source of choice pearls. Freshwater pearling in China has been known from before 1000 BC.[22]

The Qur'anic statement in our *sūra*, then, stands with its manifest meaning, supported by other Qur'anic references, and in harmony with the duality of the context, without need of emendation or forced interpretations, and in spite of the belief current amongst commentators, that pearls come only from salt water.

His are the ships that run,
Raised up in the sea like mountains;
Which, then, of your Lord's bounties do you deny?[23]

VV.24–25

This is the third and last pair of bounties connected with the sea. In spite of their size and weight, ships do not sink but sail along. The condensed description, *al-jawāri'l-munsha'āt* ('running' and 'raised') – two words in Arabic – is expanded in 42:32–34 which brings out its full significance – one part of the Qur'an explaining another.

This principle of intertextuality helps us to understand how the part of our *sūra* already discussed relates to the next. We often find elsewhere in the Qur'an that when people are on a journey by sea or on land they are reminded of their final return to God (10:23; 36:44; 43:14). Comparison (e.g. with 10:24) also reveals that just when the earth looks at its best and becomes 'adorned and its people think they are its masters', all this can vanish away. This leads on to an explanation of the relative permanence of the next life. The eschatological part of this *sūra*, therefore, follows logically in the same way as in other *sūras* and need not (as Bell suggested without any substantiation) have been composed at a later time.

All that dwells on the earth is perishing
Yet the Face of your Lord shall remain, Glorious, Bestowing Honour
Which, then, of your Lord's bounties do you deny?

vv.26–28

One would have expected this statement to read 'all of you, men and *jinn*, are perishing', but the reference to earth makes this encompassing statement more emphatic and recalls the earlier reference to earth, in v.19 as stabilised and provided with all that is necessary for life. This binds the structure firmly in keeping with the Qur'anic pattern noted above, where the flourishing of the earth is followed by reference to the Last Day (c.f. 10:24; 57:20).

Verses 26–31 here conclude the earlier part of the *sūra* and preface what remains of it – Majesty and Honouring – reiterating the qualities of God mentioned in the first and again in the last verses of the *sūra*. Translators render *al-ikrām* inadequately as 'honour'. Its root verb, *akrama* is, however, in the causative form, meaning 'to give honour and bounty'. The contrasting pair in 26–27 is composed of the world perishing and God's face abiding. A further pair is made up of Majesty on the one hand and bestowing of honour on the other (c.f. 17:70; 21:26; 37:40–43). Indeed, the structure of the rest of the *sūra* is determined by this particular pair: the passing away of those on earth and the permanence of God necessarily mean, as witnessed elsewhere in the Qur'an, that all will return to Him for judgement. 'All things shall perish except His Face, His is the judgement and to Him you shall return' (28:88; also 10:23–30). Indeed *jalāl* and *ikrām* herald the variety of fates resulting from the judgement to which the repeated *'ālā'*' (bounties) and *tukadhdhibān* (do you deny) was bound to lead. This reinforces our statement that Bell's conclusion, that the eschatological section was added later, cannot stand.

All who dwell in heaven and earth entreat Him,
Every day He attends to some matters;
Which, then, of your Lord's bounties do you deny?

vv.29–30

The pairing here is between the entreaties and God's attention to them. This particular bounty is described in more detail in *Sūra* 14, v.34, which similarly concludes an enumeration of God's bounties in this world. The entreaties and God's answer in our *sūra* follow the part dealing with this world and precede the one leading to the next (a further pairing), to suggest that the needs and His attention to them exist in both worlds.

Section II: Eschatology: Punishment

We shall surely find the time to [judge] you -
You two weighty armies (of men and jinn);
Which, then, of your Lord's bounties do you deny?

vv.31–32

The previous pair might have suggested to them that God is engaged every day in attending to entreaties; this one stresses that He will make time to judge men and *jinn*. He has the power over them, even if they gather all together as two massive armies. This echoes the challenge in *Sūra* 17, v.88: 'if all the men and *jinn* were to gather to... they would not be able to ...'.

Arberry translates *al-thaqalān* as 'you weight and you weight', but *thaqal* also means a massive, heavily-moving army (see Lane's *Lexicon*). The challenge supports this. Being weighty is an element of strength for men and *jinn* here, but it will prove a hindrance in the following verse where they are shown to be too cumbersome to escape. The shift (*iltifāt*) from talking about God, to Himself challenging them, speaking in the first person divine plural makes the challenge awesome and all the more effective.

The pairing here is of the army of men and the army of *jinn* gathered, and God attending to deal with them. Commentators had to ask themselves: where is the bounty here and in the following verses, about punishing the sinners (and, even in 26–28), in which the refrain is maintained after each pairing? Zamakhshari's answer is typical. There is a blessing in the judgement, for those who are saved from punishment, and a blessing for everybody in being warned beforehand: out of His benevolence He did not leave them in darkness about the fate that awaits sinners. However, we need not necessarily take this view. The punishment will be for those who deny (77:15 passim), and the challenge: 'Which, then, of your Lord's bounties do you deny?' is in fact for those who may deny the encompassing bounties. It is ungrateful and futile to deny such encompassing bounties. It is, moreover, foolish to deny and rebuff such a bounteous and powerful Lord who will certainly judge them, where denial will have due punishment. The bounties in the section (31–45) can, I suggest, be understood to be the bounties God has given them in the world. Had the question in this section been 'which of these two bounties...' we would have been forced to interpret what is in every pair in this section as bounties. The refrain is maintained in the punishment section to emphasise their foolishness in addition to their ingratitude, and the challenging question carries threat and mockery in it, c.f. (44:47–50; and 53:50–56). Twice in this *sūra al-Raḥmān* is described as being *Dhu'l-jalāli wa'l-ikrām*. Punishing the sinners has to do with *jalāl* (majesty), while *ikrām* shows itself in the bounties He has shown men and *jinn* in this world and will show the believers in the next.

> *O company of jinn and men, if you have power to penetrate the confines of heaven and earth, penetrate them:*
> *You shall not penetrate them except with (Our) authority;*
> *Which, then, of your Lord's bounties do you deny?*
> *Against you shall be loosed a flame of fire and molten brass,*
> *And you shall not be helped;*
> *Which, then, of your Lord's bounties do you deny?*
> *And when heaven is split asunder*
> *And turns to crimson like red leather -*
> *Which, then, of your Lord's bounties do you deny?*
> *The guilty shall be known by their mark,*
> *And they shall be seized by their forelocks and their feet;*
> *Which, then, of your Lord's bounties do you deny?*
> *This is the Hell which the guilty deny,*
> *They go round between it and hot, boiling water;*
> *Which, then, of your Lord's bounties do you deny?*
>
> vv.33–45

With all their might men and *jinn* cannot run away when God attends to their judgement. The context requires the introduction of the *jinn* first, since they seem to have more power to penetrate heaven and earth (c.f. 17:88). The heavens which He has raised up and made firm and comely in this world will split and redden in the new order of things in the next. In this world they have been asked again and again in this *sūra*: 'Which of your Lord's bounties do you deny?' – in the next they will no longer be asked: the guilty will be known by their marks. The pairing structure is maintained throughout: the guilty will be seized by the forelocks and the feet, and will wander between Hell fire and boiling water. There is no refrain between 43 and 44 because the pair has not been completed (c.f. Bell). It is important to note that the context of *Sūrat al-Raḥmān* has affected the way the treatment of the guilty is presented. They are surrounded: held by forehead and feet and roam 'between ... and ...'; in other contexts they are 'in' hell (c.f. 18:29; 56:41). Being surrounded in this way calls to mind their being surrounded in this world from all directions by the bounties they presumed to deny. It will be observed that their treatment is dealt with briefly in this *sūra*, unlike in many others, before a longer description of what is a more important matter in *sūrat al-Raḥmān*: the reward of the believers.

Section III: Eschatology: Rewards

But for him who fears the time when he will stand before his Lord;
There are two gardens;
Which, then, of your Lord's bounties do you deny?
Wherein are two fountains flowing;
Which, then, of your Lord's bounties do you deny?
Wherein of every fruit there are two kinds.
Which, then, of your Lord's bounties do you deny?
Sitting[24] *on couches lined with brocade,*
The fruit of both gardens above them within reach;
Which, then, of your Lord's bounties do you deny?
Therein maidens restraining their glances,
Untouched before them by men or jinn;
Which, then, of your Lord's bounties do you deny?
As though of ruby
And brilliant pearls
Which, then, of your Lord's bounties do you deny?
Shall the reward of good work be anything but good?
Which, then, of your Lord's bounties do you deny?

vv.46–60

The believers are divided into two classes: the first is the pious with whose rewards we will deal now. The structure of pairs is maintained, and so is the refrain. As the guilty who deny the judgement and punishment will suffer between the two torments of fire and boiling water, those who fear standing before their Lord for judgement will enjoy two gardens. (In his Companion to Arberry's translation, W. M. Watt comments, 'Why two, it is not clear' (II, p.250). The bounties are shown on two sides of the believers, as an example of perfect bliss. In discussing the significance of the dual we should compare such expressions as: *labbayka wa-sa'dayka* (I respond to you twice) and *ḥanānayka!* (be kind/have pity twice) where it is used as an intensive to express fullness and completeness.

We have seen in the earlier part of this *sūra* that the Lord's bounties surround them from above and below (heaven raised, with the Qur'an and the balance 'coming down' from it and earth stabilised with plants coming up from it), from east and west, on land and sea. Here the two gardens are on the right and left; from above them there are abundant branches for shade and fruits (c.f. 76:14). Each has a running fountain from below (c.f. 85:11) and in each garden every fruit is of two kinds. The inhabitants sit on couches under them with the fruit of both gardens hanging within reach above them. The lining of the couches is brocade – and the exterior is left to the imagination. They will be there with their spouses (c.f. 36:56). The spouses are chaste and untouched by any before them; and they have the lustre of ruby and the whiteness of brilliant pearls.[25] Verse 58 here and its parallel (56:23) confirm that *marjān* here, as in v.22, means small pearls, not corals as thought by most translators.

The guilty will suffer from above and below, seized by the forelocks and the feet; and suffer from two sides hell-fire and boiling water. The pious will find enjoyment on both sides – in the two gardens – and from above and below. Whereas the guilty will 'roam' between hell-fire and seething water, the pious will be 'sitting'. There are no spouses for the guilty, and the contrast with the pious is obvious. The rewards for pious souls are concluded with the testimony of their Lord that they have done good work: 'Shall the reward of good work be anything but good?'

And below these two
There are two [other] gardens
Which, then, of your Lord's bounties do you deny?
Two green, green gardens;
Which, then, of your Lord's bounties do you deny?
Therein are two fountains of bubbling water;
Which, then, of your Lord's bounties do you deny?
Therein are fruits,
Date-palms and pomegranates;
Which, then, of your Lord's bounties do you deny?
Therein goodly, beautiful ones;
Which, then, of your Lord's bounties do you deny?
Dark-eyed, sheltered in pavilions;
Which, then, of your Lord's bounties do you deny?
Untouched before them by man or jinn;
Which, then, of your Lord's bounties do you deny?
Sitting on green cushions and fine carpets;
Which, then, of your Lord's bounties do you deny?

vv.61–77

The two gardens described here are for the second class of believers and are lower in rank or quality – *min dūnihimā* – as shown by the comparison: these gardens are 'green'; the first are 'abounding in branches'. The water here is 'bubbling', not 'flowing'; there is only 'fruit' here, whereas in the other there is 'of every fruit two kinds'. The descriptions of the damsels[26] and the cushions, too, are of a lesser order.[27] The bounties in the earlier gardens are more encompassing from above and below. There are couches rather than cushions, and the fruit in the branches above them is within reach rather than simply being fruits in the garden; the divine testimony of their having done well is reserved for those in the first gardens. The pairing structure is, nevertheless, maintained throughout, as is the refrain.

That there are two classes of gardens, for two classes of believers, fits the pairing scheme evident in this *sūra*. It is also confirmed by the next *sūra* (56:10–38) where there is a parallel description of two classes of garden, one for 'those nearest to God' and the other for 'the Companions of the Right Hand'. Some commentators[28] have thought that the four gardens in our *sūra* could be for the same believers. This is refuted by the categorical distribution in *Sūra* 56. Moreover, it does not make sense: how can the Lord (*dhu'l-jalāli wa'l-ikrām*) say to a favoured believer: 'I have given you these two excellent gardens as a reward for your good work' (46–60) and in addition: 'I am giving you these two inferior ones' (63–77)? Wansbrough questioned the 'two gardens' in v.46 and suggested that the total number in this *sūra* should be halved. This was based on a quotation from the early commentator al-Suyuti attributing to al-Farra' the view that the dual form *jannatān* was demanded by the rhyme-scheme, but in fact represented the singular *janna* as in Q. 79:41.[29] However, at the end of the same paragraph in Suyuti, from which Wansbrough took this quotation, there is another statement attributed to Farra' to the effect that it was *jannāt* in the plural (not dual) that was meant.[30] By comparing what Farra' had actually said with what Suyuti and earlier authors have attributed to him it becomes clear that he was in fact misrepresented. Commenting on v.46 he said:

> Commentators have said they are two of the gardens [*bustānān*] of Paradise *wa-qad yakūn fi'l-'arabiyya janna tuthannīha'l-'arab fi ash'āriha.* In Arabic you may come across the word '*janna*' which the Arabs in their poetry put in the dual. [two lines of verse quoted]: *wa-dhālika ana'l-shi'r lahu qawāfin yuqīmuha'l-ziyāda wa'l-nuqṣān fa-yaḥtamil mā lā yaḥtamiluh al-kalām.* Because verse has rhyme which can be produced by addition and omission. Thus it allows situations not normally allowed in prose.[31]

Farra' did not state that the dual was inserted 'for the rhyme', nor did he state that the gardens were plural '*jannāt*'. He also misunderstood the meaning of the lines of verse he quoted. The dual is, in fact, intended by the poet, the point being that the character in the poem exaggerates the value of his tree, seeing it not just as a whole garden but as two, the notion of two gardens obviously representing perfect bliss. In any case Farra's, original statement about v.46 is, at most, very tentative and it is clear that authors after him blew it out of proportion.

Moreover, in discussing the number of gardens and whether there are one or two in vv.46–67, we must not lose sight of two important factors. First, the context of the whole *sūra* which has been demonstrated from the beginning to be of bounties encompassing from above and below, right and left – semantically, and not, as claimed by Wansbrough, grammatically, for verse juncture this demands two encompassing gardens. Second, internal relationships in the Qur'an confirm that two gardens are intended here. As in the line quoted by Farra', two encompassing gardens in this world,[32] one on the right and one on the left, represent perfect bliss. Such bounties should be met with gratitude; denial and ingratitude incur punishment (c.f. 34:15–17, and 18:32–43).[33]

In view of these examples one cannot understand the difficulty Wansbrough finds in having two gardens, one on the right and one on the left. It is clear that there is a difference between *janna*, and *al-janna* in the next life. The first means a garden, *bustān* as in Farra's passage. The second means Paradise, as opposed to Hell. In this sense we can talk about the believers being contained, all of them in *al-janna*, each one of them having within it *al-Janna* or *jannatayn* or *jannāt*. As witnessed by a glance at any concordance, the Qur'an itself speaks in scores of instances about the believers being in *al-Janna* or in *jannāt* (or *jannatayn* in our *sūra*).

Thus, the two factors of the context (duality and encompassing bliss), and intertextuality (confirmation in Sura 56), in addition to our discussion of what has been attributed to Farra', lead to a conclusion contrary to Wansbrough's. 'It may well be that the dual *jannatāni* of Q.55, 46, and 62 was, implicitly, never understood as anything but singular.'[34] The dual is meant in the Qur'an to be a dual, not just a rhyming device.

It has already been stated that vv.46–61 and 62–77 represent two sets of gardens for two classes of believers. Wellhausen, however, suggested that in these two more or less similar descriptions of two gardens we have a case of duplication due to varying recollections on the part of those from whom the compilers got the *sūra*.[35] Commenting on Zamakhshari's statement that the descriptive components of the second set 'version B' are inferior to those of 'version A', Wansbrough states:[36]

That implied, of course, acceptance of the canonical order of the two descriptions, but from the same evidence it could be argued that version 'A' represents an elaboration of version 'B', both by rhetorical device and exegetical gloss. Whether the embellishment is to be understood as purely literary or as a reflex of what may have been the liturgical function of these verses, is difficult to determine. If a cultic context can be envisaged, it would seem that the descriptions of paradise were recited in inverse order to the canon. More likely, however, is juxtaposition in the canon of two closely related variant traditions, contaminated by recitation in identical contexts, or produced from a single tradition by oral transmission.

Like all translators, Wansbrough translates *min dūnihimā* as 'besides them'. This suits a juxtaposition theory but it is difficult to see from the context or Qur'anic reference the basis for such a translation.

The speculation of Wellhausen and Wansbrough, however, disregards Qur'anic evidence concerning this matter. Such evidence occurs no further away than the beginning of the next *sūra*, two and a half lines down the page. There we have a division of three groups: those on the right, those on the left, and the foremost in the race who will be brought near. Speculation about juxtaposition of material deriving from variant transmissions, or version A elaborating version B, cannot stand: there is a governing sentence announcing from the beginning that there are three divisions: *wa-kuntum azwājan thalāthatan* – and you are three classes. Then it deals with the three groups in detail – 56:7–44ff; 88–95.

In *Sūra* 55 the guilty are dealt with first, together with the challenge to escape the judgement. That group is dispensed with quickly (three verses and refrains), in order to get back to speak at length of bounties of *al-Raḥmān*, the Bountiful One – an example of how the context affects the treatment of the material. In *Sūra* 56, on the other hand, the foremost in the race, 'those who will be brought near', are dealt with first, clearly to highlight their distinction, followed by those on the right hand.[37] In *Sūra* 56 the treatment of those on the left hand comes last. This fits the sequence of the verses that follow. They are dealt with there in a much longer passage than that of the guilty in our *sūra*, again context affecting the treatment and order of material. In fact Wansbrough himself refers, in another context, to the verses cited above as evidence: 'The notion of propinquity to God as a reward for piety is clearly conveyed, expressed in 56:7–11 as a tripartite distribution of benefit, of which *muqarrabūn* (those brought near) represents the highest order.' (p. 30)

As in *Sūra* 55, the proportion of excellence in the descriptions of the abodes of the two classes of believers is kept in *Sūra* 56. Parallel descriptions and contrasts are also evident. A few examples will suffice: (1 refers to the better class; 2 to the second).[38]

	Sūra 55	*Sūra* 56
1.	*min kull fākihatin zawjān* Of every fruit two kinds	*wa fākihatin mimmā yatakhayyarūn* with fruits, any that they may select
2.	*fākihatun wa-nakhlun wa-rummān* fruits, palm trees and pomegranates	*wa fākihatin kathīra* and plenty of fruit
1.	*wa-jana'l-jannatayn dān* the fruit of the two gardens near at hand	*wayuṭuf 'alayhim... bi... wa fākihatin* youths will go round serving them with fruit
2.	*fīhimā fākihatun* in both gardens there is fruit	*wa-fākihatin* and fruit
1.	*hal jazā' al-iḥsān illa'l-iḥsān* Shall the reward of good work be any but good?	*jazā'an bi-mā kānū ya'malūn* a reward for what they have done
2.	none	none

The select class has a special reward – 'Shall the reward of good work be anything but good?' (55:60) – that is paralleled by 'a reward for what they used to do' (56:24). This comment is not made on the rewards of class II in either *sūra*. This 'extra' reward is confirmed by such Qur'anic statements as (10:26) *li'ladhīna aḥsanu'lḥusna wa ziyāda* 'For those who do right is a goodly reward, and more!' Such a comment does not always, or often, come as a rhetorical question (c.f. 76:22; 77:44; 78:36 and *passim*). The above theory of the juxtaposition of different versions appears to imply that at some stage, before the second pair of gardens, there was inserted the mention of reward in v.60 at the end of the *sūra*. However, evidence from other places in the Qur'an, such as those cited here, show that this could not have been the case. Wansbrough's suggestion that the question of v.60 'would belong to the exegetical tradition ...' (p.29) lacks any support from Qur'anic usage. His suggestion of the possibility of a cultic context or liturgical origin is like his insistence upon the term 'litany' rather than 'refrain' which we said was quite alien to the Qur'an and the way Muslims read it in their prayers. The result of Wansbrough's earlier suggestions would be to reduce the four gardens to two and to reduce the two to one. Qur'anic references cited earlier leave such a conclusion without support.

Commenting on Wellhausen's suggestion that the description of two sets of gardens was a case of duplication due to varying recollections, Bell says: 'The frequent use of the plural "gardens" in the Qur'an, and the plural pronoun, here in vv.56 and 70, suggest that Muhammad did think of a number of Gardens, perhaps through confusion with the four rivers of the Garden of Eden mentioned in Genesis.' His 'perhaps through confusion ...' etc. is so extraordinary that it does not warrant any consideration.

A single verse (v.78) concludes the *sūra*: 'Blessed is the name of your Lord, the Lord of Glory and Bestower of Honour.' It is addressed in the second person singular to the Prophet/reader/listener; accordingly it is not followed by the refrain addressed in the dual to both men and *jinn*. As already stated, the first time the refrain was introduced was when men and *jinn* – to whom it was addressed – were referred to in the word *al-'anām* v.10. The only factors that decided that the occurrences of the refrain would number thirty-one were the pairing scheme and the sequence of the specific themes developed within the context of the *sūra*. The sequence having been completed within the pairing scheme, the refrain need not occur any more (or less) times. The final verse is a comment glorifying God's name *al-Raḥmān* above their denial of His bounties. Such a comment is observed in the Qur'an in other similar situations such as 36:83; 37:180–82; 56:96. Even in this final comment we find a pair of adjectives maintaining the scheme to the last: Lord of Majesty and Honouring, (Honouring with bounties in this world and the next, Majesty shown in His creation and in disciplining those that deny His encompassing bounties). Verse 1, verse 27 and this final verse 78 fuse the whole *sūra* into one solid unity.

Al-Raḥmān and Psalm 136

As mentioned in the introduction to this chapter, it has been conjectured[39] that *Sūra* 55 is an imitation of Psalm 136. Such conjecture seems to be based on three things:

1. The *sūra* is entitled *The Merciful* and the psalm repeats 'for His Mercy endureth for ever';
2. The 'bounties' in the *sūra* seems to parallel the 'great wonders' in the psalm;
3. There is a refrain in both.

Without wishing to make a comparison between the two scriptures or faiths, I will examine some points of similarity and difference between the two texts, which could be taken as a comment on the conjecture of imitation.

In the Qur'an, the name 'The Merciful' occurs only once, in v.1 in the *sūra* while 'His Mercy' is repeated throughout the psalm, twenty-six times in all. In any case the Merciful occurs in the *basmala* of every *sūra* in the Qur'an (except *Sūra* 9) as well as in other places.

The bounties in *Sūra* 55 are also listed in other places in the Qur'an, e.g. 14:32–34; 16:10–18; 27:60–64; 30:20–27. Eschatological bounties – of which there are none in the psalm – are abundant in the Qur'an. The refrain device, too, is used in other *sūras* of the Qur'an (e.g. 26, 37, 54, 77). In the psalm, the refrain occurs at the end of every verse, while in the *sūra* it starts after verse 12 and, as has been explained, does not occur at the end of every verse nor at the end. In the psalm it takes the form of an assertion, while in the *sūra* it is a question. The addressees in the psalm are the Israelites – a limited group of men – while in the *sūra* it is all men and *jinn.*

Compare also 'raising the heaven up' (so that it does not fall down on them) and stabilising the earth (under them) (*Sūra,* vv.7–10) with 'made the heavens' and 'stretched out the earth' (Psalm, vv.5–6). As we have seen, the bounties in the *sūra* are encompassing throughout. They are not only for Arabs or Muslims, or even for mankind alone, but universal. The eschatological bounties are for the believers among all men and *jinn.*

In the psalm that is not the case. The universal bounties are confined to the creation of heaven-earth, sun-moon etc. (vv.4–9), and then v.25 'giveth food to all flesh' – separated as it is from the earlier universal group. For the most part, the psalm expresses the concerns of the specific group of people it addresses. Accordingly the list includes:

(v.10) 'To him that smote Egypt in their first-born; for His mercy endureth for ever.'
(v.11) 'And brought out Israel from among them: for His Mercy endureth for ever ...'
(v.16) 'To Him which led His people through the wilderness: for His mercy endureth for ever ...'
(v.17) 'To Him which smote great kings: for His mercy endureth for ever.'
(v.19) 'Shi'hon, King of Amorites: for his mercy endureth for ever:'
(v.20) '... and Og the King of Ba'shan: for His mercy endureth for ever ...' etc.

Compare these punishments with those in the *sūra,* where the basis on which punishment is inflicted is – as always in the Qur'an – identified: it is the fate of those who deny the bounties of God (*yukadhdhib biha'l mujrimūn* – which the guilty deny).

As we have seen in our discussion of the *sūra*, the material relates firmly to the specific context there and to other parts of the Qur'an. In the *sūra*, the bounties start with the spiritual and educational, which is not the case in the psalm. The psalm consists of twenty-six verses, the first and last of which are didactically imperative: 'give thanks', whereas the *sūra* consists of seventy-eight verses, the first and last of which are celebratory: '*al-Raḥmān*' and 'Blessed is the name of your Lord, Lord of Majesty and Bestower.'

13
Dynamic Style

In a study which has been described as 'pioneering', *Neue Beiträge zur Semitischen Sprachwissenschaft*,[1] Theodor Nöldeke 'discussed in detail the "Stylistische und Syntaktische Eigentümlichkeiten der Sprache des Korans" (pp. 5–23) thereby collecting together everything that had occurred to him in this respect during his protracted and intensive study of the Holy Book of the Muslims.'[2] Among the examples Nöldeke discusses (pp. 13–14) are Q.7 (not 77 which is clearly a misprint in his text): 55,[3] 27:61; 35:27, 6:99, 20:55, 10:23, etc. where there is a sudden shift in the pronoun of the speaker or the person spoken about, known as *iltifāt* in *balāgha* (Arabic rhetoric), though Nöldeke does not refer to the term here. Introducing his discussion, Nöldeke remarks that 'the grammatical persons change from time to time in the Qur'an in an unusual and not beautiful way (*nicht schöner Weise*)' (p.13). This is a personal value judgement. Arab writers, in contrast see the matter differently. Ibn al-Athir, for instance, after studying this stylistic feature as we shall see below, classed it among the 'remarkable things and exquisite subtleties we have found in the Glorious Qur'an.'[4] It will be seen that the examples Nöldeke cites immediately following the statement quoted above do not occur haphazardly in the Qur'an but follow a pattern. Examination of where exactly the shift occurs and why, will show how effective the technique is in these examples and why Muslim literary critics and exegetes greatly admire *iltifāt* and its related features. Nöldeke further remarks (p.14) that in a few places the second and third person plural are exchanged abruptly: 30:38, 49:7, 10:23. Here again it will be seen that the changes are made according to an effective pattern and that the frequency of occurrence is much greater than is indicated by Nöldeke.

The impression that the incidence of *iltifāt* in the Qur'an is low can also be gained from books on *balāgha* in Arabic.[5] These tend to confine themselves to specific examples, including, for instance Q.1:4, 36:22, 10:22, 35:9, 108:2, repeated with little variation[6], to represent the various types of *iltifāt* between first, second and third persons. That these only represented a small sample is made clear by reference to the books[7] of Ibn al-Athir (637/1239)[8] who discusses some twenty examples, Suyuti (911/1505), who deals with about thirty-five examples[9] of *iltifāt* and related features, and Badr al-Din al-Zarkashi (794/1391) who provides the most extensive treatment of this phenomenon and includes about fifty examples.[10] Still, it will be seen from our treatment below that the feature occurs much more extensively in the Qur'an than even these figures suggest. Accordingly, the way it is treated in these works does not give an accurate picture. We are told there are six types of change in person, but for one of these (first to second person) they all give just one example – Q. 36:22 and indeed, as we shall see, even that is doubtful. The change from second to first person does not occur in the Qur'an. However it will be seen that other types are used far more frequently, for instance the change from third to first person is represented by well over 100 examples. Identifying the precise extent of each type will help us to understand the nature and function of the feature under discussion.

It has, moreover, been argued that almost all examples of *iltifāt* in the Qur'an are to be found in the Meccan *sūras.*[11] This conclusion was perhaps based on surveying examples used in *balāgha* books. It will be seen that a survey of the Qur'anic text itself gives a different picture.

Iltifāt has been called by rhetoricians *shajā'at al-'arabiyya*[12] as it shows, in their opinion, the daring nature of the Arabic language. If any 'daring' is to be attached to it, it should above all be the daring and dynamic quality of the language of the Qur'an since, for reasons that will be shown below, it employed this feature far more extensively and in more variations than did Arabic poetry. It is, therefore, natural to find that *al-Mathal al-sā'ir* of Ibn al-Athir which deals with *adab al-kātib wa'l-shā'ir,* (literary prose and poetry) uses mainly Qur'anic references in discussing *iltifāt.* No one seems to quote references in prose other than from the Qur'an: and indeed a sampling of *ḥadīth* material found not a single instance.[13] It is hoped that our discussion will explain why this should be so.

Nöldeke treated the verses referred to above as peculiarities in the language of the Qur'an. As will be seen below, it would not be correct to assume that this stylistic feature is exclusive to the Qur'an in Arabic, though it is an important feature of the style of the Qur'an. As has been noted, in his discussion Nöldeke did not mention the term *iltifāt.* Nor did Wansbrough who dedicated a section to 'Rhetoric and Allegory'[14] under the 'Principles of exegesis', list *iltifāt* in his 'Index of technical terms'.[15] Likewise, Bell and Watt dedicated a section to 'Features of Qur'anic Style';[16] the author of the article on 'Kor'an' in the *Encyclopaedia of Islam* has a section on 'language and style'[17] and the author of the article on the 'Qur'an – I' in *The Cambridge History of Arabic Literature* includes a section on 'language and style'[18], but none of these writers mentions the word *iltifāt.* This is surprising and makes it necessary to deal with this important feature of Arabic literary and Qur'anic style.

In this chapter I shall discuss the meaning of *iltifāt*, and the types of *iltifāt* in general (giving the extent of each). Along with *iltifāt* I shall discuss analogous features of this nature, involving grammatical shift for rhetorical purposes, though some of these were not generally labelled as *iltifāt* they were nonetheless considered as related to it. In our discussion of specific examples I shall point out where these shifts occur and attempt to explain their effects. Finally I shall deal with the function of *iltifāt* and its related features in general. It is hoped that all this will help to clarify the nature of this stylistic feature and explain its use in the Qur'an.

The Meaning of *Iltifāt*

Lexically, *iltifāt* means 'to turn/turn one's face to'. There is the famous line: 'My eye turned (*talaffatat*) to the remains of (my beloved's) encampment; when they passed out of sight, my heart turned to them.'
After earlier attempts,[19] we find fuller definitions of *iltifāt* in Ibn al-Athir (637/1239) and Zarkashi (794/1391). The former considered *iltifāt* part of the essence of *'ilm al-bayān* and the basis of *balāgha.* 'Its meaning (of turning) is taken from the turning of a person from his right to left as he turns his face once this way and once the other; such is this type of speech since one turns in it from one form to another. One would for instance turn from addressing a person to talking (about him) in the third person; or from third to second person; or turn from perfect to imperfect verb or vice versa; or turn in such other ways as will be detailed below.' *'Iltifāt,'* he continues, 'is also called *shajā'at al-'arabiyya*' (the daring of the Arabic language). 'A daring person,' he explains, 'undertakes what others do not dare, and such is *iltifāt* in speech, which', he thinks, 'is peculiar to Arabic.'[20]
Al-Zarkashi for his part defined *iltifāt* as:

... the change of speech from one mode to another, for the sake of freshness and variety for the listener, to renew his interest, and to keep his mind from boredom and frustration, through having the one mode continuously at his ear.

He goes on in the following paragraph to say:

Each of the first, second and third persons, has its appropriate context in which it is used. The general opinion is that *iltifāt* is 'transition' from one of them to another after using the first. Sakkaki said it is either this or it is using one in a place where another ought to have been used.[21]

After dealing with all types of transition in persons Zarkashi concludes with a section on transition to other than persons under the heading, *yaqrub min al-iltifāt naql al-kalām ilā ghayrih,* making these related to *iltifāt.* Of the two it is Ibn al-Athir's definition that is the more precise and his explanation more lucid. Other accounts include those of Sharaf al-Din al-Tibi (743/1342)[22] and al-Khatib al-Qazwini (793/1395), both concise, and the rather more extensive but unoriginal one by Suyuti (911/1505). The treatment by Ibn al-Athir as a writer on the rhetoric of prose and poetry, and by Zarkashi as a writer on *'ulūm al-Qur'ān,* have thus remained the best examples on the subject.

Conditions of *Iltifāt*

In discussing *iltifāt* as it has become well established in *balāgha,* all authors begin with types involving transition in persons and, indeed, some of them stop there. It is with this kind only that authors mentioned conditions of *iltifāt.* The first condition is that the pronoun in the person/thing one turns to should refer to the same person/thing from which one turned. Thus there is no *iltifāt* in: 'you are my friend' but there is *iltifāt* in Q. 108:2 – 'We have given you abundance, therefore pray to your Lord' – since the reference here is to one and the same, i.e. God. Another suggested condition stipulates that the transition should be between two independent sentences. This perhaps resulted from the observation of a limited number of examples, and was thus rightly refuted by reference to many other examples that do not involve two independent sentences, for example Q.25:17.[23]

Types of *Iltifāt* and Related Features

These can be of the following types:

1. Change in person, between first, second and third person which is the most common and is usually sub-divided into six kinds.
2. Change in number, between singular, dual and plural.
3. Change in addressee.
4. Change in the tense of the verb.
5. Change in case marker.
6. Using a noun in place of pronoun.

No. 1 is the most commonly known and was called *iltifāt* before other types were labelled as such or as related to *iltifāt.*

Nos 1–4 were dealt with by Zarkashi and Suyuti, for instance, each in a chapter entitled *al-iltifāt,* though some of the types were considered only as related to *iltifāt.* No. 5 was considered as *iltifāt* by some, according to Zarkashi. No. 6 was dealt with along with *iltifāt* by Qazwini, Subki and Hashimi for instance, under a general heading combining them both: *khurūj al-kalām 'alā muqtaḍa'l-ẓāhir* (departure from what is normally expected). In fact in all these types we have a departure from the normal expected usage of language in a particular context for a particular rhetorical purpose.

Change in person is sub-divided as follows:

(i) Transition from third to first person. This is the most common type I have come across over 140 instances in the Qur'an.
(ii) From first to third person is second with nearly 100 instances.
(iii) From third to second person – nearly 60 instances.
(iv) From second to third person – under 30 instances.
(v) From first to second person – of which there is only one example which is quoted by every author above, but which one could argue is not *iltifāt.*
(vi) From second to third person, of which there is no example in the Qur'an as Suyuti himself pointed out (*Itqān* III, 254).

Types (v) and (vi) need only a brief mention here so that we may return to deal with the other more important cases. For (vi) Imru' al-Qays's lines about his long sleepless night were quoted by Zamakhshari. The poet here talks *to* himself in the second person, saying that 'your night at al-Ithmid has been long, others without cares did sleep, but you did not'. Then he speaks *about* himself, 'He spent that night like someone with diseased eyes.' Finally, he returns to speak in the first person, saying 'That is because the news came to me, what I have been told about Abul Aswad'.[24] It is noteworthy that these lines are always quoted to illustrate this type of *iltifāt.*

For (v) it is Q. 36:22 that is always quoted: 'Why should *I* not worship Him who created me? and to Him *you* shall return'. It was suggested that 'you' is in place of 'I shall return'. This, however, does not have to be so, as indeed Suyuti said (p. 253). The speaker could simply be warning his addressees that they shall return to God, in which case the condition of *iltifāt* does not obtain here. Suyuti also quotes Q.6:73 but this will be discussed under changes in tense.

It will be observed for examples of other kinds of *iltifāt* that a great many of them involve God talking in the first person or about Himself in the third person; but He does not talk *to* himself in the second person. Examples from poetry suggest that a poet talks to himself when he reproaches, pities or encourages himself, which clearly does not befit God as seen in the Qur'an, where 'He has power over all things' (2:20); 'has knowledge of everything' (4:176); he is 'Performer of what He desires' (85:16) and is 'the Creator of all things' (39:62). This may explain the lack of examples in the Qur'an of types (v) and (vi).

I shall now list occurrences of the four remaining sub-types of *iltifāt* in person. These lists, are not meant to be final but to give what is hoped will be a fair picture of the use of *iltifāt* in the Qur'an. It should be pointed out that the word containing the pronoun from which the transition took place does not necessarily immediately precede that to which the transition occurs, but in any case nobody makes proximity a condition of *iltifāt*.

1. Third – first person:
   2:23, 47, 73, 83, 118, 160, 172; 4:30, 33, 37, 41, 64, 74, 114, 174; 5:14, 15. 6:97, 98, 107, 126; 7:37, 57; 8:41; 10:11, 21, 22, 23; 13:4, 14:13, 16:66, 75; 17:1, 33, 97; 19:9, 21, 58; 20:53; 21:29; 22:67; 24:55; 25:32, 45, 48; 27:60; 28:75; 29:4; 23; 30:34; 31:10, 32:16; 33:9, 31; 35:9, 27; 39:2, 3, 16; 41:12, 28, 39; 42:13, 23, 38, 45:31; 48:25; 49:13; 52:48; 54:11; 55:31; 58:5; 61:14; 65:8; 66:10; 67:17; 68:15, 35; 69:11 72:16; 80:25; 87:6; 88:25.
2. First – third person:
   2:5, 23, 37, 161, 172; 3:57, 151; 4:30, 33, 69, 122; 6:90, 95, 111, 112, 127; 7:12, 58, 101, 142; 8:4; 10:22, 25; 14:46; 15:28, 96; 16:52; 17:1; 20:4; 21:19; 22:6; 23:14, 57, 78, 91, 116; 24:35, 46; 25:31, 47, 58; 26:5, 9, 213; 27:6; 28:13, 59, 62; 29:3, 40, 67, 69; 30:54, 59; 31:11, 23; 32:25; 33:9, 46, 50; 34:21; 35:31, 32, 38; 36:36, 74; 37:33; 38:26; 40:61, 85; 41:19, 28, 40, 45, 53; 44:6; 45:22, 30; 48:2; 51:58; 53:30; 54:55; 57:27; 60:3; 65:10; 66:12; 67:19; 68:48; 76:6, 24, 29; 87:6; 94:8; 95:8; 97:4; 108:2

3. Third – second person:
1:5; 2:21, 25, 28, 60, 83, 214, 229, 233; 3:180; 4:11; 6:6; 8:7, 14 9:19, 69; 10:3,68; 11:14; 16:55, 68, 74; 19:89; 21:37; 23:15, 65; 27:90; 30:34; 31:33; 33:55; 34:37; 35:3; 36:59; 37:25; 38:59; 43:16; 47:22, 30; 50:24; 52:14, 19, 39; 55:13; 56:51, 91; 57:17, 20; 67:13; 75:34; 76:22, 30; 77:38, 43; 78:30, 36; 80:3; 87:16
4. Second – third person:
2:54, 57, 85, 88, 187, 200, 216, 226, 229, 286; 4:9; 10:22; 16:69, 72; 24:63; 28:16; 30:38; 31:32; 32:10; 45:35; 47:23; 67:18; 75:31.

1. Change in Person

Third–first person

In the first kind (third–first person) we notice that in the great majority of verses, God is involved in the speech. The transition in this type introduces two powerful elements that accord with the dramatic nature of the language of the Qur'an, that is: the first person itself (which is more powerful than the third as it brings God Himself to speak), and secondly, the element of plurality which expresses more power than does the singular.

We may begin by considering the first example Nöldeke introduced after his remark that 'the grammatical persons change from time to time in the Qur'an in an unusual and not beautiful way', Q.27:61: '*Who* created the heavens and the earth and sent down for you water from the sky wherewith *We* caused to grow joyous garden?' The point of emphasis here is the great power which caused joyous gardens to grow, a contrast between the abstraction of creative power and the personal involvement of aesthetic creativity. This is not a matter of my personal taste or opinion; it is clear from the rest of the verse which goes on to emphasise the point and describe the garden: 'whose trees you could never cause to grow'. Here God reserves for Himself the power to cause them to grow and hence the shift at this point from third person singular to first person plural. As it comes suddenly the shift makes the listener feel afresh the true meaning of the concepts of both first person and of plurality, so that the grammatical forms are here given much more weight than they normally carry.[25] A longer statement in place of this concise powerful one would have been required if 'normal' grammatical rules had been used without the change in person commented on by Nöldeke. The effect in this example is, moreover, achieved with no loss of clarity since it is obvious that the verse speaks about God before and after the transition. Interestingly, such a technique is also often used with other verses dealing with water, with the shift always occurring at a semantically important point as in Q:6:99, 7:57, 13:4, 15:66, 20:53, 25:48, 31:10, 35:9, 41:39. In 13:4, for instance, the shift does not occur at making the plants grow but at making their produce different in taste, which is the point in context:

It is He that … In the land there are adjoining plots: vineyards and cornfields and groves of palms, the single and the clustered. Their fruits are nourished by the same water: yet We make the taste of some more favoured than the taste of others. Surely in this there are signs for men of understanding.

13:4

In the first set of examples cited above as discussed by Nöldeke (7:55; 35:27; 6:99; 20:55; 10:23) all but the last deal with water (Nöldeke does not seem to have noticed this), and exhibit the same feature for the same effect. 10:23 also involves water, but in a different context that will be explained later.

The shift to first person of majestic plural is also suitable for expressing might, e.g. 14:13: 'Then *their Lord* revealed to them: *We* will surely destroy the evildoers.' The effect of the particle of oath '*la*' and that of emphasis, *nūn al-tawkīd*, is made much more powerful by the presence of God to announce (in direct speech) the punishment Himself in the plural; see also 32:16, 33:9. Abundant giving is also expressed in first person plural as if to emphasise multiplicity of giving. For example:

There is no good in much of their conferences except in his who enjoins charity, kindness, and peace-making among the people. He that does this to please God, We shall bestow on him a vast reward.

4:114

See also 2:172; 32:16, 42:38. Similarly reassuring the Prophet, who was anxious that he might forget the Qur'an, was suitably expressed by a shift to the first person divine plural: '… *your Lord* who … *We* shall make you recite so that you shall not forget.' Also 75:16–19.

It should be pointed out that in pre-Islamic literature, and during the time of the revelation of the Qur'an, pronouns do not appear to have been used as indicative of status; they did not change with social status, and the plural of majesty in particular does not appear to have been used by, or for addressing or referring to, kings or chiefs. The Prophet and early successors did not use it for themselves or in their letters to kings or governors.[26] It was clearly in the Qur'an that such usage was introduced, as has been shown, on the basis of a highly sophisticated application of the concept of plurality.

First – third person

This category is second in number but it is still large compared to those remaining. It is noteworthy that, with the exception of a small number of cases, the person involved in *iltifāt* in categories 1 and 2 is God, while in 3 and 4 this is less commonly the case. Again with the exception of a few cases, we find that when God speaks in categories 1 and 2, He speaks in the first person plural; in the other part of the transition, He is in the third person singular, referred to either as 'God', 'He', 'He it is who' or '*rabb*' in the form of 'Your/their/his Lord, Lord of'. Two related questions should be discussed here:

1. Who speaks in the Qur'an?
2. How is it that God, who is believed in Islam to be the author of the Qur'an, speaks about Himself in the third person?

While admitting that it is allowable for a speaker to refer to himself in the third person occasionally, Bell and Watt find that the extent to which the Prophet is being told about God as a third person is unusual.[27] Although 'it will be found that much of the Qur'an is thus placed in the mouth of God speaking in the plural of majesty' (p. 65) they consider that:

> difficulties in many passages are removed by interpreting the 'We' of angels rather than of God Himself speaking in the plural of majesty. It is not easy to distinguish between the two and nice questions sometimes arise in places where there is a sudden change from God being spoken of in the third person to 'We' claiming to do things usually ascribed to God, e.g. 6:99b, 25, 45:7. (p. 67)

It is difficult to agree that the 'We', in the two examples Bell and Watt give, refers to the angels since the acts referred to (bringing forth the plants and bringing water down from the sky) are definitely ascribed to God in other parts of the Qur'an (cf. 50:67; 16:65). Examination of the examples of *iltifāt* shows that it is difficult from the grammatical point of view to conclude – as Bell and Watt seem to do – that a part of the statement is spoken by one person (God) and the rest by another (the angels). Bell and Watt conclude: 'In the later portions of the Qur'an, it seems to be an almost invariable rule that the words are addressed by the angels or by Gabriel using the plural "We" to the Prophet.'

No examples are given to substantiate this statement. Does it include a passage like 'O Messenger, We have sent you' (33:46)? But we have to understand this in conjunction with Q.61:9, 'It is He Who sent His Messenger' – both verses are taken from 'the later portions of the Qur'an'. Such a procedure should be applied to any passage that may be cited as spoken by the angels.

Commenting on Horovitz's observation that all of the Qur'an must be regarded as the utterance of God,[28] Wansbrough states:

> Less dogmatic than Horovitz, Suyuti adduced five passages in Muslim scripture whose attribution to God was at least disputed: Q. 6:104,114 were the words of the Arabian Prophet; 19:64 (but curiously, not 19:9, 21 and 51:30) were the words of Gabriel; 37:164–66 were ascribed to the angels; finally verse 4 of the *Fātiḥa* may have been uttered by the faithful (*'ibād*) or could by insertion (*taqdīr*) of the imperative *qūlū* be attributed to God.[29]

Suyuti, however, did not consider 6:104, 114 as 'the words of the Arabian Prophet'. He discussed the five passages at the end of a chapter entitled *Fīmā unzil min al-Qur'ān 'alā lisān ba'ḍ al-ṣaḥāba* ('On Qur'anic passages that have been sent down [revealed], put in the mouth of some of the companions'). The examples include, for instance, passages introducing institutions such as the *ḥijāb* for the Prophet's wives, which 'Umar had wished the Prophet would adopt. Suyuti introduced the five passages referred to above by saying: *yaqrub min hādha mā warad fi'l-Qur'ān 'alā lisān ghayr-illāhi*, which again means they were revealed placed on the tongue of other than God. Suyuti introduces 6:114 thus: '*kaqawlihi*', (i.e. 'as His [God's] saying'), then comments: '*fa-innahu awradahā ayḍan 'alā lisānihi*' (i.e. 'He presented this verse also placed on his [the Prophet's] tongue'). The *Fātiḥa* is an important example of *iltifāt* (third–second), being the first in the Qur'an and much quoted.

Before we discuss this verse we must deal with the question of why God is referred to, and so frequently, in the Qur'an, in the third person. The first and most important reason for God's speaking about Himself in the third person relates to the fundamental message of the Qur'an – which is calling men to the religion of *tawḥīd* according to which 'there is no god but Allah (God)'. The Islamic testimony begins with the negation of any other god, then moves on to except only one, who is named Allah. No pronoun, even of the first person, will do here in place of the name. ('Call not upon another god with Allah, lest you incur punishment' 26:213). This is clear in verses that show the contrast between Allah – in this particular name – and any other assumed deity. In successive verses, for instance (27:60–4) we have a structure such as:

... Who created the heavens and the earth and brought down for you water from the sky ... another god besides Allah? Yet they make others equal [to Him].

27:60–4

The sequence ends with 'Say: "No one in the heavens or on earth has knowledge of the unseen except Allah'." The Qur'anic message is meant to be communicated to men naming Allah as the Lord they should serve. Knowledge of the unseen, creation and judgement are the prerogative of Allah in the religion of *tawḥīd* and as such frequently accompany His name which is considered in Arabic grammar as *a'raf al-ma'ārif* (the most definite of all definite pronouns). Similarly, in the Qur'an *ḥamd* truly belongs to Allah and it occurs in the text forty odd times together with the name Allah or, if it is with His pronoun, coming very soon after the name and in a few cases it combines with *rabb* (cf. also *hudā*). The Qur'an describes Allah, in His particular name, to believers and non-believers: He does such and such, e.g. 16:65–81; it is He Who e.g. 16:10–20. Adjectival structures, ordinary or relative, require a noun before them – in this case, Allah. Such combinations occur frequently in the Qur'an. (e.g. 1:1–4, 59:22–4). The name of Allah is also used in verses (frequently at the end, commonly introduced by *kan*) indicating that such is His way, e.g:

That was Allah's way with those who passed away of old – and the commandment of Allah is certain destiny.

33:38

Give ... before death comes to one of you and he says 'Reprieve me, Lord a while'... But Allah reprieves no soul when its term comes; Allah has knowledge of all your actions.

63:10–1

The Qur'an, it should be remembered, is not an autobiography of Allah, which would cast it in the form of 'I' and 'me'; it is revealed for men who will speak in their prayers and to each other about Allah. It urges the believers: 'Call, then, unto Allah, making your religion His sincerely, though the unbelievers be averse.' (40:14). It teaches them how to call upon Him in this way: *al-ḥamdu li'llāhi rabbi'l-'ālamīn* (40:65).

It is not surprising, then, that this comes at the beginning of the *Fātiḥa* to be repeated in the obligatory prayers at least seventeen times a day.

It should also be noted that in some verses God is mentioned more than once, and is depicted from different perspectives so that we have multiplicity of viewpoints:

We suffice you against the mockers who serve another god with Allah. Certainly they will soon know. We know you are distressed by what they say. Proclaim your Lord's praise and prostrate yourself and worship your Lord until the certain end comes to you.

15:95–99

Here Allah Himself speaks in the first person plural of majesty to assure the Prophet. From the point of view of the mockers, they serve another god beside Allah; and from the point of view of the Prophet, he should serve his caring, reassuring Lord. 'All that is in the heavens and the earth magnifies Allah' (57:1, 59:1, 61:1, 62:1, 64:1). From God's point of view, He proclaims to all that this is the prerogative of Allah, shared by no other deity, and believers read this from their point of view, which is that of glorifying Allah. It is important, then, when discussing reference to God in the third person in the Qur'an to bear in mind two things: the principle of *tawḥīd* and the multiplicity of viewpoints observed in the language of the Muslim scripture.

In the following examples of the second category of *iltifāt* we see that there is a shift from the first person to the third, in which God is referred to as Allah or *rabb*, emphasising *tawḥīd*, and showing the multiplicity of viewpoints: 'Eat of the good things wherewith *We* have provided you, and render thanks to *Allah* if it is *He* whom you worship' (2:172). '*We* shall cast terror into the hearts of those who disbelieve, because they ascribe partners to *Allah*' (3:151). 'David, *We* have appointed you a viceroy in the land; therefore judge between men justly and follow not caprice lest it leads you astray from the way of *Allah*' (38:26). '*We* have given you a manifest victory, that *Allah* may forgive you, ... that *Allah* may help you.' (48:1–3) (in this connection we should remember that the Prophet used to repeat *astaghfir Allah* – I seek the forgiveness of Allah) (cf. also Q.4:106, 8:10). Finally: '*We* have given you abundance; Pray then to *your Lord* and sacrifice to Him – it is he that hates you who is cut off' (108).

Third – second person

The shift in most examples of this kind appears to be for the purpose of honouring, reproach, threat and sometimes request. The first example of *iltifāt* in the Qur'an, much quoted in *balāgha* books, is of this kind: verse 4 of the *Fātiḥa*, coming after praise in the third person:

Praise belongs to Allah, the Lord of all Being, the Most Beneficent, the Most Merciful, the Master of the Day of Judgement. You only we serve, You alone we ask for help

Zamakhshari explains (and he is repeatedly quoted) that when the servant talks about Allah Who is worthy of praise and of the great qualities mentioned, his mind thinks of this great God who is worthy of praise, of full submission to Him and whose help should be sought in important matters. The servant then addresses this distinguished Lord '*You* alone do we worship'; after the introduction which demonstrates that He is truly worthy of being worshipped, direct address is more indicative of the fact that He is being worshipped for that distinction.[30]

One may add that the shift to second person is also important here as the servant is going to ask Him: 'Guide us....' The third person was suitable at the beginning to name the Lord Who should be praised and served at the beginning of the book of *tawḥīd* (the oneness of God). No pronoun of any kind would have served here, and praise, as we said, truly belongs in Islam to that particular name – Allah.

Honouring by addressing is observed in such examples as those speaking of the blessed in Paradise: 'Happy in what their Lord has given them ... "Eat and drink in health as a reward for what you used to do."' (52:18–19). The address here is announced without such an introduction as 'it will be said to them' – a feature of Qur'anic style known as *ḥadhf al-qawl* which gives a statement immediate and dramatic effect.[31] Examples of this are, particularly in the kind of *iltifāt* under discussion, used for various effects. Thus in 'Their Lord shall give them to drink a pure draught: this is a reward for you and your striving is thanked,' (76:22) the address is honorific while in 'They say: "The All-Merciful has taken unto Himself a son"; you have indeed advanced something hideous! ...' (19:88ff) the address is a rebuke followed by a threat, as also in 16:55, 36:59. In Q.2:28, 10:3, 37:25 it is rebuke and scorn. The effect of *iltifāt* in such examples is that it makes God appear Himself in the middle of a situation to address a particular group at a crucial point.

The shift to second person can be for request as in:

And your Lord inspired the bees: 'Make your homes in the mountains, trees, and what men thatch. Feed on every kind of fruit and follow the ways of your Lord, easy to go upon.' From their bellies comes forth a syrup of different hues wherein is healing for men. Surely in this is a sign for those who would give thought.

16:68–69

The switch back to third person in 'from their bellies comes forth …' emphasises to men the wondrous act. In Q.80, 1–3, we have an example of how the Qur'an revitalises grammatical forms by drawing attention to them afresh. The passage is clearly addressed to the Prophet for reproach but it begins:

He frowned and turned away that the blind man came to him. How could you tell? He might have sought to purify himself … but to the one who reckons he is self-sufficient you pay attention?

By merely using the third person at the beginning, God is already expressing displeasure at what the Prophet did and upbraiding him in front of all listeners; turning to second person after that is in itself a reprimand; the shift is sudden and powerful. The grammatical concept of second person is here given an added effect which is maintained in a number of the following verses.

Second–third person

This is less frequent than the previous three kinds. We have had in 16:69 an example of how the use of the third person expresses wonder and in 80:1 displeasure, making listeners a witness to this. 16:72 shows a similar effect:

Allah has given you spouses from among yourselves and through them has given you sons and grandsons. He has provided you with good things: will they then believe in falsehood and deny Allah's favours?

In 47:23 we have:

If you turned away, would you then haply work corruption in the land and break your bonds of kin? Those are they whom Allah has cursed …

The indicative pronoun *ulā'ika* (those) expresses *ib'ād li'l-taḥqīr* (distancing for humiliation). But distancing can also be for honouring, as is recognised in virtually all *balāgha* books[32] as a feature of Arabic rhetoric. Thus in 30:38, cited earlier by Nöldeke, we have an example of honouring:

That which you give in usury, that it may increase upon the people's wealth, increases not with Allah; but what you give in alms desiring Allah's face, those [who do it for the face of God] – they receive recompense manifold!

Nöldeke also cited 10:22. This reads:

It is Allah that conveys you by land and sea, and when you are in the ships – and the ships run with them rejoicing in a favouring wind, a raging tempest overtakes them. Billows surge upon them from every side and they fear they are encompassed by death. They pray to Allah with all fervour, saying: 'Deliver us from this peril and we will be truly thankful.' Yet when He does deliver them, they rebel in the earth wrongfully. O Men, your insolence is only against yourselves.

Here, the shift to third person adds another dimension, making the sea travellers seem truly helpless, far away, cut off from anyone to aid them except the Lord they feel they have to turn to. This would have been lost if the verse continued in the initial second person. Moreover, had the verse continued to address them in the second person, then listeners to the Qur'an who sit in the security of their homes, some never going to sea, would have been less convinced and less affected. He shifted to addressing them again only when the sea travellers landed and began, in safety, to rebel wrongfully. Moreover, as Arab writers of *tafsīr* (Qur'anic exegesis) and *balāgha* observed, when He spoke about them in the third person, He made others witness how they behaved in their helplessness and they can compare this to their subsequent behaviour in safety.

In *tafsīr* and *balāgha* books writers are moved to high praise of *iltifāt* in this verse, which Nöldeke, clearly viewing it from a purely formal standpoint, was unable to appreciate. Nor is this verse unusual in the Qur'an: the same idea of riders on the sea is expressed in 31:31–2 with *iltifāt* to third person producing the same effect, and the theme of helplessness at sea is particularly emphasised in such verses as 17:69, 36:43, 42:32–4.

2. Change in Number

The shift here is between singular, dual and plural. I list over fifty examples: 2:34, 38,40,106, 123, 217; 7:24, 127; 14:31, 37; 15:49; 16:65; 17:36; 20:37, 40, 41, 81, 124; 22:45; 23:51, 66; 27:84; 29:8, 57; 31:15; 32:13; 34:12, 45; 35:40; 43:32, 69; 46:5; 50:30; 54:17, 22, 32, 40; 55:31; 65:11; 68:44; 69:44; 70:40; 73:12; 74:16, 31; 75:3; 77:39; 90:4; 98:8; 100:11.

In many of these examples it is God that is involved in *iltifāt*; the shift to the plural of majesty expresses power with remarkable effect, e.g.:

No! I swear by the reproachful soul! What does man reckon? We shall not gather his bones? Yes indeed; We are able to shape again his fingers.

75:1–4

It is the singular that is fitting for 'I swear'; the sudden shift to the plural expresses, as it were, multiplicity of power in answer to the pre-Islamic Arabs' incredulity at the idea of putting scattered bones together again at the resurrection. The sudden shift recharges the concept of plural as a grammatical form with its full sense of majesty (see also 55:31, 73:22, 2:39, 13:30, 43:32). The Qur'an uses the singular pronoun for God particularly in such contexts as those expressing worship (*yā 'ibādī* – O, my Servants), prohibition of *shirk* – serving others beside God, and wrath; the use of the singular is clearly important in such contexts and when there is a sudden shift to the plural of majesty it sharpens the listener's sense of the contrast between the two grammatical forms investing 'we' when it comes after 'I' with enhanced meaning. The Qur'an thus revitalises grammatical forms (2:23, 14:31, 20:53, 29:8, 31:10).

This type was regarded as *yaqrub min al-iltifāt* (related to *iltifāt*) by such writers as Zarkashi[33] and Suyuti.[34]

3. Change of Addressee

Various addressees within the same or adjacent verses are sometimes spoken to in the Qur'an. *Iltifāt* in such verses has the original lexical meaning of actually turning from one direction/person to another. In these examples we normally find the first addressee addressed again with others when there is a request that applies to them all. Thus in 2:144 the Prophet, in answer to his personal prayer to be directed to a new *qibla* (prayer direction), is requested to turn his face to the mosque in Mecca. Then he and all the Muslims are requested to do so wherever they may be. In 10:87 there is more than one shift:

We revealed to Moses and his brother: 'Take you [dual] for your people in Egypt certain houses; and make your [pl.] houses a direction for prayer and perform the prayers; and do thou give good tidings to the believers'.

The second addressee may not have been there at the moment the first was originally spoken to, but a shift is made as when God, in the Qur'an, addresses Moses and his people. Satan is addressed, when he requests a respite in order to tempt the children of Adam (who were not yet born).

He is told: 'Depart (sing.)! Those of them that follow thee – surely Hell will be your (pl.) recompense.'

The shift has a powerful effect: those who follow Satan at any time or place are thus addressed directly by God with this strong warning, not simply informed that any one of 'them' will meet with such a reward. Although *iltifāt* of this kind has its real lexical meaning, it has, in addition, a rhetorical effect, since a person in the second group of addressees can see that he is connected with what has been requested of the first addressee, be it favourable or otherwise. Since the person in the first addressee is normally included in the second address, this type meets the condition of *iltifāt* mentioned earlier. God as seen in the Qur'an has access to everybody and may address them whenever He wishes. Since no distinction is shown in contemporary English between singular, dual and plural second person pronouns, in translations of such Qur'anic passages the shift may go unobserved and its effect be lost.

Here is a list of over twenty examples of this type: 2:144, 148, 150; 4:109; 5:48; 6:133; 7:3; 10:87; 12:29; 16:2; 17:63; 27:93; 28:35; 29:46; 31:31; 33:4; 19, 51 39:31; 42:13; 48:9; 58:2; 65:1; 69:18; 73:20.

This category was considered *yaqrub min al-iltifāt* by such writers as Suyuti,[35] Zarkashi[36] and Subki.[37] In fact, the name *iltifāt* fits this category well, as it is turning from one person to another.

4. Change in Verb Tense/Mood

A shift to the imperfect (present) tense serves a number of purposes. It may conjure an important action into the mind as if it were happening at present:

Remember Allah's favour when there came against you hosts ... from above you and from below you, when eyes grew wild and hearts reached the throats and you think [wa taẓunnūn] vain thoughts about Allah. There were the believers sorely tried.

33:10–11

He it is Who created you from dust, then from a drop [of seed] then from a clot, then He brings you forth as a child.

40:67

The shift may take place because the second remarkable action continues to happen at present:

He sent down water from the sky ... and then the earth becomes green upon the morrow.

22:63

Allah has made all that is in the earth subservient to you and the ships run upon the sea by His command.

22:65

A shift to the perfect tense has the effect of making the act appear already done, hence its frequent use in talking about the hereafter:

On the day when We shall set the mountains in motion ... and We mustered them [ḥasharnāhum] ...

18:47

When the trumpet is blown and all in heavens and earth became terrified [fazi'a] ...

27:87

A shift from the indicative to the imperative mood highlights a requested act:

We appointed the House to be a place of visitation for the people, and a sanctuary and: Take to yourselves Abraham's station for a place of prayer!

2:125

Say: 'My Lord has enjoined justice, and set your faces upright (toward Him) at every place of worship!'

7:29

As prayer is a pillar of Islam, the imperative here is more effective than the indicative – which is a piece of information. Similarly, highlighting a good thing is sometimes effectively achieved by a shift from the indicative to the imperative mood:

... the fire which has been prepared for the disbelievers, whose fuel is men and stones; and give glad tidings to those who believe and do good works!

2:23–4

The shift to the imperative *bashshir* is employed in such other instances as 36:11, 39:17, 61:13. Here are more examples of this category: 2:25,125; 7:29; 11:54; 16:11; 18:47; 22:25, 31, 63, 65; 27:87; 33:10; 35:9; 36:33; 39:68; 40:67.

The shift in the verb tense was considered *iltifāt* by Sakkaki, as mentioned earlier and also by Ibn al-Athir.[38] It was considered related to *iltifāt* – (*yaqrub min al-iltifāt*) by such other writers as Qazwini,[39] Zarkashi,[40] Suyuti[41] and al-Hashimi.[42] What is involved in this and in the earlier types of *iltifāt* is the same phenomenon, a grammatical shift for a rhetorical purpose.

5. Change in Case Marker

This category differs from other categories discussed here in three respects:

1. It involves only a very limited number of examples: two have been called *iltifāt* by some (2:177; 4:162). What is said of these two applies also to 5:69;
2. It was said to be *iltifāt* only according to one reading which involves a shift in the words concerned, but in each case there is another reading (if less common) that does not involve a shift;
3. According to the reading involving a shift, explanation of the shift on other grammatical grounds have been advanced; but explanation on the ground of *iltifāt* remains at least as strong as, if not stronger than, other explanations.

In spite of these restrictions, examples of this type have been called *iltifāt* and, at the very least, we may legitimately recognise that such a construction has the right to be considered in terms of *iltifāt* by its very nature. It should be pointed out again that this is the only group in which different readings were involved and grounds proposed for the shift other than *iltifāt* and related features.

Zarkashi reports that 2:177 and 4:162 have been considered *iltifāt* according to some,[43] and the claim appears to have justification, as it involves a shift, and appears to be employed for rhetorical effect. Q. 2:177 counts those who are truly pious, who believe, keep the prayers, give of their substance, however cherished:

... and those who fulfil their covenant [al-mūfūn] when they have one and endure with fortitude [al-ṣabirīn] misfortune, hardship and peril [of conflict], those are they who are true in faith.

Al-ṣābirīn is parallel with *al-mūfūn*, which is a nominative and should therefore be nominative (*al-ṣābirūn*), but there is a shift to the accusative case. How is this to be explained? According to the reports of Zarkashi, it is *iltifāt*. As will be seen below, departure from what is normally expected is done only for a special consideration. Here it can be seen to emphasise the importance of *al-ṣābirīn*. The need to emphasise the importance of this particular class of people is borne out by the fact that *al-ṣābirīn* is mentioned four times in the same *sūra*, being associated particularly with misfortune, hardship, and battlefield (2:153, 155, 177, 249). The verse following our example of *iltifāt* here speaks of retaliation in homicide, and fighting comes in the *sūra* not long afterwards.

The shift in the case marker did not cause any confusion about the role of the word involved and its relationship to other parts of the sentence. The case marker is only one of many (stronger) indications of that relationship, including the order within a series of conjunctions, the adjectival form in the masculine plural.[44]

6. Using a Noun in Place of a Pronoun

This is a substantial category of which I have recorded well over 100 examples from the Qur'an; in fact there are many more. Writers on *balāgha* place it along with *iltifāt* under the broader heading of *al-khurūj 'alā muqtaḍa'l-ẓāhir* (departure from what is normally expected).[45] In both, there is actually a departure of one kind or another, be it in person, number, addressee, case, reference (noun/pronoun), or tense/mood of a verb. There is no difference between replacing a pronoun by a noun for special effect and replacing first person by the second, or singular by plural, for a similar effect. The condition of *iltifāt* pertains to the present category since the person is the same in the noun used and the pronoun it has replaced. To that extent, there is no reason to treat examples of this category in the Qur'an differently from those treated under *iltifāt* and related features. In fact, when Zarkashi was discussing the reasons for *iltifāt* and giving examples to illustrate his point he included an example [46] involving the use of a noun in place of a pronoun (Qur'an 44:4–6).

This category comprises the following: 2:59, 60, 64, 105, 107, 109, 112, 115, 153, 157, 207; 3:5; 4:26, 27, 28, 32, 80, 81, 84, 87, 88, 92, 94, 95, 99, 100, 103, 104, 106, 110, 113, 176; 5:39, 40, 54, 83, 97, 98; 6:1, 21; 8:13; 12:87, 90; 13:2,3; 14:1, 6, 11, 20, 21, 25, 27, 34, 47, 51; 16:18, 19, 84; 17:22; 19:19, 56, 69, 91, 92, 93; 20:130; 21:39; 22:31, 58, 60, 61, 62, 72, 78; 23:27, 58, 59; 24:38, 62, 64; 25:17; 28:46, 56, 68, 70, 75, 87; 29:5, 10, 20, 45, 63; 32:3; 33:2, 13, 17, 25, 50; 35:3, 28; 38:4, 26, 27; 39:2, 3, 22; 40:6, 21, 44; 41:27; 42:5, 47, 49, 53; 46:11; 47:4; 57:9, 21, 29; 59:18; 60:1; 61:13; 63:1, 9; 67:11; 74:31; 110:3

A large number of the examples involve substituting the name of Allah (sometimes *rabb*) for His pronoun. Thus: 'To Allah belongs the East and the West; whithersoever you turn there is the face of Allah: Allah is All-Embracing, All-Knowing' (1:115). Instead of 'His Face' and 'He is' we have the name, which is more important than the pronoun; it makes the matter explicitly exclusive to Allah. Stating the name of Allah, moreover, in the three successive statements make each of them absolute, independent and quotable. This is a common feature in the language of the Qur'an, and appropriate to a book which asserts that it is the word of God for all times and places. A great many verses end with such absolute, independent, quotable statements as: 'Allah is with the steadfast', 'Allah is Merciful, Compassionate,' and the like. Such an ending gives the statement in the verse force and conclusiveness. There are, moreover, certain words in the Qur'an that tend to collocate specifically with the noun Allah (and less frequently with *rabb*) rather than with the pronoun. We have already mentioned *al-ḥamd* (praise); other such words are: *faḍl* (bounty) *rizq* (provision) *sabīl* (the way) *ajal* (the term set by Allah) *ba'th* (resurrection) and, to a certain extent, *hudā* (guidance). This collocation highlights exclusivity and a contrast with other than Allah is normally implied.

When a derived (*mushtaqq*) noun is used instead of a pronoun, it indicates causality. Thus in Q.38:27:

We have not created the heaven and the earth and all that is between them in vain. That is the opinion of those who disbelieve, and woe to those who disbelieve from Hell-fire.

Repeating the noun (*li'lladhīna kafarū*), instead of using a pronoun (*lahum*), indicates that their disbelief is the cause of their opinion and their doom. Indication of causality in such cases is expressed in Islamic jurisprudence in a formula linking a proposition to a derived noun (rather than a pronoun) that indicates the causality of the noun from which the derivation was made.

A frequently quoted example of the technique of using a noun in place of a pronoun is 33:50:

O Prophet, We have made lawful for you … and a believing woman, if she gives herself to the Prophet, if the Prophet desires to take her in marriage, this is for you only, not for the rest of the believers.

If she offers herself 'to the Prophet' rather than 'to you'. This restricts the ordinance to the person of the Prophet, emphasised by the repetition of 'the Prophet'. Q.110:2–3 gives us two examples of this technique.

When Allah's help and victory come, and you see men entering the religion of Allah in throngs, then proclaim the praise of your Lord …

In 'the religion of Allah' in place of 'His' there is emphasis and contrast with the religion of others; 'the praise of your Lord' instead of 'His' reminds the Prophet at the time of victory of the care of his Lord and echoes the request made repeatedly early in his career: 'Be thou patient under the judgement of *your Lord'* and 'proclaim the praise of your Lord'. (15:98, 52:48, 68:48).

Iltifāt and Related Features: A characteristic of the style of the Qur'an

There are examples of *iltifāt* in pre-Islamic Arabic. In fact nearly all authors on *iltifāt* as well as early writers on the Qur'an, and Zamakhshari in his *Tafsīr*, who was quoted by subsequent authors, state that it is a well-known feature in Arabic and well-established in pre-Islamic poetry. Yet even what these authors themselves say makes it clear that the extent and variety of *iltifāt* in the Qur'an goes far beyond what they have cited in poetry. In fact even Ibn al-Athir, whose book was not on the Qur'an but on *adab al-kātib wa'l-shā'ir*, recognised this: 'If you examine the text of the Qur'an you will find much *iltifāt* (*ashyā' kathīra*); something of this (*shay' min dhālik*) is also found in poetry.'[47]

The overwhelming majority of his examples are from the Qur'an. The lists we have included above give a clear picture of the extent of the feature in the Qur'an. As explained earlier, it has been suggested that almost all examples of *iltifāt* in the Qur'an are to be found in the Meccan *sūras*. In fact this is not so. As is clear from the lists provided, *Sūra* 2 (which was revealed over a long period in Medina) contains many instances of *iltifāt* (see also *Sūras* 6 and 8). Even in a very late, very short, Medinan *sūra* (110) we find *iltifāt.*

As God speaks in the Qur'an, He is seen to have access to everybody present or absent, in time (past or future) and place. We have seen in examples of Type I (*iltifāt* in person) how God addressed generations that were not yet born (to warn them about following Satan, for instance). Only limited kinds of *iltifāt* can be expected in poetry, as observed in examples quoted in *balāgha* books: Imru al-Qays' lines, for instance, are a form of monologue. This may partly be explained by the fact that, with a few exceptions, such as the poetry of 'Umar b. Abu Rabi'a, there is very little dialogue in Arabic poetry. In the Qu'ran God also speaks about Himself in various ways:

A book We have sent down to thee that thou mayst bring forth mankind from darkness to light by the leave of their Lord to the path of the All-Mighty, the All-Laudable, Allah, to Whom belongs all that is in the heavens and all that is in the earth.

14:2

Here we have various aspects, shown in bold, each with a shift – either in number, person or reference (noun in place of pronoun). In the Qur'an Allah speaks to the Prophet, the believers, the unbelievers, and sometimes to things; and He speaks about them, sometimes commenting or addressing them at an important point with approval or disapproval. He informs, orders, prohibits, urges, reprimands, promises or warns, all with reference to this world and the next. The limits of a Qur'anic verse are different from those of an ordinary sentence and may encompass a number of sentences, with different persons, with Allah in the middle of the whole situation having access to all, speaking from the point of view of various aspects of His Godhead about the various persons/things or talking to them from their multiple viewpoints – this can hardly be expected in poetry. Qur'anic material is complex and intense: in addition to *al-jumla'l-khabariyya* (declarative statement) there is an unusually high frequency of *al-jumla'l-inshā'iyya* (affective statement). All this facilitates the frequent use of *iltifāt* and its related features.

The use of direct speech is, moreover, an obvious feature of the style of the Qur'an; so is the omission of the introductory 'he says'. Thus God addresses bees (16:68–9) and mountains (34:10) for instance. The use of the direct speech of the unbelievers in the Qur'an is important as it records exactly what they utter so that they may be judged by what they themselves have professed rather than by what anybody has reported (see for instance 22:51–69, 26:16–31). Such techniques frequently give rise to the employment of *iltifāt*.

We have also seen how, for various theological and rhetorical reasons, certain words collocate in the Qur'an with others; how the principle of *tawḥīd* and the technique of contrast, and the multiplicity of viewpoints, and the use of independent quotable statement together affect grammatical forms and give rise to shifts in these in a way that could not be expected in Arabic poetry or prose other than the Qur'an, even in the *ḥadīth* of the Prophet or *Ḥadīth Qudsī*.[48]

As attested by the Arabic text of the Qur'an and such books on *balāgha* and *tafsīr* as those by 'Abd al-Qahir al-Jurjani and Zamakhshari, there are two general features that mark the use of language in the Qur'an: conciseness of statement, and loading economy of statement with maximum effect. These, together with the other factors mentioned, account for the high frequency of the employment of *iltifāt*, and its related features.

The Functions of *Iltifāt* and its Related Features

Iltifāt and the related features discussed above involve a grammatical shift. As we have seen, they are discussed in *ma'ānī* under the general heading of *khuruj al-kalām 'ala muqda'l-ẓāḥir.* Departure from what is expected is done *li'qtiḍā' al-ḥāl lidhālik li-'urūḍ i'tibār ākhar alṭaf min dhālik al-ẓāhir* (because the situation requires such departure, to meet a consideration more subtle than is normally expected).[49] Departure from the normal without benefit is forbidden in *balāgha, mumtāni' fī bāb al-balāgha.*[50] Ibn al-Athir explains that the shift from one form to another is only done for some special reason that requires it: *al-'udūl 'an ṣīgha min al-alfāẓ ilā ukhrā lā yakūn illā li-naw' khuṣūṣiyya iqtaḍat dhālik.*[51] With every shift, then, it is only natural to question the reason for such a departure from the norm. Thus Muslim writers on *iltifāt* normally include a section on *asbāb/fawā'id al-iltifāt* (the reasons for/beneficial effects of *iltifāt*).

Zarkashi gives a representative section on the functions of *iltifāt* (pp. 325–33). After noting the general benefit of raising interest and the objections levelled at it by some authors, he gives examples of specific benefits. There is, for instance, the intention to honour the addressee as in Q.1:4; adding a useful piece of information contained in a noun used in place of a pronoun (44:6); showing others by change from second to third person how badly the original addressees behaved so that they are turned away from (10:22); expression by the speaker, through change from first singular to first plural, that the action is exclusively his (35:9); showing a particular interest in something at which the shift took place (41:12) and scolding by suddenly turning to address someone you have been talking about (19:99).

Muslim writers on *balāgha* and *tafsīr* and Arab literary critics who discussed examples of *iltifāt* in the Qur'an (including those cited by Nöldeke and mentioned at the beginning of this chapter) showed the beneficial points and powerful effect of *iltifāt.* It has been suggested earlier that Nöldeke appeared to view the examples he cited from a purely formal and grammatical point of view. Recognising that this is a very old feature in Arabic and is still used in modern Arabic,[52] has a technical name and countless examples (there are hundreds in the Qur'an itself), and recognising further that a shift or departure from what is normally expected for no reason is inadmissible (*mumtāni'*) in *balāgha,* Arab critics, rhetoricians and exegetes have considered the rhetorical purpose of the grammatical shift. Nöldeke, it has been observed, did not mention the term *iltifāt* in discussing the examples he cited. It should be pointed out that the finer points of certain types of *iltifāt* may not appear in the translation of the Qur'an into a European language (like English or German) which naturally differs from Arabic in certain aspects of style. This, however, is a problem of translation for which a solution should be sought. We are here discussing Qur'anic material in Arabic and a feature of style of the Arabic language in general. We have seen how prevalent the feature of grammatical shift is. This feature is discussed in all *balāgha* books in Arabic. The shift is done only for a special reason, otherwise it is *mumtāni'* in *balāgha.* To stop at the shift and not look at the reason is to see only part of the picture. Material in any language should not be considered without regard to the stylistic norms of that language.

Other Stylistic Features

As we have seen, God speaks directly in the Qur'an, not the Prophet, or anyone else talking about Him. This gives the text of the Qur'an a very special authority. We have also seen that *iltifāt* marks the text of the Qur'an with obvious dynamism. The following features enhance this dynamism:

1. Omission of the verb 'say' and its derivative. Thus in the Qur'an 2:186, we read 'When my servants question you about me, I am near. I answer the prayer of the supplicant when he calls to me'. Instead of asking the Prophet to tell the servants, God Himself answers directly and immediately, 'I am near'.
2. Dialogue is an important feature of the Qur'an, and in narratives we find extensive examples. Qur'an 26:16–66 gives an example of both extended dialogue and speed of action. Not only is dialogue frequently used in discussions in this world but on the day of judgement, and in Paradise and Hell.[53]
3. The comments that the Qur'an frequently makes on various situations further enhance the interactive nature of its style. For instance, when the believers are earnestly asking God to forgive them, perhaps worried that they were not good enough, He interrupts their prayer saying, 'God does not charge a soul save to its capacity; standing to its account is what it has earned, and against its account what it has merited'. Then the prayers of the believers continue (2:285–6).
4. The vitality of the language is also noticed in the high frequency of the affective sentence (*al-jumla al-inshā'iyya*) as opposed to the indicative sentence (*al-jumla al-khabariyya*). The difference between the two is an important feature discussed in Arabic *balāgha* books. An indicative sentence is one that can be said to be false or true, whereas the affective

sentence cannot. It comes in the form of an interrogative, command, urging, persuading, etc. Rather than making an assertion to the listener or reader, it involves him or her by questioning, commanding and so on. The Qur'an abounds in such affective sentences. Thus 52:30–43 consists entirely of an extended series of questions which corners the unbelievers and shows their position to be completely untenable. See also 27:59–64, 56:58–72. The second person pronoun 'you' is very frequently used in the Qur'an, to engage the addressee and maintain dynamism.

5. Emphasis adds to the intensity of the language in the Qur'an. Because the Qur'an was addressing non-believers of various creeds and ideologies who denied or were doubtful about its message, it employs the various degrees of emphasis used in the Arabic language. The more doubt addressees show, the more emphasis the Qur'an employs in answering them, as scholars of Arabic rhetoric make clear.[54] Some English translators of the Qur'an render emphasis by saying 'verily', but this is outdated and adequate only for certain degrees of emphasis. Unfortunately many translators overlook the emphasis in the Arabic text altogether, which is misleading since it serves an important function in the sentence.
6. Another type of emphasis in the text of the Qur'an, especially in the Meccan period, are the oaths. This may appear unusual in modern English, but it is very effective; as God Himself swears as to the validity of the statements and the truth of the message. He swears by phenomena such as the night, the day, the sun and the moon, which awakens the awareness of the reader to the importance of these natural elements, as signs of God's power and grace in maintaining them in perfect order:

> *The Sun is not allowed to overtake the Moon, nor does the Night outpace the day. Each in its own orbit runs.*
>
> 36:40
>
> *Say: 'Think! If God should shroud you in perpetual night until the Day of Resurrection. What other God could give you light. Will you not hear? Say: 'Think! If God should give you perpetual day until the Day of Resurrection, what other God could bring you the night to rest in? Will you not see?'*
>
> *Of his Mercy he has given you the night that you may rest in the day, that you may seek his bounty and give thanks.*
>
> 28:71–3

Even when the word, 'sun', 'moon', 'night' etc. is merely mentioned in the oath, it recalls, through intertextuality, the elaboration about the phenomena in other parts of the Qur'an.[55] The injunction 'think' seen above occurs in various forms in the Qur'an over sixty times; so does 'have you seen?', 'see how' and 'have they not considered?' which keeps the listener/reader in an interactive state.

7. Another feature that adds vibrancy to the language of the Qur'an is the high frequency of the employment of adjectives and especially in the intensive forms in Arabic. This is particularly noticed in mentions of God, showing His boundless power and grace, rendered by some in English as 'The Almighty, the All-Merciful, the All-Wise' etc.

We have noted in the previous chapters of this book some of the dynamic and lively language of the Qur'an. In the *Fātiḥa* there is *iltifāt*, a shift between talking about God to addressing him. In 'Water' we witnessed the movement and vitality showing the generation and effects of water. On the theme of war, there was urging and restraining; in marriage and divorce, freedom and limitation. In 'Life and Beyond' and 'Paradise' there is action and shifts in tense to show how interrelated they are in the Islamic concept. In the stories of Adam and Joseph, there is continuous action, dialogue and swift change of dramatic scene. In 'The Face' we saw how faces reflect the inner feelings and their changes in this world and the next. This exemplifies a general feature of the Qur'an, where sometimes abstract concepts are usually presented in visual and auditory imagery rather than in abstract language. Indeed imagery has been identified as a main vehicle enhancing the power of expression the Qur'an.[56] Together with all the other features it contributes to the dynamic style which is an inseparable part of the power and effect of the Qur'anic message.

Notes

Preface

1. Fazlur Rahman, *Major Themes of the Qur'an,* (Maryknoll, 1979).

2. The approach of translating passages of the Qur'an on different subjects, such as that of Henry Mercier, trans. L. Tremlett, Luzac & Co (London, 1956) is a very useful one, but is not comprehensive enough to show the full picture on any of the themes and also cuts the passages off from their context.

3. This is in addition to many conferences and symposia on the Qur'an and Science held in Egypt at al-Azhar and at other Arab universities.

4. Fazlur Rahman, *Major Themes of the Qur'an,* 2nd edition, (Maryknoll, 1989) p. xiii.

Chapter One

1. E.g. S. Quṭb, *Fī ẓilāl al-qur'ān,* Cairo 1985, vol. 6, p. 399.

2. 9:43; 80:1–11.

3. Poetry or prose. Eloquence of speech was the most prized artistic talent among the Arabs.

4. See Ṣubḥī al-Ṣāliḥ, *Mabāḥith fī 'ulūm al-qur'ān,* (Beirut, 1981) p. 65–7.

5. M. A. Diraz, *al-Madkhal li dirāsat al-qur'ān al-karīm,* (Kuwait, 1981) p. 120.

6. M. A. S. Abdel Haleem, 'Qur'anic Orthography: The Written Representation of the Recited Text of the Qur'an', *Islamic Quarterly,* (London, 1994) XXXVIII, 3, pp. 171–92.

7. See Chapter 7 below.

8. *A Concise History of Islamic Legislation* (in Arabic) by A. Khallaf, (Kuwait, 1968)

pp. 28–9.

9. See Muḥammad al-Zifzāf, *al-Ta'rīf bi-l qur'ān wa'l ḥadīth,* (Kuwait, 1979) pp. 99–105.

10. See Chapter 2 below.

11. Even though, according to one religious interpretation, it is permissible for those who cannot read Arabic to read the prayers in a foreign tongue.

12. The Protestant missionaries who translated Sale's *Preliminary Discourse* into Arabic, (Cairo, 1909) p. 400.

13. *The Quran Translated* 1960 vol. 2, p. 667.

14. In two volumes published by the University of Manchester 1991.

15. See T. Ḥassān, *al-Bayān fī rawā'i' al-qur'ān,* (Cairo, 1993) pp. 443–53.

16. Similarly, the Anglo–Saxon epic *Beowulf* starts with 'Hwaet!'.

Chapter Two

1. See Chapter 12 below.

2. He is Merciful – the Judgement itself is a manifestation of God's mercy as there He will right the wrongs that have been inflicted on the oppressed. In the world while they endure, they are aware that the Mercy of God will not leave them under oppression, and He will see that Truth will eventually be asserted. The wrong-doer will not get away scot free both in this world and the next. That is why in the Qur'an the people of Paradise will declare, when Judgement has been passed in justice, '*al-Ḥamdu li-Llāhi Rabb al-'Ālamīn* (Praise belongs to Allah the Sustainer of the worlds' (39:75).

3. Moses, for instance, on being told by his followers, who could see Pharaoh closing down on them with his army at the sea, 'They will overtake us', said to them 'No, my Lord is with me and will guide me' (26:61–2). Obviously he meant that God would guide him to a way out of the predicament. At this point he was inspired by God to strike the sea with his staff and it split open, showing a path for them to cross.

4. *Tafsīr* (Beirut n.d.), vol. I, p. 257.

5. An excellent comparative study, was conducted by S. Sperl, 'The Literary Form of Prayer: Qur'an *Sūra* One, the Lord's Prayer and a Babylonian Prayer to the Moon God' in *BSOAS*, p. 218.

6. Ibid.

7. 'Lord's Prayer', *The Interpreter's Dictionary of the Bible,* vol. 3, 154–8. (New York, 1962).

Chapter Three

1. See Chapter 8 below.

2. See Chapter 13 below.

3. See A. Yusuf Ali, *The Holy Qur'ān: Text, Translation and Commentary,* note

5149 to 54:28 and note 1044 to 7:73; and the commentary by al-Jammāl, Sulaymān b. 'Umar, *al-Futuhāt al-ilāhiyya,* on 54:28; and M. B. al-Sadr, *Iqtiṣādunā,* (Beirut, 1981) pp. 519 and *passim.*

4. A. M. A. Maktari, *Water Rights and Irrigation Practices in Lahj,* (Cambridge, 1971) p. 28.

5. Ibid., p. 21.

6. S. A. 'Ishār, 'Social Life in the Islamic City', *'Ālam al-Fikr,* vol.11, no.1, Kuwait, June 1980, pp.85–126.

7. N. M. Titley, *Plants and Gardens in Persian, Mughal and Turkish Art,* (London, 1979).

Chapter Four

1. It sets strict penalties for infringing this code.

2. Qur'an 24:32.

3. Ibid., v.33.

4. 57:27, *Musnad Aḥmad* 5:162.

5. 4:21.

6. 2:187.

7. A. M. al-'Aqqād: *Ḥaqā'iq al-Islām wa-abāṭil Khuṣūmih,* (Cairo 1969) pp.147–52).

8. Al-Fayrūzabādī, *al-Qāmūs al-muḥīṭ.*

9. Bukhārī, *Ṣaḥiḥ,* Chapter on Sales, *Ḥadīth* of Jābir b. 'Abdallāh.

10. Al-'Ajlūnī, I., *Kashf al-khafā',* 1, (Cairo, n.d.) p. 562.

11. e.g. 2:233.

12. The lexical meaning is 'rising above', so a wife in this situation puts herself above, not just equal to, her husband.

13. The translator is too polite, using the expression 'they should not behave with open unseemliness'; it should read: 'They should not commit flagrant lewdness.'

14. *The Life of Muhammad,* by Ibn Isḥāq, tr. Guillaume, OUP 1974, p. 651.

15. Even in cases of disagreement (33:29–31; 66:6).

16. I. al-'Ajlūnī, *Kashf al-khafā',* op.cit., pp. 187–91; A. M. 'Aqqād op.cit., pp. 155–7; & S. Quṭb, op.cit., commenting on Qur'an 4:34.

17. Ibid.

Chapter Five

1. See Chapter 6 below.

2. 'Slay them wherever you find them: Humanitarian Law in Islam,' by James J. Busuttil, Linacre College, Oxford, in *Revue de Droit Penal Militaire et de Droit de la Guerre,* 1991, pp. 113–40.

3. See Chapter 6 below.

4. See A. M. al-'Aqqād, op.cit. (Cairo, 1957) pp. 187–91, quoting a survey by Aḥmad Zaki Pasha.

5. See for example 3:169–72; 9:120–1 and many *ḥadīths* in the chapters on *Jihād* in the various collections of *ḥadīths.*

6. Busuttil, p. 127. The rendering he uses runs: 'Idolatry is worse than carnage'. This corrupts the meaning. It is clear from the preceding words, 'those who have turned you out' that *fitna* means persecution. This meaning is borne out by the identical verb (turning out/expelling) preceding the only other verse (2:217) where the expression, '*fitna*' is worse than killing' appears. Here the statement is clearly explained: 'Fighting in [the prohibited month] is a grave (offence) but graver is it in the sight of God to prevent access to the path of God, to deny Him, to prevent access to the Sacred Mosque and drive out its people.'

7. 'Aqqād, op.cit., pp. 204–9.

8. See Chapter 6.

9. In the New Testament Jesus gives the high ideal that if someone hits you on one cheek, you should turn the other cheek. Pardon and forgiveness on the individual level is also highly recommended in the Qur'an. 'Good and evil deeds are not alike. Requite evil with good, and he who is your enemy will become your dearest friend, but none will attain this attribute save those who patiently endure; none will attain it save those who are truly fortunate' (41:34–5). And see 45:14. But when it comes to the places of worship being subjected to destruction and when helpless, old men, women and children are persecuted and when unbelievers try to force believers to renounce their religion, the Qur'an considers it total dereliction of the duty for the Muslim state not to oppose such oppression and defend what is right.

10. See Chapter 6.

11. Red camels were proverbial in Arabia as the best one can have.

Chapter Six

1. *Encyclopaedia of Religion and Ethics,* vol.12, 1921, p. 360.

2. *al-Qāmūs al-muḥīṭ* of al-Fayrūzabādī.

3. For example 11:118, 18:29–30, and see any concordance of the Qur'an.

4. Friedman, Y. (trs), *The History of Tabari,* vol. 12, (New York, 1992) pp. 191–2.

5. T. Jones and A. Ereira, *Crusades,* BBC Books, (London, 1994) p. 75.

6. See Y. al-Qaraḍāwī, *Non-Muslims in Islamic Society,* (Arabic edn), (Cairo, 1977) pp. 35–9.

7. The reported Turkish genocide against the Armenians during the first world war was committed by the secularist Turks who ended the Islamic state in Turkey and continue to deprive the Turks of their basic human right to practise their religion.

8. See also 17:2–7.

9. *The Redefining of Tolerance* http:\\ www.ezllink.com%7Extrbranch/toleranc.htm.

10. Document ref: PE 223 423/def. 23 October 1997.

Chapter Seven

1. M. F. 'Abdel-Bāqī: Qur'an Concordance (in Arabic), (Cairo, many editions).

2. See for instance: Qur'an 3:55, 26:82; 40:27; 71:17–18.

3. 'The Hour' is a term frequently used in the Qur'an meaning the ending of the world, at which begin the resurrection and the after-life.

4. See for instance M. A. Khalīfa: *al-Ḥayāh al-barzakhiyya,* (Cairo, 1983).

5. Ibn Rushd, *Manāhij al-adilla fī 'aqā'id al-milla,* ed. M. Qasim, 3rd edition, (Cairo, 1969) p. 246.

6. Ibid., pp. 246–7.

7. Ibid., p. 245.

8. See 39:67–75; 56; 75:81; 33:40.

9. 76:22, 89:27–30.

10. Qur'an 83:15, 35:54; 3:192; 9:63; 11:60. There is an excellent and comprehensive exposition of the whole question of recompense in the Qur'an in Chapter 3 of *La Morale du Quran* by M. A. Diraz, al-Azhar University, (Paris, 1951).

11. 55:37 ff.; 56:1ff.; 69:13 ff.; 78:18 ff.; 79:34 ff.; 81:1 ff.

Chapter Eight

1. In addition to the above figure, the Qur'an uses the same word *janna* in the sense of an earthly garden 26 times and for the original garden in which Adam and Eve lived before the 'fall', six times.

2. Of Persian origin, etymologically related to the word 'paradise'.

3. Dictionary of Qur'anic Words prepared by the Arabic Language Academy of Cairo, 1989, p. 247.

4. See Rāzī, *Tafsīr* at 2:25.

5. See Chapter 12 below.

6. The importance of the face as reflecting the psychological state (joy or torment) in the hereafter has been examined elsewhere, see Chapter 9.

7. In the *Encyclopaedia of Religion* (p. 239) it is 'in no way lacking the enjoyment of sensuous pleasures and bountiful surroundings'.

8. See al-Jalalayn at 37:42; M. Diraz, *Dustūr al-akhlāq fi'l-Qur'ān* translation (of his distinguished work in French, *La Morale du Kuran*) by A. Shahīn, (Kuwait, 1985) p.385 to whom I am indebted in this chapter; Abu'l-Ḥasan al-'Āmirī, *Kitāb al-i'lām bi-manāqib al-Islām,* ed. A. Ghurāb, (Cairo, 1967) pp. 136–7.

9. Ibid., p. 378.

10. See *Ni'ma*: Concordance of the Qur'an by M. F. 'Abd al-Bāqī, (Cairo, many

editions).

11. This affects the Islamic attitude towards marriage and the relationship between members of the family, which is seen here and in other places to continue after death.

12. The angels are also described in the Qur'an as being 'made pure'; so is Mary, mother of Jesus, and Jesus himself (56:79; 3:42 and 55).

13. This affected the concept of the garden among Muslims, and particularly in the arts.

14. See Chapter 3 above.

15. See for example 36:54–5; 34:70,72; 56:1,12; 88:1,9 etc.

16. See Chapter 9.

17. c.f. M. Dirāz, ibid., pp. 375 and 380.

18. Ibid., p. 245.

19. See M. Abdel Haleem, 'al-Sayyab: a Study of his Poetry', in *Studies in Modern Arabic Literature,* ed. R. Ostle, (Warminster, 1975) pp. 78–9.

20. See Chapter 13 below.

21. Al-'Āmirī, op.cit., p. 136.

22. See Tabarī, *Tafsīr,* (Cairo, 1994) Vol. 1, p. 174.

Chapter Nine

1. We shall see later in a tradition of the Prophet relating to prostration in prayer that the ears are counted as part of the face.

2. M. Argyle, *Bodily Communication,* (London, 1975) p. 214.

3. Ibid. p. 223.

4. A. J. Wensinck, *Ḥadīth Concordance* see under *wajh.*

5. See, for instance, *Ṣaḥiḥ al-Tirmidhī* (Cairo, 1934) vol. 13, pp. 116–21.

6. See the views of the Karramites in *Ghāyat al-marām fī 'ilm al-kalām,* by Sayf al-Dīn al-Āmidī ed. H. M. 'Abd al-Laṭīf, (Cairo, 1971) p. 180.

7. Ibid., p. 138.

8. Ibid., 1971, p. 179.

9. Abū Bakr al-Bāqillanī (d.403/1012).

10. See M. Abū Zahra, *Tarīkh al-madhāhib al-islāmiyya,* I, (Cairo, 1976) p. 186.

11. Ibid., p. 187.

12. Ibn Fūrak, *Kitāb mushkil al-ḥadīth,* (Hyderabad, 1362/1943) p. 131.

13. M. Sheikh, *A Dictionary of Muslim Philosophy,* (Lahore 1976) p. 119.

14. See al-Bāqillānī, ibid., pp. 297–9; Ibn Furak Ibid. pp. 131–2, 167–8.

15. *Maqālāt al-islāmiyyīn,* I, (Cairo, 1969) p. 290.

16. See *Aqwāl al-thiqāt fī ta'wīl al-asmā' wa'l-ṣifāt,* by al-Mar'i b. Yūsuf, Karmī, (Beirut, 1985) p. 139.

17. Rāzī's *Tafsīr.*

18. Zamakhshari, *Kashshāf.*

19. Tirmidhi *Ṣaḥiḥ, adab*; see Wensinck's *Concordance* under *wajh,* and under

nasab.

20. Ibn Fūrak, Ibid., p. 89.
21. Ibn Isḥāq, tr. A. Guillaume *The Life of Muhammad,* (Oxford 1970) p. 193.
22. Ghazālī, *al-Da'awāt al-mustajāba,* (Cairo 1985) p. 125.
23. See *Tafsīr al-Jalalayn* at Qur'an 10:26.
24. Āmidī, Ibid., pp. 159–78.
25. *Al-Taṣwīr al-fannī fi'l-qur'ān,* (Cairo 1966) p. 73.
26. M. N. Albānī, *Ṣifat ṣalāt al-nabiyy,* (Beirut 1983) p. 128.
27. Bukhari, *Ṣaḥiḥ, wuḍū,* 3.
28. Nawawi, *Forty Ḥadīth,* (Damascus, 1979) p. 79.
29. Ibn Māja, *Sunan, iqāma,* 50.
30. It is wrong to assume that the word *aswad* in classical Arabic means 'black' and nothing else. The 'colour field' in Arabic is different from that in English. In classical Arabic they may talk about white as being red; about black as being green; about green as being black. (T. Ḥassān, *al-Usūl,* (Casablanca 1981) pp. 321–32.) Dates have been described in *ḥadīth* and other literature as being *aswad* when in fact they were dark/brown. In Arabic grammar books we find the example: *mā kull sawdā' tamra* 'not everything black is a date'; in *ḥadīth,* we find that the Prophet's house sometimes had no food other than *al-aswadān* – dates and water. The fertile land between the two great rivers in Iraq was known as *sawād al-'irāq,* referring to the mud, or the dark green vegetation.
31. In fact, under the word *aswad* in classical Arabic dictionaries we find a range of colours, certainly much wider than the English 'black', and when the colour of *aswad* is intense we find that an adjective is added as in *aswad ghirbīb* or a different word is used, like *aḥwā* (See Ibn Sīda, *al-Mukhaṣṣaṣ,* under *al-alwān*).
32. The word *aswad* as an original colour occurs in the Qur'an only twice: 'When you can tell a white thread from a black on in the light of the approaching dawn (2:187) and 'black mountains' (35:27).
33. The difference in the 'colour field' between one language and another is an area that could lead translators to fall into error. Translators of the Qur'an into English have been inconsistent, arbitrary and maybe misleading in translating the very same word *muswadd* as 'dark-faced' when it describes 'fathers of daughters', and 'black' on the Day of Judgement (Arberry, Dawood, Pickthall and Yusuf Ali).
34. E. W. Lane, *Lexicon.*

Chapter Ten

1. Perhaps that is why Christians find it difficult to accept the idea of carnal knowledge in Paradise.
2. E.g. to show that all human beings come from the same father and mother, and that there is no ground for discrimination or oppression (49:3; 4:1).
3. Later (7:27; 36:60–64) the Children of Adam are warned that Satan will cause them to be expelled from the second Paradise (in the hereafter) in the same

way.

4. See discussion in *The Story of Joseph,* Chapter 11, below.
5. See Chapter 4 above.
6. See Chapter 8 above.
7. See Chapter 7 above.

Chapter Eleven

1. See for instance *The Encyclopaedia of Islam,* 1st edition, IV (2), under 'Yusuf', pp. 1178–9; Encyclopaedia *Judaica,* Vol. 10, (Jerusalem 1991) pp. 212–3; E. I. J. Rosenthal, *Judaism and Islam,* (London 1961) pp. 15–16; H. Speyer, *Die Biblishcen Erzahlungen im Quran,* New York 1961, pp. 187–224. However, a different approach from all these was taken by A. H. Johns in 'Joseph in the Qur'an: Dramatic Dialogue, Human Emotion and Prophetic Wisdom', *Islamochristiana,* 7, 1981, pp. 29–55.
2. *E. J.* 10, p. 209.
3. Ibid. p. 203.
4. Compare 12:102 with 11:49.
5. S. Quṭb, *al-Taṣwīr al-fannī fi'l-qur'ān,* op.cit., pp. 148–9.
6. *E. J.*, p. 209.
7. *E. J.*, p.209.
8. Reuben also rent his clothes when he returned to the pit and found Joseph was not there (37:29), and Joseph's brothers rent their clothes in Egypt when the cup was found in Benjamin's sack (44:13) – clearly an interesting (and expensive!) custom of the time.
9. Oxford, 1871, p.63.
10. *E. J.*, 10, p. 212. See also *E.I.*, IV(2), 1178.
11. See for instance Q.2:128–33; 6:161–63; 26:69–89.
12. 11:120; 12:109–10.
13. *E. I.*, 1st edition, IV (Part 2), p.1178.
14. 9:40; 24:22.
15. In Islam similar lists are given in *sira* books: compare for instance the list of Muslims who emigrated from Mecca to Abyssinia in *The Life of Muhammad* translated by A. Guillaume, (Oxford 1970) pp. 146–8.
16. In connection with the story of Joseph in the *Encyclopaedia of Islam* the writer makes the extraordinary claim that 'the Shi'is do not recognise *Sūra* XII'.
17. This was observed by the late S. Quṭb, op.cit. p. 154; *Fī ẓilāl al-qur'ān,* vol.4, (Cairo, 1985) p. 1962. See also Johns, op.cit.
18. A. Johns remarked that 'as a first encounter, the Qur'anic presentation of the material may to the westerner appear disjointed and incomplete, requiring its readers to supply out of their imaginations or prior knowledge, both the links between the events occurring in the narrative and the framework in which they are set, without which the story could not exist.' op.cit. p.30. This is certainly not the

case with the Arabic version. Everything that has been left out has been alluded to in the scenes. What may appear to the Westerner as disjointed and incomplete is the poor translations. But the reason for this is also likely to be connected to what Johns has rightly observed: for anyone brought up in the ambience of the Judaic or Christian tradition, the Genesis version of the story is inevitably regarded as the norm.

19. S. Quṭb observed that the technique of scenes and gaps is followed in nearly all Qur'anic stories. *al-Taṣwīr al-fannī fi'l-qur'ān*, p. 154.

20. *E. J.* op.cit. 10, p. 208.

21. *The Problem of the Hexateuch and Other Essays*, Edinburgh and London, 1966, p. 292.

22. Better appreciated in the Authorised Version than the New English Bible). The latter has flattened much of the freshness, beautifully simple statements and local colour found in the former.

23. *E. J.* op.cit., p. 208.

24. Wolfhart Pannenberg remarked: 'Within the reality characterized by the constantly creative work of God, history arises because God makes promises and fulfils these promises. History is even so suspended in tension between promise and fulfilment that through the promise it is irreversibly pointed toward the goal of future fulfilment. This structure is pregnantly expressed, for instance, in Deuteronomy 7:8ff: '… it is because the Lord loves you, and is keeping the oath which he sware to your fathers, that the Lord has brought you out with a mighty hand, and redeemed you from the house of bondage, from the hand of Pharaoh, King of Egypt. Know therefore that the Lord your God is God, the faithful God who keeps covenant and steadfast love with those who love Him and keep His commandments to a thousand generations.' 'Redemptive Event and History', in *Essays on Old Testament Hermeneutics*, ed. Claus Westermann, (Atlanta, 1979) pp. 316–17.

25. *E.J.* (see note 21 above).

26. *The Problem of the Hexateuch and Other Essays*, see note 22 above.

27. 'Thus a scholar of the stature of Torrey treats it almost frivolously.' Of the vision which warns Joseph against adultery when Zulaikha tempts him, he remarks 'This is characteristic of the Angel Gabriel's manner of spoiling a good story'. A. H. Johns, op.cit., p. 30.

Chapter Twelve

1. *Al-Itqān*, IV, Cairo, 1967, pp. 24–37.

2. Muḥammad b. 'Abd al-Raḥmān al-Qazwīnī, *Sharḥ al-talkhīṣ*, (Damascus, 1970) p. 14.

3. *Al-Lughat al-'arabiyya, ma'nāha wa-mabnāha*, Cairo, 1973, pp. 337 and 372.

4. Abū Isḥāq al-Shāṭibī, *al-Muwafaqāt fi uṣūl al-aḥkām*, III, (Cairo, 1342 AH).

5. *Muqaddimat al-tafsīr*, Vol. VIII, in *Majmū' fatāwa' Ibn Taymiya*, (Riyadh, 1382 AH) p. 362.

6. Ibid., p. 254.
7. Ibid., p. 353.
8. I. Anis, *Min asrār al-lugha,* (Cairo, 1966).
9. See Zamakhsharī's and Rāzī's *Tafsīrs.*
10. Regrettably I was told the publisher would not accept material in Arabic. I believe any study of the Qur'an must centre on the Qur'anic text itself, in Arabic; a reader who knows Arabic and wishes to appreciate the Qur'an should refer to the Arabic text.
11. *Al-Kashshāf,* 55:6.
12. *The Quran Translated with a Critical Rearrangement of the Suras,* II, (Edinburgh, 1960) p. 548.
13. His numbering system is one verse short of the system we follow according to editions of the Qur'an printed in Arabic countries.
14. *Quranic Studies,* (Oxford, 1977) p. 26.
15. *Shorter Oxford Dictionary.*
16. Aḥmad b. Yūsuf al-Tifāshī (d. 651/1253), *Azhār al-afkār fī jawāhir al-aḥjār,* (Cairo, 1977) pp.42, 242. See also *Kashshāf,* 55:58 and Bayrūnī, *al-Jamāhir fī ma'rifat al-jawāhir,* (India, 1355 AH).
17. I, 15; II, 244. See also Wansbrough, op.cit., p. 221.
18. *Majāz al-qur'ān,* I, 14–15.
19. Wansbrough, op.cit., 221.
20. *Ta'wīl mushkil al-qur'ān,* ed. Saqr, Cairo, 1954, pp. 221–2.
21. See for instance, Tabari and Qurtubi.
22. *Encyclopaedia Britannica, Micropaedia,* VII, (Chicago, 1977) p. 821.
23. c.f. 17:70; 31:31.
24. See chapter on 'Paradise' – not reclining as in many translations.
25. Al-Bayrūnī, op.cit., p. 190.
26. *Qāṣirāt al-ṭarf* is used in the Qur'an three times only, always for the select: *al-mukhlaṣīn* (37:40–48); *al-muttaqīn* (38:49–52); and *man khāfa maqāma rabbihi* (55:46–56).
27. See *Kashshāf.*
28. See for instance Qurtubi and Jalalayn.
29. Wansbrough, op.cit., p. 25.
30. *Itqān,* iii, 299.
31. *Ma'ānī'l-qur'ān,* (Cairo, n.d.) 3, p. 118.
32. The Qur'an here speaks of incidents that happened in this world. That is why the imagery did not evoke eschatological speculation, c.f. Wansbrough, op.cit., p.27.
33. See also Qur'an 16:48.
34. Ibid.
35. Apud Bell, *The Quran Translated,* II, 548.
36. Ibid., pp. 26–7.
37. This confirms, as also does 4:95–6, that there are two categories of the blessed,

in the same order as in Ch. 55, leaving no room for Wellhausen's and Wansbrough's speculation that in *al-Raḥmān* there are two variant versions of one category.

38. See the original of this chapter in *Approaches to the Quran*, ed. Hawting and Sharif, (London, 1993) pp. 71–98.

39. See for instance E. M. Wherry: *A Comprehensive Commentary on the Qur'an*, 1896, IV, 104; I use the Authorised Version of the Old Testament.

Chapter Thirteen

1. Strassburg, Verlag von Karl J. Trübner (1910).

2. R. Paret (ed.), *The Cambridge History of Arabic Literature*, I, (Cambridge, 1983), 205.

3. According to the numbering system used in the Egyptian edition of the Qur'an which I follow, this is 7:57; similarly, there is a slight difference in some other numbers; but with reference to the Arabic version of the Qur'an there should be no risk of confusion.

4. *Al-Jāmi' al-kabīr fī ṣinā'at al-manẓūm min al-kalām wa'l-manthūr*, eds M. Jawad and J. Sa'id, (Iraq, 1956) pp. 98.

5. See for instance, *al-Tibyān fī 'ilm al-ma'anī wa'l-badī' wa'l-bayān* by Ḥusayn b. Muḥammad al-Tībī (743/1342) (Baghdad, 1987) pp. 284–8; *al-Īḍāḥ fī 'ulūm al-balāgha*, by M. M. A. al-Qazwīnī (793/1338) (Cairo, 1971) pp. 43–5.

6. This was a general practice for centuries, in writing textbooks on various subjects in Arabic, and not just *balāgha*, where some striking examples were simply copied by successive writers who found these age-old examples adequate and saw no need to depart from them.

7. *al-Mathal al-sā'ir fī adab al-kātib wa'l-shā'ir*, II, ed. M. M. 'Abd al-Hamīd, (Cairo, 1933) pp. 4–19; *al-Jāmi' al –kabīr fī sinā'at al-manẓūm min al-kalām wa'l-manthūr* (Baghdad, 1956) pp. 98–105.

8. A. Maṭlub, *Mu'jam al-muṣṭalaḥāt al-balāghiyya wa-taṭawwurha*, I, (Baghdad, 1983) pp. 302.

9. *Al-Itqān fī 'ulūm al-qur'ān*, III, (Cairo, 1967) pp. 253–9.

10. *Al-Burhān fī 'ulūm al-qur'ān*, III, (Cairo, 1958) pp. 314–37.

11. M. Abū 'Alī, *Dirāsāt fi'l-balāgha*, (Ammān, 1984) p. 127.

12. See Ibn al-Athir, *al-Mathal al-sā'ir*, 2, 4.

13. The famous *al-Arba'īn* of Nawawi, for instance, (Beirut, 1976).

14. *Qur'anic Studies: Sources and Methods of scriptural interpretation*, (Oxford, 1977).

15. Ibid., pp. 249–51.

16. *Bell's Introduction to the Qur'an: completely revised and enlarged*, by W. Montgomery Watt, Islamic Surveys, (Edinburgh, 1970) pp. 79–85.

17. *E.I.* (2nd ed.), V, 419–21.

18. Ibid. pp. 196–202.

19. See M. Abdel Haleem, 'Grammatical Shift for Rhetorical Purposes: *Iltifāt* and related features in the Qur'an', *BSOAS*, LV,3, London 1992, pp. 409–10.

20. *Al-Mathal al-sā'ir*, II, (Cairo, 1939) p. 4.

21. *Al-Burhān*, III, pp. 314–15.

22. *Al-Burhān fī wujūh al-bayān*, (Baghdad, 1967) p. 152.

23. See Zarkashi's *Burhān*, III, 31–2; Suyuti, *Itqān*, 3, p. 257.

24. See M. Abdel Haleem, op.cit., p. 412.

25. If we compare the use of pronoun here to that in other types, we can observe the contrast between the use of the 3rd person – abstract power, the 1st person plural – aesthetic power, and the 1st person singular – personal feeling, the shift emphasising the quality of each.

26. M. Sa'rān, *al-Lugha wa'l-mujtama'* (Cairo, 1963), 139–58.

27. *Bell's Introduction to the Qur'an*, (Edinburgh, 1970), 66.

28. *Koranische Untersuchungen*, (Leipzig, 1926) p. 5.

29. *Quranic Studies*, p. 14.

30. Zamakhsharī, *Kashshāf*, I, (Beirut, n.d.) pp. 64–5.

31. Zarkashī, *Burhān*, 3, 196; M. Abdel Haleem 'al-Sayyab – a Study of his poetry', in R. C. Ostle (ed.) *Studies in Modern Arabic Literature*, (London, 1975) pp. 78–9.

32. See for instance Qazwīnī, op.cit., pp. 26–7; A. al-Hāshimī, *Jawāhir al-balāgha*, (Beirut, 1986) p. 129.

33. Ibid., pp. 234.

34. Ibid., pp. 258.

35. Ibid., pp. 258.

36. Ibid., pp. 334–5.

37. *Shurūḥ al-talkhīṣ*, I, (Cairo, 1937), p. 492.

38. *Al-Mathal al-sā'ir*, II, 13–19.

39. Ibid., 46–7.

40. Ibid., 336.

41. Ibid., III, 258–9.

42. Ibid., 241–2.

43. *Al-Burhān*, 3, 325.

44. See T. Ḥassān, *al-Lugha'l-'arabiyya mabnāhā wa-ma'nāhā*, (Cairo, 1976), 233–40. J. Burton dealt with some verses in this category in 'Linguistic Errors in the Qur'an' *Journal of Semitic Studies*, xxx, 2, 1988, 181–96, M. A. S. Abdel Haleem discussed Burton's views and conclusions in: 'Grammatical shift ... ', pp. 423–7.

45. Qazwīnī, 42:46; al-Hāshimī, 239:242.

46. Ibid., 392.

47. *Al-Mathal al-sā'ir*, II, 9.

48. I have checked *Forty Ḥadīth Qudsī*, selected and translated by E. Ibrahim and D. Johnson Davies, Damascus, 1980. Interestingly God speaks throughout in the first person singular pronoun.

49. Al-Maghribī's commentary on *Talkhīṣ al-miftāḥ*, see *Shurūḥ al-talkhīṣ*, 1, (Cairo, 1937), 448.

50. Ibid., II, 57.

51. *Al-Mathal al-sā'ir*, II, 14.

52. Najīb Mahfuẓ, the distinguished Arab novelist and winner of the Nobel prize for literature in 1988 uses it frequently in his novels written after his naturalistic phase, where he uses the 'stream of consciousness' technique. See H. El-Sakkout, *The Egyptian Novel and its Main Trends 1913–1952*, The American University of Cairo Press, Cairo, 1970, 115, 141.

53. See for instance: 14:21–2; 34:31–3; 37:5–7; 40:47–56.

54. Al-Hāshimī, Ahmad: *Jawāhir al-balāgha*, (Beirut, 1986) pp. 58–63.

55. See under 'Intertextual Relationships', Chapter 12 above.

56. Quṭb, S., *al-Taṣwīr al-fannī fi'l-qur'ān*, (Cairo, 1966) p. 10, pp. 193–203.

Index

Aaron, 22
Abel, 125
ablution (*wuḍū*), 8, 32, 116, 117
Abraham, 5, 22, 117, 139, 140, 141, 142, 146, 151, 152, 153, 156, 201
Abu Bakr (caliph), 4, 152
Abu Lahab, 152
Abu'l Aswad, 188
Adam, 10, 35, 49, 72, 92, 123, 124, 125, 126, 127, 128, 129, 130, 131, 132, 133, 134, 135, 136, 137, 199, 210, 215
Aeilia (Jerusalem), 75, 76
Africa, 76
afterlife, 10, 63, 82, 83, 84, 88, 90, 91, 92
ahl al-ḥadīth , 109, 110, 114
ahl al-kitāb, 73, 74, 78 *see also dhimmis*
ahl al-sunna , 110
alcohol, 76
Alcoran of Mahomet (of Alexander Ross), 9
al-Amidi, Sayf al-Din, 109
al-Amiri, 105
Amorites, 68
Angel of Revelation, 2, 6, 2, 3, 193
anthropomorphism, 110
Arabian peninsula, 7
Arabic language, 1, 2, 3, 5, 6, 7, 8, 9, 10, 11, 12, 13, 14, 16, 17, 18, 20, 23, 24, 25, 27, 32, 34, 38, 47, 48, 49, 52, 53, 56, 62, 72, 75, 87, 90, 100, 104, 105, 106, 107, 108, 110, 111, 121, 131, 144, 146, 153, 154, 159, 163, 171, 177, 184, 185, 186, 194, 197, 205, 206, 207, 208, 209, 210, 211, 214, 215, 216, 217, 218, 219, 220, 221, 222; Arabic grammar, 7, 104, 121, 194; Arabic orthography, 5
Aramaic, 25
Arberry, A. J., 9, 49, 52
Asad, 52
al-Ash'ari, 110
Ash'arites, 109, 110, 114
St Augustine, 59
Averroes *see* Ibn Rushd
Azerbaijan, 4

balāgha, 184, 185, 186, 187, 196, 197, 198, 203, 205, 206, 207
barzakh, 87, 88
bayān, 186
Baydawi, 64